Contents

D0103578

Preface

This is a book about one of the Supreme Court's most famous decisions, *Roe v. Wade*, and about what that opinion means three decades after it was first announced. The past thirty years have witnessed a continuous battle over the legitimacy of *Roe* that has shaped not only the abortion right but also the composition of the federal courts, and American politics generally. Hence, this is also a book about the role of courts in defining and enforcing fundamental rights in a constitutional democracy and how the work of courts necessarily interacts with and is affected by the work of legislatures, political parties, and social movements.

In each generation, a handful of Supreme Court decisions crystallize the problems and tensions in American constitutional theory and raise crucial questions about the proper role of the courts in interpreting the Constitution in a democracy. *Brown v. Board of Education* was such a case for the generation of the 1950s and 1960s. *Roe v. Wade* has proven to be the key case for the generation of scholars that came afterward.

Brown and *Roe* differ in many respects, but perhaps the most important difference is the degree of public acceptance each has enjoyed. Like *Roe v. Wade*, *Brown v. Board of Education* was hotly contested in the first few years after it was decided. For a decade or more, the legitimacy of *Brown* was bitterly disputed in the South. However, ten years after the decision, Congress ratified the result in *Brown* in Title VI of the Civil Rights Act of 1964. The success of the Civil Rights Movement altered the racial attitudes of most Americans. In the years that followed, *Brown* was transformed from a flashpoint of controversy into a hallowed icon that symbolized Americans' aspirations toward equality and human rights. In subsequent controversies over busing, affirmative action, and the expansion of civil rights to women and gays, people no longer disputed whether *Brown v. Board of Education* was correct. Rather, different groups of Americans, both liberal and conservative, attempted to seize the mantle of *Brown* for themselves, arguing that they were the true adherents of *Brown* and that their opponents were distorting its meaning for political ends. The political debate was framed within the parameters set by *Brown*, rather than as a debate over the legitimacy of *Brown* itself.

The story of *Roe v. Wade* would be very different. No Civil Rights Act of 1983 ratified the result in *Roe* ten years after the case was decided. The second wave of American feminism did change American attitudes about gender equality. But *Roe v. Wade* also energized conservative and religious social movements that were deeply hostile to the decision. These social movements became important features of contemporary politics and helped produce the American party system as we know it today.

In contrast to *Brown*, many Americans—and particularly many American politicians—continue to argue that *Roe v. Wade* was wrongly decided and should be overruled. Since 1980, the platform of one of the country's two major political parties—the Republicans—has called for overturning the decision. *Roe* has not become a hallowed icon like *Brown* but rather has remained a site of political and legal controversy. For this reason, the debate over abortion rights has not occurred solely within the framework set by *Roe* but has continually put the very legitimacy of the decision into question. And, since the 1980s, debates about federal judicial nominations have often focused, directly or indirectly, on the continued vitality and authority of *Roe*.

For this book, I asked a group of distinguished constitutional scholars to rewrite the opinion in *Roe v. Wade*. I asked each one of them the same question: How would you have written the *Roe* opinion in 1973, if you knew then what you know now about the subsequent history of the country? The results were staged at a special symposium at Yale Law School on January 31, 2003, to mark the thirtieth anniversary of the decision in *Roe v. Wade*. The participants assumed the roles of a mock Supreme Court; I played the role of the Chief Justice.

Each person was asked to write an opinion using only materials available as of January 22, 1973, when the opinion in *Roe v. Wade* was handed down. The opinion could be structured as a majority opinion, a concurrence, or a dissent. The participants were allowed to predict events if they chose, but they could not refer to anything in the future as fact. Thus, they could not cite to medical studies or law review articles written after January 1973, although they were free to make any arguments or predictions about the future they wanted.

Roe v. Wade, which struck down Texas's nineteenth-century prohibition on abortion, was decided together with a companion case, *Doe v. Bolton*, which struck down Georgia's abortion reform statute, passed in 1968 and based on the American Law Institute's Model Penal Code. Together, the two cases raised a number of important and difficult questions for the contributors. *Roe* presented basic questions about the constitutional status of unborn life and about whether states could prohibit abortion in all circumstances. *Doe* concerned the question of what procedural hurdles the state could put in the way of abortion once it was decriminalized. And both cases raised the issue of when and how courts should identify fundamental rights that were not explicitly mentioned in the text of the Constitution. I asked the participants to draft an opinion that addressed the legal issues raised by both *Roe* and *Doe*.

This is the second exercise of this type that I have organized. Five years ago I asked nine constitutional scholars to rewrite the decision in *Brown v. Board of Education*. The results were published in 2001 under the title *What* Brown v. Board of Education *Should Have Said*. The publisher, NYU Press, was sufficiently pleased that it asked for a sequel, and after some thought I decided that the logical candidate was *Roe v. Wade*.

Organizing a book to rewrite *Roe*, one of the Supreme Court's most controversial cases, has a very different meaning from organizing a book that rewrites *Brown*, one of the most revered of Supreme Court decisions. And it presents its own special difficulties. In the case of *Brown*, finding a legal academic to dissent from the decision was a challenge (although Derrick Bell admirably played that role). In the case of *Roe*, it was a necessity. What complicates matters is that the American legal academy is strongly pro-choice in its orientation. To counteract that tendency, I asked sixteen people to participate in this volume, divided roughly between supporters and critics of the decision. Eventually eleven people accepted, of whom seven are supporters and four are critics of the constitutional right to abortion recognized in *Roe*. That result, interestingly enough, tracks the original 7–2 split in *Roe* itself. Actually, the vote in this book is closer to 7½–3½, for one of the four critics, my colleague Akhil Amar, argues in his very interesting opinion that only abortion statutes passed before 1920, when women gained the right to vote, should be considered presumptively unconstitutional. While Amar and Jeffrey Rosen argue forcefully that *Roe* was wrongly decided because it was badly reasoned, Teresa Stanton Collett and Michael Stokes Paulsen object to *Roe* on moral grounds, offering a strong and forthright defense of pro-life principles.

*

Rewriting the opinion today, three decades after *Roe,* has three basic purposes. First, it is a good way to reexamine the premises of *Roe* and fundamental rights jurisprudence at the beginning of a new century. This is as true for defenders of the decision as for its critics.

The title of this book, *What* Roe v. Wade *Should Have Said,* might suggest that changing the language of the opinion might have changed history. That may or may not be the case. The exact language of a decision may matter much less than most people (and most legal scholars) think. Most Americans do not read Supreme Court opinions and have only the vaguest idea of their contents. Moreover, whatever the original language, no decision is immune from subsequent revision, especially a controversial one like *Roe v. Wade.* Judges and Justices reshape and transform older decisions to conform with current concerns. The meaning of *Roe* was transformed repeatedly over time, and substantial features of *Roe* were jettisoned and replaced by the 1992 decision in *Planned Parenthood of Southeastern Pennsylvania v. Casey.*

Reappraising the premises of an important decision like *Roe v. Wade* with the hindsight of three decades is a valuable exercise even if particular changes of wording might have had little effect. For the same reason, it is a valuable exercise even if no Justice living in 1973 would have or could have reasoned in the way that people now reason about constitutional law. The point of considering "What *Roe v. Wade* Should Have Said" is to ask this question from today's standpoint, and in light of the experiences —and the hard won lessons—that have produced the world in which we live today.

Second, like many great and controversial cases, *Roe* has spurred people to offer and defend different theories of constitutional interpretation. Some have tried to offer accounts of why the result (if not the precise reasoning) in *Roe* is consistent with sound constitutional interpretation, while others have pointed to *Roe* as the central example of a decision that lacks fidelity to the Constitution and sound interpretive principles. Several of the contributors to this volume have distinctive theories of how the Constitution should be read and interpreted. Rewriting *Roe* is a good way of putting those theories to the test.

This second reason leads naturally to a third: *Roe v. Wade* has become a key point of controversy in an ongoing debate about the role of courts in a constitutional democracy. *Roe* has been a central example in debates about when courts should recognize and guarantee rights that are opposed by significant segments of society, and the legitimacy of courts' trying to do so. Rewriting *Roe* is a good way to address these important questions, and many of the opinions in this book are deeply concerned with the proper role of the judiciary three decades after *Roe*.

As noted earlier, *Roe v. Wade* is a paradigmatic case for the present generation of American constitutional scholarship. It is the key case with which every constitutional theorist of this generation must eventually come to terms. There is no better way to confront the problems that *Roe* symbolizes and embodies than having to argue the issues out for oneself. It was obvious to all of the contributors that writing a decision for an hypothetical court some thirty years after the fact does not present the same experience that the Supreme Court faced in 1973. But the task of putting one's views in the form of a judicial opinion requires an intellectual discipline that has its own distinctive values. It is one thing to offer academic theories of constitutional interpretation. It is quite another to have to articulate those theories in the form of a legal opinion and to demonstrate that one's views about the Constitution really are consistent with a successful and acceptable judicial performance.

I am grateful to many different people for their help and encouragement as I prepared this book. First and foremost, I would like to thank my wife, Margret Wolfe, for her patience, her love, and her emotional support during the many twists and turns this project took. Mark Graber, Sandy Levinson, and Mark Tushnet offered helpful comments on the introduction. As she has so often, Reva Siegel provided me with valuable advice about the project as it developed. Will Baude generously offered to help prepare the book's index and table of cases. I would also like to thank the members of Yale Law Women, and my secretary Debbie Sestito, for helping to put together the conference at Yale Law School where the opinions were first delivered. Last but not least, I would like to thank the contributors themselves, who approached the project in a genuine spirit of cooperation and intellectual engagement. They have truly made this volume much more than the sum of its parts.

JACK M. BALKIN

New Haven, Connecticut

July 2004

Part I

Introduction

Roe v. Wade

An Engine of Controversy

Jack M. Balkin

If *Brown v. Board of Education*[1] is America's most hallowed modern Supreme Court decision, *Roe v. Wade*[2] is surely its most controversial. In 1973, *Roe v. Wade* struck down the abortion laws of most of the states in a single opinion, but it did not settle the question of abortion rights in America. Far from it: *Roe* was merely the opening event in a political and legal struggle over reproductive rights that continues to this day. *Roe* energized new social movements that eventually divided the two major political parties over abortion rights and reshaped their respective coalitions. Securing and expanding the right to abortion became a central concern of the women's movement, while opposition to *Roe v. Wade* awakened the sleeping giant of religious conservatives, who in turn helped shape the contemporary Republican Party. In the process, *Roe v. Wade* became a central issue in federal judicial nominations, symbolizing not only the issue of reproductive freedom but also the larger question of the proper role of courts in a democratic society. Attacking and defending the principles and reasoning of *Roe v. Wade* has been a central preoccupation of constitutional theorists ever since it was decided. It is hardly an exaggeration to say that, more than any other Supreme Court decision, *Roe v. Wade* has defined the constitutional jurisprudence and the constitutional debates of the modern era.

The State of Abortion Today

Thirty years after *Roe*, Americans remain divided over abortion rights. Polling data consistently show majority support for some form of abortion

3

right, and overwhelming majorities favor the legal availability of abortion in cases of rape, incest, or when a woman's life or health would be jeopardized. Nevertheless, many Americans remain ambivalent about giving women too free an access to abortions, and a significant minority of the public are adamantly opposed to abortion except in a small class of cases. The median position appears to be that abortion should be legal but that women should be able to obtain the procedure only for good reasons, with some dispute about what a sufficiently good reason would be. For example, in an ABC News–*Washington Post* poll conducted on the thirtieth anniversary of *Roe v. Wade,* 57 percent of respondents surveyed stated that abortion should be legal in "all or most cases." Eight in ten agreed that abortions should be available in cases of rape or incest or when the mother's life or health is endangered. At the same time, 57 percent also believed that abortion should be illegal "if the woman is unmarried and does not want the baby." That might suggest that majorities prefer much stricter regulations of abortion. Nevertheless, 56 percent wanted abortions to be as easy to obtain as they are now (including 14 percent who wanted them even easier to get), while 42 percent wanted abortions to be more difficult to obtain.[3] Finally, although Americans remain uneasy about unhindered access to abortion, a majority also oppose the idea of appointing Justices to the Supreme Court to overturn *Roe.*[4]

These conflicted feelings about abortion have been translated into government policies that maintain the formal legality of abortions but impose many practical and procedural obstacles on women who wish to obtain them. These burdens fall most heavily on poor women and women who live in rural areas.[5] In fact, since 1982, the number of abortion providers in the United States has decreased by 37 percent. In 2000, 87 percent of all U.S. counties lacked an abortion provider; 34 percent of all women between the ages of fifteen and forty-four lived in these counties. By contrast, obstetric and gynecological care is available in half of the nation's counties.[6]

Several different factors have contributed to women's lack of practical access to abortion. Physicians and hospitals have shied away from performing abortions because of repeated protests, harassment, and violence directed against abortion clinics and the doctors and nurses who staff them. Many medical schools no longer provide training in abortions for medical students, further reducing the pool of abortion providers. Consolidation of the health care industry in the late twentieth century and the rise of managed care may have produced subtle economic pressures that disfavor abortion clinics and have made abortion services in hospitals more costly.

Perhaps equally important, state and local governments have enacted abortion regulations that discourage abortion or make it harder to obtain. Several states refuse to allow abortions to be performed in publicly owned facilities that are the sole (or main) health care providers in some jurisdictions. Following the Supreme Court's 1992 decision in *Casey v. Planned Parenthood of Southeastern Pennsylvania*,[7] states have been free to impose greater restrictions on abortion. As of December 2003, twenty states require that state-directed information or counseling be provided to pregnant women and impose a waiting period (usually twenty-four hours) before women can obtain abortions. Thirty-two states (and the District of Columbia) prohibit Medicaid funding of abortion for poor women unless the woman's life is at risk or the pregnancy results from rape or incest; South Dakota makes an exception only if the woman's life is endangered. Nineteen states require parental consent before a pregnant minor may obtain an abortion, while fourteen require parental notification. Eleven states prohibit coverage of abortions in state employee insurance policies, while four states prevent even private insurers from paying for abortions as part of general health and medical coverage, instead requiring separate insurance policies or riders.[8]

Despite these limitations, more than 39 million legal abortions have been performed in the United States since *Roe v. Wade* was decided in 1973. However, the total number of abortions and the percentage of women of childbearing age obtaining abortions has declined, particularly since 1990. Although legal impediments are one cause, more likely reasons are better knowledge about and access to effective methods of contraception and lower rates of teenage pregnancy.[9] Contraception is key to reducing abortion rates: 47 percent of the 6.3 million unplanned pregnancies that occur each year in the United States occur among the 7 percent of women who do not practice contraception and are at risk of unintended pregnancy. Even so, contraception does not eliminate women's need for access to abortions: 54 percent of women who have had abortions reported that they were using contraceptives during the month they became pregnant. Lack of education about contraceptives and inconsistent or improper use remain major problems, and nonuse is greatest among those who are young, poor, or poorly educated.[10]

Public concern about abortions usually focuses on the later stages of pregnancy, when the fetus is more developed. For example, a recent poll showed that only 11 percent of Americans believed that abortions should be legal if they are performed in the sixth month or later.[11] In fact, the vast majority (88 percent) of abortions occur in the first twelve weeks of pregnancy. Only 7 percent occur between weeks thirteen and fifteen, and 4 percent between weeks sixteen and twenty. (Twenty weeks is about halfway through a normal pregnancy.) Only 1 percent of abortions occur from week twenty-one on.[12] Viability generally occurs at approximately twenty-four weeks or later. The number of postviability abortions performed in the United States is very small; a 1992 study found that after twenty-six weeks, only about 300 to 600 abortions are performed a year.[13]

The Decision in Roe

The Supreme Court's decision in *Roe* arose out of three different streams of social movement organization. Doctors and public health advocates had pushed for greater access to abortion and contraception for almost three decades before *Roe*. The medical profession, although sympathetic to the plight of pregnant women, was interested primarily in freedom to practice medicine without interference from what they regarded as religiously motivated legislatures. Public health advocates saw abortion as a public health crisis; although affluent women in the United States could obtain abortions, poor women were remitted to unsafe and dangerous methods. Public health advocates denounced the class and race discrimination they saw in existing abortion practices; they argued that poor women and minorities should have the same access to safe methods of abortion as the rich already did.[14] The third stream of politics was the second wave of American feminism in the 1960s, which was at first ambivalent about abortion as a movement issue. However, by 1970, feminists had begun to understand abortion as a basic right of women and began to press for repeal of existing abortion laws.

In 1960, all fifty states and the District of Columbia outlawed abortion except in very limited circumstances. By the early 1970s, public opinion had changed rapidly, a result of the sexual revolution and social movement activism. According to a January 1972 Gallup poll, 57 percent of Americans, and 54 percent of Catholics, believed that the abortion decision should be left to the woman and her doctor.[15] The American Bar Association endorsed the view that abortion should be left to a woman and her doctor up to twenty weeks, about halfway through the pregnancy. A presidential commission on population control reported in March 1972 that it advocated abortion by choice; the only dissenters were the four Catholic members of the commission.[16] Between 1967 and 1972, seventy-five leading national groups, including twenty-eight religious and twenty-one medical organizations, advocated the repeal of all abortion laws. These groups included, among others, the American Jewish Congress, the American Baptist Convention, the American Medical Association, the American Psychiatric Association, the American Council of Obstetricians and Gynecologists, and the YMCA.[17]

In the meantime, the Supreme Court's jurisprudence was also changing. Following the constitutional struggles over the New Deal in the 1930s, the Supreme Court had abandoned the idea of using the Fourteenth Amendment's Due Process Clause, which says that states may not "deprive any person of life, liberty, or property, without due process of law," to strike down labor laws and other economic regulations. The new Justices appointed by Franklin Roosevelt were deeply suspicious of the doctrine of "substantive due process" associated with *Lochner v. New York*,[18] the 1905 decision that struck down a maximum-hour law for bakers on the grounds that it violated employees' freedom to make contracts. The *Lochner* Court believed that it was merely enforcing implied limits on government and defending a long and hallowed tradition of individual liberty. But to its critics in the Progressive Era and the New Deal *Lochner* symbolized the early-twentieth-century Court's attempt to impose laissez-faire economic principles on the country.

Beginning in 1937, the Supreme Court repudiated the *Lochner*-era jurisprudence that protected economic rights through the doctrine of substantive due process. The Court would no longer read controversial economic theories into the Constitution. Instead, it would defer to the political branches in ordinary social and economic legislation. It would intervene only when basic civil rights and civil liberties were imperiled. However, the post–New Deal paradigm of deferring to legislatures in ordinary social and economic legislation, while acting to protect civil rights and liberties, soon proved difficult to maintain. The Supreme Court was repeatedly called on to protect civil rights and civil liberties based on the relatively abstract constitutional guarantees of equal protection and due process. It responded by creating new doctrines that protected blacks, women, children born out of wedlock, and aliens from invidious discrimination. The Court also began to recognize a new class of fundamental rights designed to protect the interests of the poor, such as the right to travel and the right to access to the courts.

In 1965, in *Griswold v. Connecticut,* the Court struck down a Connecticut statute that prohibited the use of contraceptives.[19] Anxious not to follow the logic of *Lochner v. New York,* Justice William O. Douglas, a Roosevelt appointee, argued instead that the statute violated a right of marital privacy that emanated from the penumbras of the textual commitments to liberty in the various parts of the Bill of Rights.[20] Clever as Douglas's penumbra argument was, later decisions did not follow his method. Rather, the Court recognized that it had embarked once again on the determination of which fundamental liberties were protected under the Due Process Clause.[21] The right of privacy was extended in 1971 to the right of single persons to use contraceptives in *Eisenstadt v. Baird,*[22] and extended again to include the right to abortion in *Roe v. Wade.* Although the plaintiffs in *Eisenstadt* specifically disavowed any claim that the right to contraception would lead to a right to abortion, Justice Brennan's plurality opinion in *Eisenstadt* clearly pointed in that general direction: "If the right of privacy means anything," Brennan wrote, "it is the right of the *individual,* married or single, to be free from unwarranted governmental intrusion into matters so fundamentally affecting a person as the decision whether to bear or beget a child."[23] Through this dictum, Brennan served notice that the right recognized in the *Griswold* opinion was not merely a right of marital privacy, but extended to single persons as well, and encompassed not only contraception, but the "decision whether to bear or beget a child."

The Supreme Court first heard oral arguments in *Roe* on December 13, 1971. Sarah Weddington argued before the Justices on behalf of Norma McCorvey, who had challenged Texas's 1854 abortion statute under the name Jane Roe. *Roe* was argued together with a companion case, *Doe v. Bolton,* which challenged Georgia's 1968 abortion reform statute, which was based on the American Law Institute's Model Penal Code. Margie Pitts Hames argued the Georgia case on behalf of Sandra Bensing, who brought suit as Mary Doe. Justices Hugo Black and John Marshall Harlan had recently retired, and so the Court had only seven active members. The case was reargued on October 11, 1972, after Justices Lewis Powell and William Rehnquist replaced Black and Harlan.

Justice Harry A. Blackmun, who had been appointed by President Richard Nixon in 1970, wrote the majority opinions in both *Roe* and *Doe.* He argued that the right of privacy recognized in *Griswold* and extended to single persons in *Eisenstadt* "is broad enough to encompass a woman's decision whether or not to terminate her pregnancy." Denying the right to choose would impose a "detriment . . . on the pregnant woman," including possible medical and psychological harm. Child care could tax a woman's mental and physical health. Blackmun also pointed to "the distress, for all concerned, associated with the unwanted child, and . . . the problem of bringing a child into a family already unable, psychologically and otherwise, to care for it, [as well as] the additional difficulties and continuing stigma of unwed motherhood."[24]

Nevertheless, the central problem with extending the right of contraception to abortion was that abortion ended the existence of an embryo or fetus. Counsel for Texas argued that human life began at conception, that a fetus was a person under the meaning of the Fourteenth Amendment, and therefore that a fetus had constitutional rights of its own. Blackmun responded that the fetus was not a person within the meaning of the Constitution, pointing out that in many places the Constitution referred to the rights and duties of persons that would make no sense if applied to fetuses.[25] He also noted that abortion was not a felony at common law before "quickening," the point at which a fetus's movements could be felt by a pregnant woman, which usually occurred in the fourth or fifth month of pregnancy.[26] Nevertheless, the State of Texas argued, even if the fetus was not a person, the state had a compelling interest in protecting the life of the fetus.[27] That compelling interest could be vindicated only by prohibiting abortion.

Blackmun responded that "We need not resolve the difficult question of when life begins. When those trained in the respective disciplines of medicine, philosophy, and theology are unable to arrive at any consensus, the judiciary, at this point in the development of man's knowledge, is not in a position to speculate as to the answer."[28] Nevertheless, the question simply reemerged in a different way. None of the Justices believed that the right to abortion extended to the very moment of birth. At some stage in the pregnancy, the state's interest in protecting the fetus became sufficiently compelling that states could proscribe abortion in almost all cases other than when necessary to preserve the woman's life or health. To determine when that point occurred, Blackmun effectively had to decide when the life of the fetus "began," at least to the extent of deciding when the state's interest in protecting the fetus became compelling

Justice Blackmun offered an elaborate trimester framework to solve these problems. Following the medical thinking of the day, he divided the pregnancy into three trimesters. Until the end of the first trimester, "the abortion decision and its effectuation must be left to the medical judgment of the pregnant woman's attending physician." In the second trimester until the point of viability, the state may "regulate the abortion procedure in ways that are reasonably related to maternal health." After the point of viability (between twenty-four and twenty-eight weeks, around the beginning of the third trimester), states can "regulate, and even proscribe, abortion except where it is necessary, in appropriate medical judgment, for the preservation of the life or health of the mother."[29]

The trimester system was actually the result of a compromise among the Justices. Blackmun's original idea was that a woman had the right to an abortion without interference from the state until the end of the first trimester. During the first trimester, the abortion decision was left to "the best medical judgment of the pregnant woman's attending physician." Afterward states could limit legal abortions to "stated reasonable therapeutic categories"—such as the woman's physical or mental health—"that are articulated with sufficient clarity" to give physicians fair warning.[30] The idea was that health regulations were unnecessary until the second trimester because first-trimester abortions were as safe for women as carrying the fetus to term. However, Justices William Brennan and Thurgood Marshall objected that the first trimester didn't give women enough time to discover that they were pregnant, find a doctor, and take the necessary steps to obtain an abortion. Marshall, in particular, was worried about the effect of Blackmun's rule on poor and minority women.[31] Blackmun agreed that the first trimester was an arbitrary point, and he responded by pushing the cutoff point to the moment of viability. However, Blackmun believed that states should still be able to regulate abortions for health reasons after the first trimester. In effect, this produced three different sets of rules for three different trimesters. Brennan responded that the point of viability was imprecise. The Court did not have to specify a specific cutoff point but should leave that question to "medically informed" legislatures in the first instance.[32] However, Blackmun ignored this suggestion, and the result was *Roe*'s trimester framework.

During the deliberations over *Roe*, Justice Stewart worried that Blackmun's trimester framework made the decision seem too legislative,[33] a criticism that would be echoed repeatedly in later years. In hindsight, Brennan's suggestion that the Court not draw hard and fast lines but instead wait and see what legislatures would do might have been far wiser. In any event, the Court issued its opinion on January 22, 1973, striking down Texas's virtually total ban on abortions, as well as Georgia's procedural restrictions. Seven Justices joined the opinion, with Justices White and Rehnquist dissenting. Justice Rehnquist argued that the decision was a throwback to *Lochner v. New York* and had no basis in the original understanding of the Fourteenth Amendment.[34] Justice White objected that "[t]he Court apparently values the convenience of the pregnant mother more than the continued existence and development of the life or potential life that she carries."[35]

From Roe *to* Casey

Given the rapid changes in popular and elite opinion in the late 1960s and early 1970s, the Supreme Court's 1973 decision in *Roe* was hardly unexpected. As is so often the case in American history, the Supreme Court's decisions in *Roe* and *Doe* reflected the emerging views of national majorities, and particularly national elites. Nevertheless, those views had not yet crystallized in new state laws liberalizing abortion. When *Roe* was decided, most states were considering some form of abortion reform legislation. However only thirteen states had passed abortion reform statutes, which gave doctors somewhat more discretion to perform abortions, and only four states had passed abortion repeal statutes that viewed abortion as a woman's right and allowed abortion up to a certain point in the pregnancy. In fact, *Roe* and *Doe* struck down the abortion laws of almost all the states, including abortion reform statutes like Georgia's 1968 law, which had been based on the American Law Institute's Model Penal Code. By contrast, when the Supreme Court struck down same-sex sodomy laws in its 2003 decision in *Lawrence v. Texas*,[36] thirty-seven states and the District of Columbia had already decriminalized same-sex sodomy, and in the thirteen states that still made sodomy a crime, the laws were rarely if ever enforced.

Some supporters of abortion rights, including, most prominently, Justice Ruth Bader Ginsburg, have claimed that the *Roe* decision was premature and a political mistake. *Roe v. Wade* "halted a political process that was moving in a reform direction and thereby . . . prolonged divisiveness and deferred stable settlement of the issue."[37] Opposition to *Roe* helped energize the conservative religious and social movements of the 1970s and 1980s, which argued that an unelected judiciary was imposing its personal (and immoral) views and casting aside those of democratically elected state governments. These conservative social and religious movements eventually found a home in the Republican Party; they helped elect

Ronald Reagan to the presidency and helped many other pro-life candidates gain political office. In the years following *Roe,* both Congress and state legislatures passed a series of laws that repeatedly attempted to water down and limit abortion rights.[38] As *Roe* energized pro-life conservative social movements, it simultaneously demobilized social movement support for abortion rights. Instead of pressing for abortion reform in the states and at the national level, pro-choice advocates were constantly placed on the defensive and repeatedly turned to the courts for protection. Reliance on the courts, in turn, diverted political energy away from forming a mass political movement for abortion rights that could successfully counter the burgeoning pro-life movement.

When *Roe* was first decided, the nation's two major parties were not strongly organized around abortion rights. Although Richard Nixon denounced the *Roe* decision in order to curry favor with the Catholic vote, neither party was strongly identified either with abortion rights or with the pro-life movement. Of the seven Justices in the original *Roe* majority, Chief Justice Warren Burger and Justices Harry Blackmun, Lewis Powell, Potter Stewart, and William Brennan had been appointed by Republican presidents (although Brennan was a Democrat), and Thurgood Marshall and William O. Douglas had been appointed by Democratic presidents. The two dissenters, William Rehnquist and Byron White, had been appointed by a Republican and a Democratic president, respectively. In the 1976 election, the Republican candidate, President Gerald Ford, was the relatively pro-choice candidate; the Democratic nominee, Jimmy Carter, was an evangelical Protestant who believed that abortion was immoral.

The countermobilizations that *Roe* helped energize changed all of this. The Christian evangelical movement, which had largely stayed out of politics in the decades before the 1960s, saw abortion as a threat to biblical values and began to organize against *Roe.* Members of the Republican Party's New Right, such as Phyllis Schlafly, who opposed the ERA, saw an obvious connection between their goals and those of Christian evangelicals. By the end of the 1970s, the two groups had formed an alliance that would dominate the Republican Party and revolutionize American politics. Ronald Reagan welcomed evangelical and fundamentalist Christian voters into the Republican Party and actively courted pro-life leaders. In the 1980 election, many evangelicals and fundamentalist Christians moved squarely into the Republican camp and became an important part of the party's base of support. The Republican Party became largely a pro-life party, with some moderates still favoring abortion rights, and the more liberal

Democratic Party, with Carter no longer at its helm, became strongly pro-choice. In 1980, the Republican Party platform for the first time included a call for "a constitutional amendment to restore protection of the right to life for unborn children."[39]

Once in office, Ronald Reagan sought to nominate candidates to the federal judiciary who would roll back liberal judicial decisions and promote his favored constitutional values, which included opposition to abortion. Not entirely coincidentally, the 1984 Republican Party platform "applaud[ed] President Reagan's fine record of judicial appointments, and . . . reaffirm[ed] [the party's] support for the appointment of judges at all levels of the judiciary who respect traditional family values and the sanctity of innocent human life."[40]

By the time Justice Lewis Powell retired in 1987, the Supreme Court's original seven-person majority in *Roe* had dwindled to four Justices who supported abortion rights: William Brennan, Thurgood Marshall, Harry Blackmun (the original author of *Roe*), and John Paul Stevens, who had replaced William O. Douglas in 1976. Reagan's first Supreme Court nominee, Sandra Day O'Connor, replaced Potter Stewart in 1981. O'Connor strongly criticized *Roe*'s trimester framework in her 1983 dissent in *City of Akron v. Akron Center for Reproductive Health*[41] and argued that abortion restrictions should be tested by a more lenient standard: whether they imposed an "undue burden" on women's ability to obtain abortions. In 1986, Reagan nominated William Rehnquist, one of the original dissenters in *Roe*, to become Chief Justice, replacing Warren Burger, and nominated Antonin Scalia, a vocal opponent of *Roe*, to fill Rehnquist's position as Associate Justice. These three Justices joined Byron White, the other original dissenter in *Roe*.

To replace Powell, Reagan nominated D.C. Circuit Judge Robert Bork, an outspoken critic of *Roe* who championed the jurisprudence of original intention. The choice of Bork appeared to provide the crucial fifth vote to overturn *Roe v. Wade*. The Bork nomination produced a national controversy, and ultimately the Senate failed to confirm him. Pro-choice groups mobilized to help defeat the nomination.[42] Eventually the Senate confirmed Reagan's third nominee, Anthony Kennedy, a conservative circuit judge from California who was generally regarded as more moderate than Bork.

In hindsight, the failure of the Bork nomination was a turning point in the constitutional struggles over abortion. It raised the stakes in succeeding Supreme Court nominations and showed that they could be bitter and politically costly to a president. Bork's defeat also demonstrated that pro-choice forces had considerable muscle that could be harnessed in the political arena if the public thought that abortion rights were truly threatened. It gave notice that Republican politicians might pay more heavily than they had previously believed if they tried to overturn *Roe*.

Despite the failure of the Bork nomination, by the close of 1987 President Reagan had appointed three Supreme Court Justices (O'Connor, Scalia, and Kennedy) who were widely regarded as critics of *Roe*. These Justices, together with the original *Roe* dissenters, Justice White and (now) Chief Justice Rehnquist, represented five votes for cutting *Roe* back drastically or even overturning it. The Supreme Court's decision in *Roe* had helped set off a political chain reaction that now seemed to threaten the decision itself.

In 1989, in *Webster v. Reproductive Health Services*,[43] the Court upheld a series of statutory restrictions on abortion passed by the Missouri legislature, which, among other things, prohibited the use of public employees and facilities to perform or assist abortions and included a declaration that "[t]he life of each human being begins at conception." *Webster* had no majority opinion. Justice Scalia argued forthrightly that *Roe* should be overturned. Chief Justice Rehnquist's plurality opinion, joined by Justices White and Kennedy, argued that *Roe*'s trimester framework should be jettisoned, that abortion was not a fundamental right, and that restrictions on abortion need only pass a test of minimum rationality, the same test that applied to ordinary social and economic legislation.[44] However, Rehnquist was unable to persuade Justice O'Connor, the crucial fifth vote, to join his opinion. She concurred only in the result, arguing that Missouri's law was consistent with previous precedents and did not impose an undue burden on the right to abortion.

Webster left *Roe* in a legal limbo. The trimester framework no longer commanded a majority of the Court, but it was unclear what, if any, restrictions on abortion were now prohibited. *Roe*'s fate seemed even bleaker when two of the Court's most liberal Justices, William Brennan and Thurgood Marshall, left the Court due to failing health. Brennan resigned on July 20, 1990, and was replaced by David Souter, a bookish jurist from New Hampshire about whom little was known when he was nominated. President George H. W. Bush, attempting to avoid a replay of the Bork nomination, hoped that Souter would be able to avoid a politically difficult confirmation battle.[45] Thurgood Marshall, the great civil rights lawyer who had argued *Brown v. Board of Education*, announced his retirement on June 27, 1991. To replace him, President Bush nominated Clarence Thomas, a conservative African American judge on the D.C. Circuit. Thomas was widely believed to be hostile to *Roe v. Wade* but stated at his confirmation hearings that he had never debated it and had no personal opinion on the subject.[46] The Thomas nomination was bitterly contested by senators who doubted Thomas's qualifications and his commitment to civil rights and civil liberties, including the right to abortion. Matters were thrown into an uproar when Thomas was accused of sexual harassment by a former employee at the Equal Employment Opportunity Commission (EEOC), Anita Hill. After weeks of controversy, Thomas was finally confirmed by a 52–48 vote, the narrowest margin in Supreme Court history.

Of the seven Justices who had voted with the majority, only Blackmun, the author of *Roe,* remained on the Court. Brennan, Marshall, Stewart, Douglas, Burger, and Powell were gone, replaced by Souter, Thomas, O'Connor, Stevens, Scalia, and Kennedy, all appointed by Republican presidents and all but Stevens appointed after the Republican Party became the pro-life party. Even if Stevens, whose views on abortion were variable, and Souter, whose views were completely unknown, supported *Roe,* the votes of the remaining Justices, in combination with Justice White and Chief Justice Rehnquist, were more than enough to gut *Roe* or (as most people then believed) to overturn it completely.

The expected vehicle for overturning *Roe* was a challenge to Pennsylvania's 1988 abortion regulation statute. Many of the statute's provisions were passed in fairly open defiance of the Supreme Court's 1986 decision in *Thornburgh v. American College of Obstetricians & Gynecologists.*[47] Among other things, the statute required that women seeking abortions undergo a twenty-four-hour waiting period and listen to a prepared speech detailing the nature of the procedure, the health risks of abortion, the possibility of alternatives to abortion, the likely gestational age of the fetus, and the fact that the father might be liable for child support. It also required that a married woman seeking an abortion sign a statement indicating that she had notified her husband.

On June 29, 1992, the Supreme Court delivered its decision in *Planned Parenthood of Southeastern Pennsylvania v. Casey.*[48] Departing from Supreme Court custom, Justices O'Connor, Kennedy, and Souter presented a jointly authored opinion. "Liberty finds no refuge in a jurisprudence of doubt," their opinion began.[49] They noted that the federal government had asked the Court to overrule *Roe* five times in the previous decade. The see-saw of decisions expanding and contracting reproductive rights in the 1970s and 1980s had continually put the abortion right into question; the fight over abortion politics had only grown fiercer and more bitter with each passing year. It was time, O'Connor, Kennedy, and Souter said, for "the Court's interpretation of the Constitution [to] call[] the contending sides of a national controversy to end their national division by accepting a common mandate rooted in the Constitution."[50]

The three Justices, all appointed by Republican presidents, understood that their appointments (and those of Justices Scalia and Thomas) would be widely viewed as responsible for overturning *Roe*. This, they believed, would reflect badly on the Supreme Court's authority and the independence of the federal judiciary from politics. Precisely because the fight over *Roe* had been so bitter, the decision could not be easily overruled: "[O]nly the most convincing justification under accepted standards of precedent could suffice to demonstrate that a later decision overruling [*Roe*] was anything but a surrender to political pressure and an unjustified repudiation of the principle on which the Court staked its authority in the first instance," the three Justices explained. "[T]o overrule under fire in the absence of the most compelling reason to reexamine a watershed decision would subvert the Court's legitimacy beyond any serious question."[51]

Although the joint opinion claimed to reaffirm *Roe*, in fact *Casey* significantly limited *Roe* and reformulated its doctrinal basis. In *Casey*, the Supreme Court abandoned the trimester framework. It also changed the permissible reasons for regulation. Essentially, *Casey* divided the pregnancy in two, with different rules before and after viability. Before viability, states could adopt measures designed to "to persuade the woman to choose childbirth over abortion" as long as they did not impose an "undue burden" on the woman's ability to obtain an abortion. Thus, *Casey* adopted the formulation first offered in O'Connor's dissent in *Akron*. The Court defined "undue burden" as a law whose "purpose or effect is to place a substantial obstacle in the path of a woman seeking an abortion before the fetus attains viability." Under that standard, the joint opinion upheld Pennsylvania's twenty-four-hour waiting period and prepared-speech requirements (thus effectively overruling the Court's 1986 decision in *Thornburgh*). But the joint opinion struck down the spousal consent requirement. It argued that the latter, but not the former two requirements, imposed an undue burden on women. *Casey* also held that states could pass laws designed to promote maternal health, as long as they did not impose an undue burden. After viability, states could "regulate, and even proscribe, abortion except where it is necessary, in appropriate medical judgment, for the preservation of the life or health of the mother."[52]

One problem with drawing the line at viability is that it is arbitrary and subject to changes in medical technology. In *Casey,* the Court noted that by 1992, developments in neonatal care had pushed the average point of viability back from twenty-eight weeks in 1973 to twenty-three or twenty-four weeks.[53] Nevertheless, the Court retained the viability rule: "[T]here is no line other than viability which is more workable," the Court argued. Moreover, "viability . . . is the time at which there is a realistic possibility of maintaining and nourishing a life outside the womb, so that the independent existence of the second life can, in reason and all fairness, be the object of state protection that now overrides the rights of the woman." Finally, drawing the line at viability "has, as a practical matter, an element of fairness. In some broad sense, it might be said that a woman who fails to act before viability has consented to the State's intervention on behalf of the developing child."[54]

The Democrats retook the White House in 1992, and President Bill Clinton's two Supreme Court appointments, Ruth Bader Ginsburg and Stephen Breyer, were widely believed to support the constitutional right to abortion. In 2000, when the Court struck down Nebraska's ban on so-called partial-birth abortions in *Stenberg v. Cahart,*[55] Ginsburg and Breyer formed part of the five-Justice majority, while Justice Kennedy, one of the authors of the *Casey* joint opinion, joined the four dissenters. *Stenberg* demonstrated that, despite *Casey,* controversies about abortion were far from over; they had merely shifted to a new set of questions. Equally important, however, the opinions in *Stenberg* reaffirmed that the joint opinion in *Casey* was the law of the land. For the time being, at least, the Court had recommitted itself to the preservation of *Roe* and the basic right to abortion.

Casey's call for "the contending sides of a national controversy to end their national division by accepting a common mandate rooted in the Constitution" has proved to be little more than wishful thinking. The fight over abortion rights has not gone away. Rather, it continues to be implicated in political struggles over judicial appointments and in a wide range of public policy issues, including regulation of particular medical procedures like partial-birth abortion, abortifacients like RU486, emergency contraceptives and morning-after pills, new reproductive technologies such as human cloning, and the use of embryonic stem cells for medical treatment and scientific research. Although the precise subject matter of contention has changed over the years, *Roe* and the right to abortion continue to be engines of controversy, much as they have in the past.

The Opinions in This Book

In this book, eleven constitutional scholars have rewritten the opinions in *Roe v. Wade* and *Doe v. Bolton.* I asked the participants to prepare opinions addressing what they believed were the key issues in *Roe v. Wade* and its companion opinion, *Doe v. Bolton,* using only materials available as of January 22, 1973, when the decisions were first handed down. The resulting opinions took a variety of different approaches to answering the question of what *Roe v. Wade* should have said.

Several contributors offered what they believed to be the best arguments for grounding (or rejecting) the abortion right using constitutional materials available in 1973. Some tried to improve (or, in the case of the dissenters, demolish) Justice Blackmun's arguments that abortion was a constitutionally protected liberty. Others decided to ground the abortion right in the Equal Protection Clause, taking advantage of the fact that in 1973 the Court's sex-equality jurisprudence was still relatively unformed and could have been fashioned differently from the way it is today. None of the opinions adopted Justice Blackmun's original trimester framework.

Acting as Chief Justice of this mock Supreme Court, I have issued an opinion announcing the judgment of the Court, which strikes down the Texas and Georgia abortion statutes in *Roe* and *Doe.* It is joined by two other participants, Reva Siegel and Mark Tushnet. Their concurrences mean only that they agree with the basic contours of my opinion; their own opinions address what they consider to be the key issues in *Roe* and *Doe* in importantly different ways.

My opinion argues that abortion statutes violate both women's liberty and their equality. Restrictions on abortion compel women to become mothers, with all of the social expectations and duties that come with motherhood. Whether fairly or not, women in American society still bear most of the responsibility for child care. They are expected to make sacrifices for their children, and they feel most of the brunt of social condemnation if their children are not properly cared for. Moreover, because of the strong social expectations about the duties of motherhood, women suffer stigma and shame if they give their children up for adoption. Where a woman's life or health is not at risk, the right to abortion is the right to have a reasonable time to decide whether to take on the responsibilities of motherhood. How long women should have to make that decision should be determined by legislatures in the first instance: "[L]egislatures must specify a period of time during pregnancy in which women may obtain medically safe abortions." After this point, "legislatures may restrict or even completely prohibit abortions, . . . except where an abortion is necessary, in the judgment of medical professionals, to preserve the life or health of the mother." The basic idea behind this formulation is that the right to abortion has two components: Women have a right to decide whether or not to become parents, so the state must afford them an appropriate period of time in which to make that decision. But women also have a right not to be forced by the state to sacrifice their life or health to bear children, and this right continues throughout the pregnancy. My opinion rejects the rigid trimester system in *Roe*. Instead, courts should let states try out different frameworks for abortion regulation. Over time, courts should then judge the validity of these laws based on whether they give women a reasonable time to decide and a "fair and realistic chance" to end their pregnancy.

Reva Siegel argues that the proper basis of the abortion right is women's equality and that the Court's heightened scrutiny for laws that impose sex discrimination should have begun with *Roe v. Wade*. Abortion is a constitutional right necessary to secure women's equal citizenship. Siegel argues that exemptions in abortion statutes like those in *Roe* and *Doe* demonstrate, often in quite telling ways, that abortion restrictions are deeply tied to stereotypical views about the sexes and about the duties of women: "Whatever respect for unborn life abortion laws express," Siegel notes, "state criminal laws have never valued unborn life in the way they value born life." Instead, states "have used the criminal law to coerce and intimidate women into performing the work of motherhood." "Abortion laws do not treat women as murderers, but as *mothers*—citizens who exist for the purpose of rearing children, citizens who are expected to perform the work of parenting as dependents and nonparticipants in the citizenship activities in which men are engaged." Siegel bases her opinion on the equality arguments offered in amicus briefs submitted to the Supreme Court by various women's groups. These briefs grounded the abortion right in what we would today call an antisubordination model of equality law. Siegel's answer to what *Roe* should have said is to give voice to the lawyers who were part of the legal vanguard of the second wave of American feminism and whose arguments were largely ignored by the courts.

Mark Tushnet interprets the question of what *Roe* should have said differently from all the other participants; he asks what were the best arguments that could have been generated by someone who could plausibly have been a Justice on the Supreme Court in 1973. The men who decided *Roe* (there would not be a woman Justice for almost a decade) did not understand the connection between abortion rights and the Equal Protection Clause. In his view, Justice Douglas's concurrence in *Doe* (which was drafted in conversation with Justice Brennan) was the best that the Court probably could have done under the circumstances, and it forms the model for Tushnet's opinion.

Four other participants, Anita Allen, Robin West, Jed Rubenfeld, and Cass Sunstein, concur in the judgment. This means that although they agree that the Texas and Georgia statutes criminalizing abortion are unconstitutional, they do so for different reasons.

Anita Allen grounds her opinion on women's procreative liberty protected by the Due Process Clause of the Fourteenth Amendment. She argues that, because laws that compel women to abort their pregnancies would clearly be unconstitutional, so too should be laws that prevent abortion: "Like the right to prevent pregnancy, the right to terminate pregnancy is a fundamental right."

Jed Rubenfeld argues that the constitutional right to privacy is part of a more general prohibition against totalitarian policies that take over people's private lives and impose a specific occupation on them by force of law. Restrictions on abortion are unconstitutional because they conscript women against their will and force them "to carry out a specific, sustained, long-term, life-altering and life-occupying course of conduct."

Robin West argues that restrictions on abortion violate both women's liberty and their equality. However, she does not base her argument on either sex discrimination or the right of privacy. Rather, she argues that restrictions on abortion impose duties of good samaritanship on pregnant women that states impose on no other persons. Moreover, restrictions on abortion prevent pregnant women from using self-help to avoid the consequences of pregnancies imposed on them in cases of marital rape and coerced sex. Although West believes that the courts should protect a basic abortion right, courts cannot deal with the larger structural problems of sex inequality in the United States. "Mothering children, as we presently socially construct that work," West argues, "is incompatible with the basic rights and responsibilities of citizenship," and this "incompatibility has constitutional implications." But merely striking down abortion laws is "a pathetically inadequate remedy." Emphasizing Congress's duty to interpret and enforce the Fourteenth Amendment independent of the courts, West argues that Congress is the body best able to pass legislation that protects women's equality and secures their equal citizenship.

Yet another way of answering the question of what *Roe* should have said focuses not on the best doctrinal or theoretical justifications for *Roe* but on what was the best way for the Court to perform its institutional role. Cass Sunstein has advanced a theory of judicial minimalism; he argues that in courts should usually decide cases on narrow grounds and refrain from offering comprehensive and controversial justifications for their decisions.[56] By leaving things undecided and underspecifying the grounds for decision, courts can act as catalysts for democratic deliberation and avoid provoking an unnecessary political backlash. Without specifying the exact contours of the abortion right, Sunstein decides *Roe* and *Doe* on the ground that the abortion statutes were "overbroad," that is, that they abridged too much constitutionally protected liberty.

Akhil Amar concurs in part and dissents in part in *Roe* and dissents in *Doe.* He argues that the Texas statute in *Roe* is unconstitutional because it was passed before women gained the right to vote. The Georgia abortion statute in *Doe,* passed in 1968, is another matter entirely, and Amar believes that the Court should have abstained from considering it, leaving the interpretation of the statute to the Georgia courts.

Jeffrey Rosen dissents from both *Roe* and *Doe.* Like Sunstein, Rosen focuses on the Court's proper institutional role, but he argues that the question of abortion rights should be left to legislatures. He takes up many of the arguments made against *Roe* by John Hart Ely in a famous law review article in 1973.[57] In Rosen's view, the Court should have stayed out of controversial questions like abortion because the right to privacy has no basis in the constitution's text, structure, and history and because the Court's previous precedents do not require extension of the right to privacy to abortion. Instead of holding that abortion was constitutionally protected, the Court should have allowed the political process to work out the issue of abortion rights. Rosen notes that abortion reform was just beginning in the early 1970s, and in his opinion, written from the standpoint of 1973, he predicts that the Court's hasty and ill-considered intervention will only cause severe political problems both for the protection of abortion rights and for progressive causes generally in the years to come.

Objections to *Roe* generally fall into two categories, procedural and moral. Procedural objections argue that the question of abortion rights should have been left to the political process. Moral objections argue that the right to abortion is a substantive wrong that should not be elevated to a constitutional right. Rosen's objections to *Roe* are largely procedural. Teresa Stanton Collett and Michael Stokes Paulsen offer the moral case against *Roe*. *Roe*, Collett argues, is the product of a misguided radical individualism that undermines women's liberty and equality. Making abortion freely available will allow men to escape responsibility for sex and parenthood, while "artificial birth control and abortion . . . treat women's bodies as unnatural: something to be altered to conform to the male model." "I refuse to accept," Collett declares, "that women must deny their fertility and slay their children in order to obtain equal access to the marketplace and the public square."

Michael Stokes Paulsen also offers a forthrightly pro-life opinion, arguing that abortion is deeply immoral and that the Court has severely damaged its authority by recognizing it as a fundamental right. "Abortion," he insists, "does not destroy potential life. Abortion kills a living human being." Paulsen writes in a prophetic voice, denouncing the evils of abortion and condemning the Court for having been complicit in the destruction of so many innocent human lives. Paulsen calls on the conscience of Americans to abandon what he regards as the Court's most lawless and immoral opinion, or, as he describes it, "the most awful human atrocity inflicted by the Court in our Nation's history."

Conclusion: Could the Court Have Done Better?

It is hardly surprising that critics of a constitutional right to abortion would find much to criticize in Blackmun's original opinions in *Roe* and *Doe*. But supporters of the abortion right over the years have also found them wanting. Part of the problem stems from Justice Blackmun's altogether too cursory attempts to justify and defend the abortion right, the compromises between the Justices that led to the trimester system, and the Justices' inability to imagine abortion as a question of sex equality as well as a question of liberty.[58] To be sure, Blackmun's opinion in *Roe* does advance from a purely medical model of abortion, which had dominated the conversation for decades. But that conversation was already changing rapidly by 1973, moving in a short space of time from the rights of doctors to the procreative liberty of women to the larger question of women's equal citizenship. The Justices were simply not able to traverse two revolutions in thought in a single opinion.

Moreover, the question of abortion rights is legally difficult and morally complex, bringing together issues of life and death, humanity, equality, and liberty. The problems the Justices faced in *Roe* were as trying in their own way as any set of questions that come before the courts. Given the legal and moral difficulty of the issues and the inevitable need to make compromises, it was perhaps too much to expect that the Court would get it right the first time, under almost anyone's standards of what "getting it right" might mean. That suggests that Justice Brennan's initial instincts were probably correct and that the Court should have been more reluctant to offer hard and fast rules in *Roe* and *Doe*. It might have developed its ideas more fully over a course of decisions, perhaps in tandem with its sex-equality jurisprudence. That would probably not have prevented the emergence of a powerful pro-life movement or made abortion uncontroversial. But it might have produced a fairer, more flexible, and more democratically acceptable set of legal doctrines.

Finally, although the Justices clearly understood that abortion was a controversial question, they failed to recognize sufficiently, as they had in *Brown v. Board of Education,* that whatever they did would cause a significant upheaval in American politics. In hindsight, they probably should have written the opinions in *Roe* and *Doe* with a much greater degree of care about winning public support and assuaging criticism. Chief Justice Warren's decision in *Brown* is a model of eloquence and understatement, brief and statesmanlike, fully aware of its political context and deliberately designed to avoid confrontation and to conserve the Court's legitimacy. Blackmun's opinions in *Roe* and *Doe,* by contrast, although filled with scholarship and medical history, are long-winded and devote a very significant amount of space to technical legal issues. Warren's opinion in *Brown* was written so that it could be republished in newspapers.[59] Blackmun's opinion in *Roe* was so complicated that Blackmun himself at one point contemplated writing an addendum explaining its meaning.[60]

Perhaps *Roe's* most important shortcoming was not its failure to "get it right" but its relative inattention to the interactions between courts and politics and to how courts, whether they like it or not, always work in conversation with the political branches in developing constitutional norms. Defenders of constitutional rights often argue that courts exist to protect rights from political interference. But the actual process of constitutional development is much more complicated. Courts do recognize rights and defend them from legislative abridgement. But those rights also arise out of politics; they are tested by politics, and they are modified by courts as a result of politics. The work of courts, important as it may be, is always an intermediate and intermediary feature of a much longer process of legal development that stretches back into the past and forward into the future. Despite the attention that has been paid to *Roe,* the constitutional right to abortion, as it exists today, is not solely the work of the federal judiciary. Like all important constitutional ideas, it is the work of a dialectical process that engages all of the major institutions of American lawmaking, and it has been fashioned through controversy and strife, through trial and error—and with many mistakes and hesitations along the way—out of the raw materials of American politics.

NOTES

1. 347 U.S. 483 (1954).

2. 410 U.S. 113 (1973).

3. ABC News–*Washington Post* poll, "Public Support for Abortion Depends on Why It's Done," January 21, 2003, available at http://abcnews.go.com/images/pdf/909a2Abortion.pdf.

4. CNN/*Time* poll conducted by Harris Interactive, July 17–18, 2001, available at http://www.pollingreport.com/Court.htm. According to the poll, 57 percent of respondents opposed and 33 percent favored "the appointment of Supreme Court justices who would overturn Roe versus Wade, the Supreme Court decision legalizing abortion." In the ABC News–*Washington Post* poll described earlier, 54 percent supported the *Roe v. Wade* decision when it was characterized as giving women the ability to get abortions if they want one at any time during the first trimester.

5. Compared to the national average, women with incomes under $15,000 were twice as likely as women with incomes above that level to seek abortion, but least likely to be able to afford them. See Stanley K. Henshaw and Katheryn Host, "Abortion Patients in 1994–95; Characteristics and Contraceptive Use," *Family Planning Perspectives* 28:4 (July-Aug. 1996): 140–47, 158 (available at http://www.agi-usa.org/pubs/journals/2814096.pdf).

6. These figures are taken from the Alan Guttmacher Institute, "Facts in Brief: Induced Abortion," available at http://www.guttmacher.org/pubs/fb_induced_abortion.html; Abortion Access Project, "Fact Sheet: The Shortage of Abortion Providers," available at http://abortionaccess.org/AAP/publica_resources/fact_sheets/shortage_provider.htm; Lawrence B. Finer and Stanley K. Henshaw, "Abor-

tion Incidence and Services in the United States, 2000," *Family Planning Perspectives* 35:1 (Jan.-Feb. 2003): 6–15 (available at http://www.agi-usa.org/pubs/journals/ 3500603.pdf); Lawrence B. Finer and Stanley K. Henshaw, "The Accessibility of Abortion Services in the United States," *Family Planning Perspectives* 35:1 (Jan.-Feb. 2003): 16–24 (available at http://www.agi-usa.org/pubs/journals/3501603.pdf). See also Marlene Fried, "Abortion in the United States," *Health and Human Rights* 4 (2000): 174–94; Stanley K. Henshaw, "Factors Hindering Access to Abortion Services," *Family Planning Perspectives* 27:2 (Mar.-Apr. 1995): 54–59 (available at http://www.agi-usa.org/pubs/journals/2705495.pdf).

7. 505 U.S. 833 (1992).

8. Alan Guttmacher Institute, "State Policies in Brief," at http://www.guttmacher .org/pubs/spib.html. See also NARAL Pro-Choice America, *Who Decides? A State-by-State Review of Abortion and Reproductive Rights* (12th ed. 2003). In addition, thirty-one states and the federal government have passed laws that ban so-called partial-birth abortions; the constitutionality of these laws is uncertain. Eighteen states have statutes that restrict postviability abortions in ways that appear to go beyond what is permitted by existing Supreme Court precedents, although the statutes have not been challenged. However, these last two sets of limitations on late-term abortions affect only a very small number of women.

9. Rachel K. Jones, Jacqueline E. Darroch, and Stanley K. Henshaw, "Contraceptive Use among U.S. Women Having Abortions in 2000–2001," *Perspectives on Sexual and Reproductive Health* 34:6 (2002): 294–303 (available at http://www.agi-usa.org/pubs/journals/3429402.pdf).

10. The Alan Guttmacher Institute, "Facts in Brief: Induced Abortion," available at http://www.guttmacher.org/pubs/fb_induced_abortion.html.

11. ABC News–*Washington Post* poll, "Public Support for Abortion Depends on Why It's Done," January 21, 2003, available at http://abcnews.go.com/images/ pdf/909a2Abortion.pdf.

12. Id. In addition, the overwhelming majority of available facilities provide only for early abortions: 97 percent of abortion facilities provide abortion at eight weeks, and 86 percent provide services at twelve weeks, but only 13 percent of providers offer services for abortions at twenty-four weeks.

13. The statistics for late-term abortions provided by the Guttmacher Institute and the Centers for Disease Control are compared and discussed in Janet E. Gans Epner, Ph.D., Harry S. Jonas, M.D., and Daniel L. Seckinger, M.D., "Late-Term Abortion," *Journal of the American Medical Association* 280 (Aug. 26, 1998): 724–29 (available at http://eileen.250x.com/Main/PBAinfo/jsc80006.htm).

14. See Mark Graber, *Rethinking Abortion: Equal Choice, The Constitution, and Reproductive Politics* 41–64 (Princeton: Princeton Univ. Press 1996).

15. David J. Garrow, *Liberty & Sexuality: The Right to Privacy and the Making of Roe v. Wade* 539 (New York: Macmillan 1994).

16. Id.

17. Gerald N. Rosenberg, *The Hollow Hope: Can Courts Bring about Social Change?* 184 (Chicago: University of Chicago Press 1991).

18. 198 U.S. 45 (1905).

19. 381 U.S. 479 (1965).

20. Id. at 484.

21. See Justice Stewart's remarks in *Roe,* 410 U.S. at 170 (Stewart, J., concurring).

22. 405 U.S. 438 (1971).

23. Id. at 453 (emphasis in original).

24. *Roe v. Wade,* 410 U.S. at 153.

25. Id. at 158.

26. Id. at 133, 138–39, 161.

27. Id. at 160.

28. Id.

29. Id. at 164–65.

30. David J. Garrow, *Liberty & Sexuality: The Right to Privacy and the Making of* Roe v. Wade 580–81 (New York: Macmillan 1994).

31. Id. at 582–84.

32. Id. at 584.

33. Id. at 585.

34. 410 U.S. at 173–74 (Rehnquist, J., dissenting).

35. Id. at 222 (White, J., dissenting).

36. 539 U.S. 558 (2003).

37. Ruth Bader Ginsburg, "Speaking in a Judicial Voice," 67 *N.Y.U.L. Rev.* 1185, 1208 (1992).

38. See Ruth Bader Ginsburg, "Some Thoughts on Autonomy and Equality in Relation to *Roe v. Wade,*" 63 *N.C. L. Rev.* 375, 381–82 (1985) ("Roe ventured too far in the change it ordered. The sweep and detail of the opinion stimulated the mobilization of a right-to-life movement and an attendant reaction in Congress and state legislatures. In place of the trend 'toward liberalization of abortion statutes' noted in Roe, legislatures adopted measures aimed at minimizing the impact of the 1973 rulings, including notification and consent requirements, prescriptions for the protection of fetal life, and bans on public expenditures for poor women's abortions.").

39. Republican Party platform, available at http://andrsn.stanford.edu/Abortion/Platform_Planks.html. See also Barbara Hinkson Craig and David M. O'Brien, *Abortion and American Politics* 166–68 (Chatham, N.J.: Chatham House 1993) (reprinting Republican and Democratic Party platform planks on abortion from 1980 through 1992).

40. Republican Party platform, available at http://andrsn.stanford.edu/Abortion/Platform_Planks.html. See also Craig and O'Brien at 166–68.

41. 462 U.S. 416 (1983).

42. For a history, see Ethan Bronner, *Battle for Justice: How the Bork Nomination Shook America* (New York: W. W. Norton, 1989).

43. 492 U.S. 490 (1989).

44. Id. at 520.

45. On the politics behind Souter's nomination, see David Yalof, *Pursuit of Justices: Presidential Politics and the Selection of Supreme Court Nominees* 191–92 (Chicago: University of Chicago Press 1999); David J. Garrow, "Justice Souter Emerges," *New York Times,* September 25, 1994, Sec. 6, p. 1.

46. See "Nomination of Judge Clarence Thomas to Be Associate Justice of the Supreme Court of the United States: Hearings Before the Comm. on the Judiciary, United States Senate," 102d Cong., 1st Sess. pt. 1, 222–23 (1991).

47. 476 U.S. 747 (1986).

48. 505 U.S. 833 (1992).

49. Id. at 844.

50. Id. at 867.

51. Id.

52. Id. at 878–79.

53. Id. at 859.

54. Id. at 870.

55. 530 U.S. 914 (2000).

56. See Cass R. Sunstein, *One Case at a Time: Judicial Minimalism on the Supreme Court* (Cambridge, MA: Harvard Univ. Press 1999).

57. John Hart Ely, "The Wages of Crying Wolf: A Comment on *Roe v. Wade,*" 82 *Yale L.J.* 920 (1973).

58. See, e.g., The Justice Harry A. Blackmun Oral History Project 202 (1995), in which Justice Blackmun argues that *Roe* could not have been decided on equal protection grounds in 1972 and 1973.

59. Richard Kluger, *Simple Justice: The History of* Brown v. Board of Education *and Black America's Struggle for Equality* 898 (New York: Alfred A. Knopf 1975).

60. Garrow, *Liberty & Sexuality* at 587.

Part II

Revised Opinions in *Roe v. Wade* and *Doe v. Bolton*

JANE ROE, ET AL., APPELLANTS,

v.

HENRY WADE.

NO. 70-18.

MARY DOE ET AL., APPELLANTS,

v.

ARTHUR K. BOLTON, AS ATTORNEY GENERAL OF THE STATE OF
GEORGIA, ET AL.

NO. 70-40.

ARGUED DEC. 13, 1971.

REARGUED OCT. 11, 1972.

DECIDED JAN. 22, 1973.

REHEARING DENIED FEB. 26, 1973.

CHIEF JUSTICE BALKIN announced the judgment of the
Court.

These cases present constitutional challenges to Texas and Georgia statutes
that make abortion a crime.

I.

A.

Jane Roe is a single twenty-two-year-old woman, who is proceeding in
this litigation under a pseudonym. She alleges in her complaint that she is
unmarried and pregnant and that she sought to terminate her pregnancy
by an abortion "performed by a competent, licensed physician, under
safe, clinical conditions." Roe states that she could not legally obtain an
abortion in the State of Texas because abortions are permitted only when

necessary to save the life of the mother,[1] and she could not afford to travel to another jurisdiction to obtain a safe and legal abortion. She brought a class action arguing that Texas's criminal prohibition on abortion violates her constitutional rights under the First, Fourth, Fifth, Ninth, and Fourteenth Amendments. James Hubert Hallford, a physician who performs abortions, sought and was granted leave to intervene in Roe's class action, which was also consolidated with a lawsuit brought by a married couple proceeding pseudonymously. A three-judge District Court held that the married couple lacked standing to proceed. It granted Roe and Dr. Hallford declaratory relief on the ground that the Texas statute was unconstitutionally vague and violated the "fundamental right of single women and married persons to choose whether to have children . . . protected by the Ninth Amendment, through the Fourteenth Amendment." 314 F. Supp. 1217, 1225 (ND Tex. 1970). However, because the District Court refused to issue an injunction prohibiting enforcement of Texas's abortion statute, the plaintiffs appealed to this Court.[2]

The appellant in the Georgia litigation, proceeding under the pseudonym Mary Doe, is a twenty-two-year-old pregnant woman. At the time her complaint was filed, she was nine weeks pregnant, both she and her husband were unemployed, and her marriage was disintegrating. During the course of this lawsuit, her husband abandoned her, although they subsequently reconciled. She is the mother of three other children. Her third child was placed with adoptive parents at birth. She lost custody of her previous two children because state authorities determined that she was unable to care for them. She has been a mental patient in the State Hospital.

Georgia's abortion statute requires prior approval by a board of physicians. Doe applied for permission to undergo an abortion at Grady Memorial Hospital in Atlanta. Doe stated that she sought an abortion because she was emotionally and economically unable to care for and support another child. Three weeks after filing her request, she was notified that her application had been rejected by the hospital's abortion committee because her case did not fall under one of the three reasons specified in Georgia's abortion statute: (1) that continued pregnancy would endanger her life or injure her health; (2) that the fetus would likely be born with a serious defect; or (3) that the pregnancy resulted from rape.[3] She then filed a class action against the State attorney general, the district attorney of Fulton County, and the chief of police of the city of Atlanta, seeking injunctive and declaratory relief on the grounds that Georgia's statute violated her constitutional rights. Her lawsuit was joined by twenty-one other individuals. Nine of the named plaintiffs in the complaint were described as Georgia-licensed physicians, seven as nurses registered in the State, five as clergymen, and two as social workers. In addition, two nonprofit Georgia corporations that advocate abortion reform also joined the lawsuit.

A three-judge District Court heard the case, and determined that only Doe's lawsuit was justiciable. The District Court then held that only some parts of the Georgia statute violated Doe's constitutional right of privacy and it issued a declaratory judgment in Doe's favor only as to those portions.[4] It refused to enjoin enforcement of the Georgia statute. Seeking an injunction and broader relief, Doe and the other plaintiffs appealed to this Court.[5]

B.

Before proceeding to the merits, we must decide which of the plaintiffs in the Texas and Georgia cases are entitled to bring their respective lawsuits.

Jane Roe's complaint, originally filed in March 1970, stated that she was pregnant and that she was unable to obtain a legal abortion in Texas because of Texas's abortion statute. From these facts there is no doubt that she possessed standing to challenge the statute even though Texas's criminal prohibition is directed at those who perform abortions, rather than at the women who receive them, for the law effectively prevents her from obtaining a legal abortion in Texas. Texas, however, argues that since neither Roe nor anyone in the class she represents is now pregnant, her case is moot.

Normally, we require that an actual controversy exist at the time of appellate or certiorari review, not simply at the time the action is begun. However, when the issue concerns the rights of pregnant women, the normal human gestation process (which lasts approximately 266 days) is likely to end before a case can be heard or decided by an appellate court. If we adopted the rule proposed by the State of Texas, few cases involving rights of pregnant women would be justiciable beyond the trial stage. Appellate review would effectively be denied. Moreover, although no particular pregnancy lasts as long as the normal appellate process, individual women often become pregnant more than once, and pregnancies are constantly occurring in the general population. Therefore the situation of a pregnant woman asserting her rights clearly falls into the long recognized category of cases "capable of repetition, yet evading review." *Southern Pacific Termi-nal Co. v. ICC*, 219 U.S. 498, 515 (1911). See *Moore v. Ogilvie*, 394 U.S. 814, 816 (1969); *Carroll v. President and Commissioners of Princess Anne*, 393 U.S. 175, 178–79 (1968); *United States v. W. T. Grant Co.*, 345 U.S. 629, 632–33 (1953). In such situations we hold that a litigant's action is not moot. We therefore agree with the District Court that Jane Roe retained standing to bring this lawsuit, that her case still presents a justiciable controversy, and that the termination of her 1970 pregnancy has not rendered her case moot. Because Roe has standing to raise all relevant constitutional claims in the Texas case, and to seek both declaratory and injunctive relief, we need not decide whether her fellow plaintiffs, Dr. Hallford and the married couple, may raise their claims in federal court.[6]

For the reasons discussed above, the lawsuit of the Georgia plaintiff, Mary Doe, is also justiciable and is not mooted by the fact that her pregnancy has terminated. The physicians who joined her lawsuit are not currently being prosecuted or threatened with prosecution under Georgia law, but they have alleged a credible fear of future prosecution if they participate in abortions. This is sufficient to give them standing. See *Epperson v. Arkansas*, 393 U.S. 97 (1968) (recognizing right of school teacher who had not yet been charged criminally to challenge state anti-evolution statute).[7]

The Georgia statute, by its terms, is directed at doctors, rather than at nurses, clergymen, social workers, or abortion advocacy organizations. However, we need not address the standing of the remaining plaintiffs in the Georgia litigation, as their claims are adequately addressed and represented by Doe and the physician plaintiffs. We therefore move on to consider the appellants' constitutional claims.

II.

Appellants argue that the restrictions on abortion found in the Texas and Georgia statutes violate fundamental rights guaranteed under our Constitution, and in particular the liberty guaranteed by the Due Process Clause of the Fourteenth Amendment. In general, courts do not sit to pass judgment on the wisdom of ordinary social and economic legislation. *Ferguson v. Skrupa*, 372 U.S. 726 (1963); *United States v. Carolene Products Co.*, 304 U.S. 144 (1938). However, our task is different when a violation of a fundamental liberty or a basic guarantee of equality is involved. The Texas and

Georgia abortion statutes raise questions both about women's basic civil liberties and women's equality. Moreover, as we shall see, the issues of liberty and equality are intertwined.

In assessing what rights are truly fundamental, we have looked to the textual commitments in the Bill of Rights, and to other portions of the Constitution, such as the Thirteenth, Fourteenth, Fifteenth, and Nineteenth Amendments. However, we have not construed the constitutional text narrowly, recognizing that many additional fundamental rights may reasonably be implied from textual commitments. For example, although the freedom of association is not specifically listed in the text of the First Amendment, we have reasoned that such a right flows naturally out of the rights of speech, press, and assembly. See *NAACP v. Alabama,* 357 U.S. 449, 462 (1958).

Moreover, the Ninth Amendment by its own terms enjoins us to avoid too narrow an approach to fundamental rights. It states that "[t]he enumeration in the Constitution, of certain rights, shall not be construed to deny or disparage others retained by the people." This means that merely because a right is not specifically mentioned in the constitutional text it does not follow that no such right is reserved to the people. The fundamental rights secured by our Constitution belong to the people of the United States, not to the government, and the people are the continuing source of both their content and their meaning. We have seen this repeatedly in the many political and social movements that have sought recognition of rights that made our country freer and more democratic. As times change, and the people call out for protection of their basic rights, courts, legislatures, the executive, and all who interpret the Constitution must recognize that the scope of liberty and equality in a free society is much broader and more responsive to changing circumstances than that which can be set down specifically in a short document like the Constitution. Hence, when reading the text of the Constitution, and particularly its broader and more abstract guarantees of liberty and equality, we must keep the Ninth Amendment's rule of construction in mind.

The framers of the Fourteenth Amendment, concerned that state governments would violate basic liberties, created three broad clauses to secure those rights. The amendment states that no State may deny the privileges or immunities of citizens of the United States, deny any person life, liberty, or property without due process of law, or deny to any person the equal protection of the laws. Although a clause protecting the privileges or immunities of national citizenship might seem to be the most obvious home for the articulation and development of basic rights and liberties, this Court early on read the Privileges or Immunities Clause narrowly in the *Slaughterhouse Cases,* 83 U.S. (16 Wall.) 36 (1873). As a result, we have analyzed the scope of liberty and equality secured by the Fourteenth Amendment primarily through interpretation of the Due Process and Equal Protection Clauses. We have protected basic rights under both clauses, reasoning that where governments unduly burden fundamental liberties, they violate due process of law, see, e.g., *Griswold v. Connecticut,* 381 U.S. 479 (1965), and where they make arbitrary distinctions that burden the exercise of fundamental liberties for some persons but not others, they violate the guarantee of equal protection of the laws. See, e.g., *Shapiro v. Thompson,* 394 U.S. 618 (1969).

A long line of cases has recognized and protected a general right of individual autonomy in matters related to bodily security, family, reproduction, and childrearing.

In *Meyer v. Nebraska,* 262 U.S. 390, 399 (1923), we struck down a Nebraska law that prohibited teaching foreign languages in elementary schools, reasoning that the Fourteenth Amendment protected not only "the right of the individual to contract, [and] to engage in any of the common occupations of life" but also the right "to acquire useful knowledge, to marry, establish a home and bring up children, to worship God according to the dictates of his own conscience, and generally to enjoy those privileges long recognized at common law as essential to the orderly pursuit of happiness by free men." Similarly, in *Pierce v. Society of Sisters,* 268 U.S. 510, 534–36 (1925), we held that an Oregon statute that effectively outlawed private schools violated the rights of parents to raise their children as they saw fit.

Both *Meyer* and *Pierce* were decided in the heyday of economic substantive due process, when this Court struck down a number of regulatory laws on the grounds that they violated principles of freedom of contract. See *Lochner v. New York,* 198 U.S. 45 (1905); *Adair v. United States,* 208 U.S. 161 (1908); *Coppage v. Kansas,* 236 U.S. 1 (1915). The Court has long since repudiated those decisions. See, e.g., *West Coast Hotel v. Parrish,* 300 U.S. 379 (1937) (overruling *Adkins v. Children's Hospital,* 261 U.S. 525 (1923)). Given the existing precedents of the time, both *Meyer* and *Pierce* could have been decided solely on the ground that the statutes violated a laissez-faire conception of freedom of contract, but the Court went further and emphasized "the liberty of parents and guardians to direct the upbringing and education of children," arguing that "[t]he fundamental theory of liberty upon which all governments in this Union repose excludes any general power of the State to standardize its children." *Pierce,* 268 U.S. at 534–35.

Indeed, even as this Court emphatically rejected the doctrine of freedom of contract, see *Olsen v. Nebraska,* 313 U.S. 236 (1941) (upholding a statute fixing the maximum amount that an employment agency might extract from an applicant for employment), it extended the idea of fundamental rights against government manipulation and control expressed in *Meyer* and *Pierce.* Only a year after *Olsen,* in *Skinner v. Oklahoma ex rel. Williamson,* 316 U.S. 535 (1942), the Court struck down an Oklahoma law that imposed compulsory sterilization on certain habitual offenders, while excluding those convicted of embezzlement, tax offenses and other white-collar crimes. The Court, in a decision by Justice Douglas—who was also the author of *Olsen*—argued that the Oklahoma statute violated the Equal Protection Clause because it arbitrarily denied "one of the basic civil rights of man."

> Marriage and procreation are fundamental to the very existence and survival of the race. The power to sterilize, if exercised, may have subtle, far-reaching and devastating effects. In evil or reckless hands it can cause races or types which are inimical to the dominant group to wither and disappear. There is no redemption for the individual whom the law touches. Any experiment which the State conducts is to his irreparable injury. He is forever deprived of a basic liberty.

Id. at 541. The Court held that "strict scrutiny of the classification which a State makes in a sterilization law is essential, lest unwittingly or otherwise invidious discriminations are made against groups or types of individuals in violation of the constitutional guaranty of just and equal laws." Id.

Three features of *Skinner* are worthy of note. First, it explicitly expanded the rights guaranteed by *Meyer* and *Pierce* to encompass the right to procreate and have children.

Second, the case demonstrated that where fundamental rights are involved, liberty and equality are intertwined, for laws that denied some people but not others their basic human rights may violate the constitutional guarantee of equal protection.

Third, the fact that *Skinner* and *Olsen* were decided contemporaneously by the same Court (and, indeed, were written by the same Justice) shows that the rejection of the jurisprudence of *Lochner v. New York* and *Adkins v. Children's Hospital* should not be confused with the rejection of judicial protection of fundamental rights in general. The lesson drawn from the demise of *Lochner*-era jurisprudence was that this Court had focused on protecting the wrong rights, protecting the strongest and most powerful elements of society at the expense of the weakest and most vulnerable, and obstructing democratic self-government in the process.

Responding to the demands of the people and to changing circumstances, this Court eventually recognized that its doctrine of liberty of contract in cases like *Lochner* and *Adkins* did not in fact secure basic economic freedoms for ordinary people. Instead, it remitted many of our citizens to coercive and unfair business practices that deprived them of their substantive economic liberty. See *West Coast Hotel v. Parrish,* 300 U.S. 379, 398–99 (1937). Regulation in the public interest might well be necessary to promote substantive and practical economic freedom for the average person and for the poorest elements in our society. Id. at 397–400. Therefore the state should be permitted to experiment with social and economic regulation in the public interest that sought to secure substantive economic liberty for its citizens, and this Court would not second-guess such attempts if they were rationally related to a legitimate government interest. See *United States v. Carolene Products Co.,* 304 U.S. 144, 152–54 (1938). See also *Williamson v. Lee Optical Co.,* 348 U.S. 483, 487 (1955) ("The day is gone when this Court uses the Due Process Clause of the Fourteenth Amendment to strike down state laws, *regulatory of business and industrial conditions,* because they may be unwise, improvident, or out of harmony with a particular school of thought.") (emphasis added).

None of this meant that the Court would abdicate its role of protecting the fundamental liberties that are reserved to the people. This is clear from a comparison of *Olsen* and *Skinner.* In *Olsen,* the State of Nebraska had passed legislation that attempted to prevent unemployed people—who might be down on their luck and without substantial economic resources —from being manipulated by employment agencies. Whether or not this concern was justified, and whether or not the legislation in question was the best solution to this problem, was left to the legislature to decide. 313 U.S. at 235. *Skinner,* by contrast, did not involve an attempt by a State legislature to adjust economic liberties to prevent private oppression. Rather, it involved an attempt by the State to sterilize unpopular and politically powerless members of the community while exempting those who committed acts just as criminal but who enjoyed more political clout. The

Court understood that the State's control of the right to procreate posed much greater dangers for an open and democratic society than the State's control of everyday economic and fiscal policy.[8]

In *Griswold* v. *Connecticut*, 381 U.S. 479 (1965), we reasoned that the right to have children recognized in *Skinner* included the right of married couples to use contraceptives so as to not to have children. If the state could not prevent people from having children through compulsory sterilization, it followed that it could not compel them to have children through the use of its criminal laws. Once again we explained that we were not dealing with a mere regulation of economic liberty, as was involved in *Lochner* v. *New York,* and that "[w]e do not sit as a super-legislature to determine the wisdom, need, and propriety of laws that touch economic problems, business affairs, or social conditions." 381 U.S. at 482. Connecticut, however, was not attempting to regulate the minimum wage. It had made it a crime to use contraceptives to prevent pregnancy; its ban "operate[d] directly on an intimate relation of husband and wife and their physician's role in one aspect of that relation." Id. See also *Loving v. Virginia,* 388 U.S. 1, 12 (1967) ("The freedom to marry has long been recognized as one of the vital personal rights essential to the orderly pursuit of happiness by free men.") We called the right of intimate relation recognized in *Griswold* the right of "privacy." However, this privacy was not simply a right to secrecy; it was the right to engage in deeply personal decisions about whether or not to have a child, a right with which the state should not interfere.

Last Term, in *Eisenstadt v. Baird,* 405 U.S. 438 (1972), we held that a Massachusetts law that criminalized distribution of contraceptives to single persons but not to married persons for the purpose of preventing pregnancy violated the Equal Protection Clause. We said then that "whatever the rights of the individual to access to contraceptives may be, the rights must be the same for the unmarried and the married alike. If under *Griswold* the distribution of contraceptives to married persons cannot be prohibited, a ban on distribution to unmarried persons would be equally impermissible." 405 U.S. at 452. Although the right of privacy in *Griswold* "inhered in the marital relationship," we pointed out that "the marital couple is not an independent entity with a mind and heart of its own, but an association of two individuals each with a separate intellectual and emotional makeup." Id. Thus, we concluded that "[i]f the right of privacy means anything, it is the right of the *individual,* married or single, to be

free from unwarranted governmental intrusion into matters so fundamentally affecting a person as the decision whether to bear or beget a
child." Id. (emphasis in original).

Our decisions from *Meyer* to *Eisenstadt* demonstrate a continuous concern with the right of the people to make decisions about whether to have
children and to make choices about how those children will be raised.
These two elements are necessarily connected, for parenthood is more
than biological procreation. It is a powerful set of moral and social expectations and conventions. When a child is brought into this world, both
social pressure and individual conscience demand that parents take
responsibility for their offspring, and if they fail in that responsibility they
are often condemned by others, in addition to experiencing their own private sense of guilt and inadequacy.

Living up to the responsibilities of parenthood may require considerable sacrifice. The existence of a child changes a person's life. That is so
whether the person is married or unmarried, single or divorced. Because
the choice whether or not to procreate will have lasting effects on a person's future, and will impose important responsibilities, both sought and
unsought, the justifications for the right of privacy must necessarily be
concerned with the responsibilities of caring for and raising children as
well as the possibilities of creating and giving birth to them. *Griswold* and
Eisenstadt hold that the state may not forbid the use of contraceptives to
prevent pregnancy, not only because individuals have the right to decide
whether to procreate, but because the consequences of procreation are the
responsibilities of parenthood, responsibilities that are felt most heavily by
women in our society and perhaps even more heavily by single women.
Individuals have the fundamental right to decide whether they want to
become parents and assume those responsibilities. When the state bans
contraception, it compels individuals to risk becoming parents—with all
the attendant social expectations and responsibilities—or else give up sexual intercourse. Because the state may not force people to become parents
against their will, it may not put people to this choice.

The question before us today is whether the right recognized in the
unbroken line of cases from *Meyer* and *Pierce* through *Skinner*, *Griswold*,
and *Eisenstadt* extends to a woman's right to terminate her pregnancy
through abortion. We hold that it does. What we have said about the
social expectations and responsibilities of parenthood should explain why
the right to abortion is so important for so many women. If a woman

becomes pregnant and the state prevents her from obtaining an abortion, it forces her, against her will, to be become the parent of a child, an event that will have consequences not only during the course of her pregnancy but for the rest of her life.

The decision to prohibit abortion means, first of all, that the state requires a woman's body to undergo the strains of pregnancy and the difficulties of childbirth, with all the risks to her health that may attend them.

Second, when the state compels a woman to bring a fetus to term, it forces her to become a mother, with all that this word means, socially and morally. Because the woman is the child's mother, she is responsible for its care. That responsibility may utterly transform her life. She may be emotionally or physically unable to care for the child. She may be impoverished, or the additional burdens of raising the child may send her into poverty. Her ability to care for her other children may be compromised by an unwanted pregnancy, and her marriage and relationships may suffer. Her partner may be absent or unwilling to devote significant effort to the nurturance and support of the child. She may therefore have to carry this burden alone.

In our society, women still bear the most significant share of responsibility for child care. Because of society's expectations, they, and not men, are most likely to be condemned if a child is not properly cared for. They, and not men, are expected to make the greatest sacrifices in their lives on behalf of the child's welfare. If the mother gives her child up for adoption, she may suffer enormous guilt and shame. She may feel that she was a failure as a mother, not in the sense of having failed to bring the fetus to term, but in failing to meet the social responsibilities, expectations, and pressures placed on women that constitute the social meaning of motherhood in our society.

When the state makes abortion illegal, it forces pregnant women to assume life-altering obligations, restricting their present and future liberty in the most profound way. This limitation of liberty falls on all pregnant women, but most heavily on the poor. Affluent women in our society have always had ways to end pregnancies quietly and discreetly, often outside the boundaries of the law. Less fortunate women, with fewer resources at their disposal, have been forced to adopt illegal, unsafe, and dangerous methods to end their pregnancies, often with disastrous and even fatal results. There is neither due process nor equal protection of the laws in a system that condemns the poor to a Hobson's choice of compulsory motherhood or illegal and unsafe abortion, while turning a blind eye to abortions discreetly performed for the well-to-do.

III

Criminal prohibitions on abortion not only restrict the liberty of individuals; they also violate fundamental notions of equality between men and women.

The Fourteenth Amendment was premised on the notion that all citizens should enjoy basic civil liberties and that the state should not be permitted to create or maintain an inferior caste or class of citizens. In *Strauder v. West Virginia*, 100 U.S. 303 (1880), for example, we stated that the amendment protected blacks from "legal discriminations implying inferiority in civil society, lessening the security of their enjoyment of the rights which others enjoy, and discriminations which are steps towards reducing them to the condition of a subject race." Id. at 308. Although the amendment was aimed primarily at securing rights for blacks, its language spoke in general terms of the privileges and immunities of citizenship, due process, and equal protection precisely because the framers of the Amendment sought to guarantee basic rights of civil equality to all, including women. Even so, the guarantee of equality for women was compromised by two major factors. First, the framers of the Fourteenth Amendment distinguished civil equality—which concerned basic economic rights to contract and own property—from political equality, which concerned the right to vote. Second, the Framers of the Fourteenth Amendment did not attempt to alter the common law rules of coverture, under which a married woman was held to have surrendered her basic civil rights to make contracts, own and dispose of property, and sue and be sued in her own name. The coverture rules effectively undermined the civil equality of women through the legal fiction that the identities of husband and wife were merged through marriage, and that women consented to the loss of their rights and their legal identity through agreeing to marry. Thus, despite the Fourteenth Amendment's promise of equal citizenship for all, throughout the nineteenth century and much of the twentieth, women were systematically denied basic economic and political rights. Discrimination against them was justified largely through male paternalism and the belief that women's place was in the home. This attitude was summed up in a concurring opinion by Justice Bradley in *Brad-*

well v. Illinois, 83 U.S. (16 Wall.) 130 (1873), which upheld the Illinois Supreme Court's refusal to allow women to become practicing members of the bar:

> [T]he civil law, as well as nature herself, has always recognized a wide difference in the respective spheres and destinies of man and woman. Man is, or should be, woman's protector and defender. The natural and proper timidity and delicacy which belongs to the female sex evidently unfits it for many of the occupations of civil life. The constitution of the family organization, which is founded in the divine ordinance, as well as in the nature of things, indicates the domestic sphere as that which properly belongs to the domain and functions of womanhood. The harmony, not to say identity, of interests and views which belong, or should belong, to the family institution is repugnant to the idea of a woman adopting a distinct and independent career from that of her husband. . . . The paramount destiny and mission of woman are to fulfil the noble and benign offices of wife and mother. This is the law of the Creator.

Id. at 141 (Bradley, J., concurring).

Nevertheless, through social movements, political protest, and social and economic change, women have gradually won recognition for their equal rights. One of the longest social movements in American history, begun in 1848 at the first women's rights convention in Seneca Falls, New York, culminated in the 1920 ratification of the Nineteenth Amendment, which guaranteed women the right to vote. In the twentieth century many of the remnants of the old coverture rules that denied women economic rights for so many years have been abolished by statute. In the past decade, responding to social change and to the demands of the people, Congress has shown increasing sensitivity to sex discrimination. In the Equal Pay Act of 1963, Congress provided that no employer covered by the Act "shall discriminate . . . between employees on the basis of sex." In Title VII of the Civil Rights Act of 1964, Congress expressly declared that no employer, labor union, or other organization subject to the provisions of the Act shall discriminate against any individual on the basis of "race, color, religion, sex, or national origin." In 1972, Congress extended the prohibition on sex discrimination to state and local governments. Finally, section 1 of the Equal Rights Amendment, passed by Congress on March 22, 1972, and submitted to the legislatures of the States for ratification, declares that "[e]quality of rights under the law shall not be denied or abridged by the

United States or by any State on account of sex." Thus, Congress itself has concluded that discrimination based on sex is inherently invidious.

Two years ago we held in *Reed v. Reed*, 404 U.S. 71 (1971), that a mandatory preference for males over females as administrators of estates was an irrational discrimination under the Equal Protection Clause. Because we have generally held that, absent a fundamental right or suspect classification, ordinary social and economic legislation is constitutional if there is any set of facts under which it might be justified, see *United States v. Carolene Products Co.*, 304 U.S. 144, 152–54 & n.4 (1938), our decision in *Reed* implicitly rested on conclusions similar to those of Congress: that sex discrimination is inconsistent with basic guarantees of equality in our Constitution.

The creation or perpetuation of a socially subordinate group through law violates the most central command of the Fourteenth Amendment, and any law or practice that creates or maintains such subordination is contrary to the spirit of our Constitution. *Strauder v. West Virginia*, supra, see also *Brown v. Board of Education*, 347 U.S. 483 (1954). The social movements that led to the ratification of the Nineteenth Amendment and the contemporary actions of Congress show a growing recognition on the part of Americans that laws and practices that discriminate against women treat women as second-class citizens and help maintain and reinforce their lower status vis-à-vis men. We therefore hold that state laws or practices that discriminate against women or that help maintain their subordinate status are constitutionally suspect under the Equal Protection Clause. The question before us is whether laws that prohibit abortion violate this constitutional guarantee.

Restrictions on abortion impose a burden suffered only by pregnant women and by no men. One might object that this in itself does not violate the equality of women because men and women are not similarly situated. Men are not burdened by abortion laws in the same way that women are because only women can get pregnant, and it might be contended that this biological difference justifies the law's different treatment. But the idea of equality enshrined in our Constitution is one of equal citizenship. The question therefore is not whether men and women are different in their capacity to bear children but the difference this difference should be permitted to make in terms of their enjoyment of basic rights of citizenship. If the state uses the capacity of women to become pregnant as a justification for assigning women a second-class status in society, or denies them the full and equal enjoyment of the rights of citizenship, it violates the principle of equal citizenship.

The forms and practices of state action that violate the principle of equal citizenship may be different in the contexts of sex and race. Traditionally, the lower status of blacks has been enforced by separation of the races, degradation, and abuse of the powers of the criminal justice system. As the quote from *Bradwell* suggests, however, the lower status of women in society has largely been achieved through role differentiation, which has been justified by paternalism and appeals to nature and biological differences. The inequality of women in our society has been maintained by ensuring that they are remitted to traditional occupations of home and family and by denying them opportunities beyond those activities socially marked as "women's work."

As we have seen, restrictions on abortion require pregnant women to bear children and become mothers whether or not they wish to. They force women either to devote themselves to traditional roles and responsibilities of child care that lack both status and economic remuneration or else to suffer the stigma and shame of admitting their inability to care for their own children by placing them up for adoption. Restrictions on abortion thus employ basic social expectations about the duties and responsibilities of motherhood as a lever to pressure women into traditional roles of child care. By doing so, they make it more difficult for women to aspire to other opportunities in the public world of work that are structured in ways that are inconsistent with being the primary caregiver of a child (or a number of children, for that matter). Denying women the choice to end unwanted pregnancies thus pushes more women into low-status occupations and conditions of economic dependence. By refusing women a significant choice in the direction of their lives, as well as by denying them control of their bodies, restrictions on abortion reinforce women's subordinate status in society and therefore deny them equal citizenship.

In sum, women's rights to reproductive freedom are secured by the guarantees of liberty and equality in our Constitution. This reproductive freedom has two different aspects: First, women have the right to decide whether or not to become parents and to take on the obligations and responsibilities of motherhood. Second, women have the right not to be forced by the state to sacrifice their lives or their health in order to bear children.

IV.

In order to rebut the liberty and equality arguments for a woman's right to choose an abortion, counsel for the State of Texas offers its own liberty and equality arguments. It asserts that from the moment of conception the fetus is a person under the meaning of the Due Process Clause of the Fourteenth Amendment, which states that the states may not deprive "any person of life, liberty, or property without due process of law." In addition, it maintains that failure to protect the fetus would deny the fetus equal protection of the laws. Hence, Texas argues, granting women a right to an abortion would deny the fetus's constitutional rights.

For three reasons, we think that Texas's substantive due process and equal protection arguments are untenable. First, although the text of the Constitution refers to the word "person" at several points, by and large these references do not make sense when applied to fetuses. It is hard to see, for example, how a fetus could be compelled to testify against itself in violation of the Fifth Amendment.

Second, at common law, abortion was not a felony before "quickening," the point at which a fetus's movements could be felt by a pregnant woman, which usually occurred in the fourth or fifth month of pregnancy. Although Texas's abortion statute was passed in 1854,[9] most states retained the common law rule until well after the Civil War. This suggests that neither at the time of the ratification of the Fifth Amendment's Due Process Clause in 1791 nor at the time of the ratification of the Fourteenth Amendment in 1868 was the word "person" understood or intended to include fetuses. Otherwise, the common law rule that distinguished between fetuses before and after quickening would make no sense and would itself probably be a violation of due process or equal protection, for it is not clear why states could constitutionally have lesser penalties for murdering persons too young to kick.

Third, we may assume that the word "person," like the words "due process" or "equal protection," should not be confined to the original understanding but rather interpreted in light of changing times and circumstances. Even under this assumption, however, there are considerable problems with interpreting the word "person" to include fetuses from the moment of conception. Several statutes, including Georgia's, allow abortions in cases of rape, others in cases of incest. If we were to hold that a fetus was a person under the meaning of the Equal Protection and Due

Process Clauses, it would be very difficult to justify exempting a person's murder from criminal sanction merely because the victim's life arose out of coerced sex or an incestuous union. Many states, including Texas, punish abortion less severely than murder, some do not punish abortion at all before a certain point in the pregnancy, and still others, like Texas, do not hold the mother who seeks an abortion criminally liable but only the doctor. All of these distinctions would be constitutionally problematic under the assumption that from the moment of conception the fetus is a person just like anyone else and that the act of abortion is the deliberate ending of a human life. Although states punish negligent homicide and murder committed in the heat of passion less severely than other forms of murder, abortion involves a premeditated act with the specific intent of ending the fetus's life and therefore would seem to fall into the category of homicide most severely punished in virtually all jurisdictions. Given Texas's argument that "it is surely a denial of equal protection for either the state or the federal government to distinguish between a person who has been born and one living in the womb of its mother," Brief for Appellees at 56, it is not clear that states could constitutionally refuse to outlaw virtually all abortions from the moment of conception if they also punished other forms of murder.[10] We think therefore, that the argument proves too much.

V.

Appellees next argue that even if there is a fundamental right to choose whether to have an abortion, the state has compelling reasons to restrict it. Appellees offer three basic state interests that justify regulation of abortion. The first is the state's interest in protecting the life of the fetus. The second is the interest in preserving the life and health of the mother. The third is the interest in regulating the medical profession in order to promote the professional practice of medicine and the public's health and safety. All three of these interests are legitimate—and the state's interest in potential human life becomes increasingly important to vindicate as the pregnancy proceeds. We do not agree, however, that these interests are sufficient to extinguish the fundamental right in the vast majority of cases, as the Texas and Georgia statutes purport to do.

Appellees argue that even if the fetus is not a person under the meaning of the Constitution, human life begins from the moment of conception, and therefore the state has a compelling interest in its protection from the moment of conception. Alternatively, they argue that even if it cannot be determined when life begins, the state has a compelling interest in the protection of potential human life from the moment of conception.

A fetus is composed of human cells, so from conception we may assume that what is growing in the mother's womb is a potential member of the human species. A different question is at what point the fetus is sufficiently differentiated from the mother that it should be regarded as a separate entity, and still another question is when the fetus is sufficiently developed that it should be regarded as a separate human being with a separate personal identity deserving of protection. Philosophers and theologians over the centuries have offered different answers to these last two questions, and it is by no means clear that they can be resolved merely as matters of scientific fact. However, states often assert interests that combine facts and value judgments. Therefore, for purposes of this case, we may ask whether the state may assert an interest in the fetus's life based on a moral view of when human life begins, or, at the very least, an interest in the potential human life of the fetus. We agree that the state has such an interest, in addition to the interests in maternal health and in the proper regulation of the medical profession to secure public health.

Texas and Georgia, however, do not merely assert that the state has a legitimate interest in the potential human life of the fetus. They assert that it is a compelling interest that allows them to criminalize virtually all abortions. Furthermore, they do not assert that the state's interest becomes more important as the fetus develops during pregnancy, with the idea that women might exercise their fundamental right earlier in the pregnancy. Rather, they assert that the interest is equally compelling at all times from the moment of conception onward. Therefore they argue that even abortions in the earliest stages of pregnancy may be subject to criminal penalties.

Where the state seeks to impose significant restrictions on a fundamental constitutional right, a statute must be narrowly tailored to achieve state interests of the utmost importance. A statute is not narrowly tailored when it is significantly overinclusive, restricting much more than the state's asserted interest would justify, or when it is underinclusive, prohibiting much less than the state's asserted interest would demand. See *Kramer v. Union Free School Dist.* 395 U.S. 621, 632–33 (1969); *Shapiro v. Thompson,* 394 U.S. 618, 631–33 (1969). When the state insists that it must burden a fundamental right because of a compelling interest but its legislation is not narrowly tailored to achieve that interest, this is evidence that the state's asserted interest is not as compelling as it claims—because it is so easily sacrificed to other goals—or that the legislation serves other, unstated purposes that are not so compelling, or may even be impermissible. The last concern is particularly important in the context of abortion, because, as we have seen, restrictions on abortion tend to reinforce the subordinate status of women in society by compelling women to become mothers against their will.

A careful examination of the Texas and Georgia statutes involved in this case undermines the states' claims that these statutes are narrowly tailored to achieve a compelling state interest in preserving potential human life from the moment of conception.

Georgia's abortion statute, like many others, permits an exception for pregnancies due to statutory or forcible rape. 26-1202(a)(2). If Georgia is asserting an overriding interest in the life of human beings from the moment of their conception, it is not clear why fetuses conceived through rape are any less valuable to the state than fetuses conceived through consensual sex by adults. Surely the circumstances of the pregnancy do not make these fetuses less human or less valuable as human beings. Compelling interests may be sacrificed to achieve other interests equally compelling, but Georgia has offered no equally compelling reason to permit the intentional destruction of what it understands to be human lives. Rather, the exemption for rape suggests that the state's interest in the fetus is strongly connected to beliefs about maternal responsibility—that women who are the victims of statutory or forceable rape are not responsible for engaging in sexual intercourse that led to their pregnancy, and for that reason they should have a right to abortion. In the context of its more general prohibition on abortions, Georgia's exemption for rape seems to be premised on the notion that adult women who engage in sex are responsible for the pregnancies that result, even if they are due to contraceptive failure, and even if the sex was the result of coercion that falls short of the legal definition of rape in the relevant jurisdiction. Viewing the state's asserted interests from the standpoint of the pregnant woman, they take on a somewhat different cast, which, given our previous discussion of the relationship between abortion regulation and the maintenance of sex inequality, raises considerable qualms, if not outright skepticism. We do not think that Georgia has a compelling interest in forcing women who have sex to become mothers unless they have been raped.

At oral argument, counsel for Georgia informed us that the exception for rape is also intended to permit abortions for pregnancies resulting from incest. Tr. of Oral Rearg. 32. Although there is some evidence that children born of close relatives have a slightly higher chance of birth defects, most are perfectly healthy. If the State is truly asserting that every fetus is a human life from the moment of conception, it is not clear why fetuses produced through incestuous sexual relations are less worthy of protection than any others. To be sure, in some cases the life of pregnant minors may be endangered by bringing a fetus to term, but not all cases of incest involve minors, and Georgia already has an exemption for situations in which the mother's life would be endangered. Once again, Georgia's exemption undercuts its claim that the interest in fetal life is so compelling from the moment of conception that a woman must be forced to bear a child under all circumstances.

Texas's statute, by contrast, makes no exception for rape or incest. It permits abortion only to save the life of the mother, and it might be justified on the grounds that the compelling interest in preserving potential human life may yield only to the equally compelling interest in preserving existing human life.

Although Texas's law appears to make fewer exceptions than Georgia's and therefore seems more devoted to the principle of fetal life,[11] it actually contains a different sort of exemption. It holds doctors liable for performing abortions, but not pregnant women for having them. This exemption cannot be justified as an incentive for women to turn in the doctors who performed abortions on them, for it also applies to women who ingest abortifacients or otherwise perform abortions on themselves.

Texas's statute is thus conspicuously underinclusive given the state's asserted interests in the protection of fetal life. The most likely reason for the failure to hold women liable is that protection of fetal life was not in fact the statute's actual purpose. When the statute was originally passed in 1854, its goal was to prevent unscrupulous doctors from injuring women through botched abortions. Medicine was a largely unregulated profession at the time, and quacks abounded, preying on the vulnerabilities and fears of pregnant women. If the original purpose of the statute was the protection of maternal health and safety, Texas cannot justify a total ban on abortions today, for abortions can be performed safely by licensed physicians and are often less dangerous to the woman's health than carrying the fetus to term.

If we assume, however, that Texas had passed the identical law today for the asserted purpose of protecting the life of the fetus from the moment of conception,[12] the statute would remain significantly underinclusive. This lack of fit undercuts Texas's claim that protection of fetal life is so compelling that it must override the fundamental rights of women in all circumstances, particularly if Texas is willing to compromise this asserted interest for reasons that are far less compelling.

It is not readily apparent why the State's compelling interest in the life of the fetus is furthered by exempting self-abortions. The fetuses destroyed are just as human as those removed by physicians. One possibility is that the State thinks it hardhearted to prosecute women so desperate that they attempt to perform abortions on themselves. But if such charity is sufficient to trump the compelling interest in fetal life, it is not clear why other women, just as desperate, but who sought the aid of a physician for a safer procedure, should be penalized. Indeed, the incentives produced by the exemption are perverse, directing women toward unsafe methods of self-abortion that escape criminal penalties or toward equally unsafe methods of illegal abortion. And, we might add, neither of these possibilities seems well tailored to promote the life or the health of the fetus.

A second possibility for the exemption is that Texas finds it politically unpalatable to prosecute pregnant women for obtaining or attempting to obtain an abortion. It would rather have pregnant women go outside the state to procure abortions and look the other way at self-abortions performed within the state than face the widespread condemnation that would follow a public prosecution against a woman in such straitened circumstances. But if the State is willing to compromise its interest in fetal life in this manner, we cannot conclude that its asserted interest is as compelling in practice as it claims in theory. Rather, the very fact of Texas's hesitation at prosecuting women—including women who have become pregnant through contraceptive failure or coerced sex—suggests that at some level it too recognizes the deep unfairness of restricting access to abortions from the moment of conception. Where a fundamental right is involved and basic issues of equality are at stake, Texas may not maintain a dual system in which abortions are officially illegal but some are discreetly tolerated for purposes of political expediency.

For this reason we conclude that although Georgia and Texas may assert a legitimate interest in the preservation of potential human life, that interest may not fully extinguish the right to abortion. Instead, that interest must be balanced against the fundamental right of women to control their own lives. It follows a fortiori that the interest in regulation of the medical profession cannot extinguish the fundamental interest of the

woman. Finally, the interest in maternal health actually cuts in both directions. At various points in a woman's pregnancy, particularly the early
stages, some forms of abortion may actually be safer than carrying a fetus
to term.

VI.

A woman's constitutional right to obtain an abortion is subject to reasonable regulation. The scope of permissible regulation is determined by the
underlying purposes of the right. These purposes are twofold, and thus
the right to abortion has two aspects: one concerns a woman's control
over her body; the other concerns her control over the decision to become
a parent. First, women have a right not to be forced by the state to sacrifice
their lives or health in order to bear children against their will. Second,
women have a right to choose the conditions under which they will take
on the responsibilities of motherhood so as to facilitate and secure their
equal citizenship. Therefore, the key question is whether the state's regulatory scheme gives the woman the ability to protect her health and safety,
and offers her a fair and realistic chance to decide whether to become a
parent, through a safe and realistically available method of abortion.

Because many people find abortion morally repellant, there will be
strong pressures for elected officials to restrict the right of abortion under
the guise of health and safety regulation. However, because the woman's
right is fundamental, the state may not impose an undue burden on it or
seek to discourage the woman in order to prevent her from exercising it.
The state may act to protect her health and to inform and educate her
choice, but it may not deliberately place roadblocks in her way or use her
poverty or lack of education as a means of preventing her from making a
choice. The state may not use the interest in maternal health to discourage
or prevent women from obtaining abortions, and the state may not
require women to use a less safe method of abortion in order to discourage or prevent them from obtaining an abortion.

At the same time, a woman's right to abortion is not unlimited. The
state has a legitimate interest in potential human life. Moreover, as the
fetus develops during the later stages of pregnancy, abortion comes more
and more to resemble infanticide.[13] Thus, the state's interest in protecting
unborn life becomes increasingly important to vindicate as the pregnancy
proceeds, and it is strongest in the later stages of pregnancy. Allowing

states to recognize that interest when it is at its strongest is not necessarily inconsistent with the constitutional right to abortion. Where a woman's life or health is not in danger, the right to abortion is the right to a fair and realistic opportunity to choose whether or not to become a mother. In most situations, that choice can and will be exercised in the earlier stages of pregnancy.

A line must be drawn at some point to enable the state to express its sincere and legitimate interest in the human potential of the fetus. But the line must not be drawn so early as to effectively extinguish the constitutional right to choose. There is no magical formula for demarcating such a line with mathematical precision. The balance between the competing factors is essentially legislative, and must be drawn by legislatures themselves.

We hold today that the constitutional right to abortion requires that legislatures must specify a period of time during pregnancy in which women may obtain medically safe abortions. During this period, legislatures may require that abortions be performed by a licensed physician. Legislatures may restrict or even completely prohibit abortions performed after the end of the statutorily defined period, except where an abortion is necessary, in the judgment of medical professionals, to preserve the life or health of the mother. This formulation recognizes the two aspects of the right to reproductive freedom: A woman's right to choose whether to become a parent requires that she be given a reasonable time to decide, but a woman's right to protect her life and health continues throughout the pregnancy.

In deciding upon the appropriate length of the statutory period, legislatures must choose a date that vindicates the woman's fundamental rights under the Fourteenth Amendment, and this choice is subject to judicial review. We have held that women's rights to reproductive autonomy and equal citizenship require that pregnant women have a fair and realistic opportunity to obtain a medically safe abortion. Therefore legislatures must demonstrate that the period they have chosen gives pregnant women such a fair and realistic opportunity. Some women in some circumstances may need additional time, and legislation may take these special circumstances into account. Different combinations of factors and background conditions in different jurisdictions may lead democratically elected legislatures to different judgments about how and where to draw lines. Nevertheless, the basic constitutional obligation remains the same: The pregnant woman must be given sufficient time to recognize the fact of her pregnancy, weigh the difficult moral issues that abortion inevitably involves, consult with those friends and family members she chooses to confide in, locate a physician she trusts to perform the procedure, and travel to the place where the procedure will be performed. The legislature must take these factors into account in defining the length of the statutory period, and it may not use the poverty of pregnant women as a lever to obstruct their practical ability to obtain abortions.

Before the end of the statutorily prescribed period, the state's interest in the potential life of the fetus must yield to the fundamental right of women to choose whether or not to become mothers. Nevertheless, the state may prescribe reasonable health and safety regulations during this period as long as they are tailored to furthering the interest in the woman's health and do not unduly burden her fundamental right to choose. With these guidelines in mind, we now consider the two state statutes before us.

VII.

Texas's criminal prohibition bans virtually all abortions performed by a licensed physician at any point in a pregnancy, except when necessary to save the mother's life. For this reason alone, it is overbroad and therefore unconstitutional.

The Georgia statute, by contrast, imposes a number of substantive and procedural restrictions on abortions. The three-judge District Court in the Georgia litigation struck down the three statutorily specified reasons for permitting an abortion, so that § 26-1202(a) of the statute now provides that it is criminal for a physician to perform an abortion except when it is "based upon his best clinical judgment that an abortion is necessary." Appellants argue that because of the way that the District Court severed portions of the statute, the law no longer gives fair warning as to what conduct is required and therefore is unconstitutionally vague. We need not decide that question, because the Georgia statute is unconstitutional for other reasons.

Even if Georgia's statute were interpreted to allow abortions through-out pregnancy, the statute also imposes three procedural requirements that restrict access to abortions. First, the Georgia statute demands that all abortions must be performed in a hospital accredited by the Joint Commission on Accreditation of Hospitals. Second, it requires that the procedure be approved by an abortion committee composed of members of the hospital staff. Third, it requires that the performing physician's judgment be confirmed by independent examinations of the patient by two other licensed physicians.

For Georgia's statute to be constitutional, Georgia must show that its regulations materially further the woman's interest in health without significantly burdening her right to an abortion. None of these three requirements meet this standard.

Georgia requires abortions to be performed in hospitals, but it has not demonstrated that licensed physicians cannot perform safe abortions in properly licensed clinics. It has not provided substantial evidence to show that the full resources of a licensed hospital are necessary to protect women's health. Appellants and *amici,* by contrast, have provided considerable evidence that the state's interests in maternal health are well served by licensed clinics equipped with staff and services necessary to deal with the complications that arise from abortions, or by clinics that have made arrangements with a nearby hospital to provide those services in case of an emergency. Georgia's hospital requirement unnecessarily limits access to safe abortions for women who are not located near hospitals that perform abortions; it also limits access for poorer women who cannot afford the cost of a hospital stay. Georgia may not impose unnecessary costs on abortion that are unrelated to a woman's health.

Georgia's requirement that the hospital also be licensed by the JCAH only compounds the obstacles placed in the path of the pregnant woman. The JCAH is a nongovernmental organization devoted to articulating optimal standards for medical care rather than minimum standards. Georgia does not require that other forms of surgery be performed only at JCAH-accredited hospitals. Indeed, we were informed at reargument that only 54 of Georgia's 119 counties have a JCAH-accredited hospital. Tr. of Oral Arg. 19. Perhaps equally important, the JCAH's standards are directed at medical and surgical practices generally, and pay no specialized attention to issues of abortion. Georgia has not explained how this requirement furthers its interests in maternal health and safety.

Georgia also requires that a hospital committee composed of members of the hospital staff approve all abortions in advance. Georgia has not informed us of any other surgical procedures, including life-threatening ones, where it requires that a physician's judgment be approved by a hospital committee. Rather, this rule seems designed to supervise and restrain both women who seek abortions and physicians who regularly perform them. Georgia has offered no basis for believing that women will seek abortions for frivolous reasons. Indeed, it is more likely that the decision to have an abortion is one of the most serious and heart-rending decisions that a woman may make in her lifetime. In addition, Georgia has offered no reasons to believe that physicians who perform abortions are more likely than other surgeons to encourage their patients to engage in unnecessary surgery.

For similar reasons, Georgia's requirement that the performing physician's judgment be confirmed by independent examinations of the patient by two other licensed physicians also falls afoul of the Constitution. Georgia does not impose this requirement for any other medical procedures or surgeries, even life-threatening surgeries. If attending physicians are duly licensed by the State, they are presumed capable of deciding what their patients' needs are. If they fail in the exercise of their medical judgment, they may be sanctioned or censured and their licenses revoked. Physicians are trained and encouraged to consult with other physicians as a matter of course in difficult cases, and Georgia has offered no reason to think that physicians will not follow this practice in cases of abortion. Rather, in this as in the other challenged regulations, Georgia appears to be treating abortions as a special kind of medical procedure that should be discouraged through a series of procedural hurdles. It may not burden the exercise of a fundamental right in this fashion.

Appellants also challenge Georgia's requirements under §§ 1201(b)(1) and (b)(2) that the pregnant woman be a resident of the State and that she swear an oath to that effect. Georgia's prohibition is not an internal regulation of its own hospitals; it applies alike to public and private facilities throughout the State, all of which are forbidden to perform this particular medical procedure for nonresidents. Georgia has made no showing that there is a crisis in the delivery of health care for citizens or a shortage of available clinics and hospitals. Under Article IV, § 2, states must provide to citizens of other states the same the privileges and immunities as are enjoyed by its own citizens. We do not think that Article IV § 2 allows a state to prohibit the provision of medical care to noncitizens. See *Toomer v. Witsell*, 334 U.S. 385 (1948). We therefore hold the residency requirement unconstitutional.

VIII.

In both the Texas and Georgia cases, the lower courts granted declaratory relief but not an injunction. We need not decide whether this was error, since we may assume that authorities in both States will not initiate further prosecutions on the basis of statutes that have been declared unconstitutional by this Court.

The decision of the District Court in the Texas case is affirmed. The decision of the District Court in the Georgia case is affirmed in part and reversed in part.

It is so ordered.

N O T E S

1. Texas's abortion statute, codified in Chapter 9 of Title 15 of the Penal Code, Art. 1191-1196, Vernon's Ann.P.C., provides:

Article 1191. Abortion
If any person shall designedly administer to a pregnant woman or knowingly procure to be administered with her consent any drug or medicine, or shall use towards her any violence or means whatever externally or internally applied, and thereby procure an abortion, he shall be confined in the penitentiary not less than two nor more than five years; if it be done without her consent, the punishment shall be doubled. By "abortion" is meant that the life of the fetus or embryo shall be destroyed in the woman's womb or that a premature birth thereof be caused.

Art. 1192. Furnishing the means
Whoever furnishes the means for procuring an abortion knowing the purpose intended is guilty as an accomplice.

Art. 1193. Attempt at abortion
If the means used shall fail to produce an abortion, the offender is nevertheless guilty of an attempt to produce abortion, provided it be shown that such means were calculated to produce that result, and shall be fined not less than one hundred nor more than one thousand dollars.

Art. 1194. Murder in producing abortion
If the death of the mother is occasioned by an abortion so produced or by an attempt to effect the same, it is murder.

Art. 1195. Destroying unborn child
Whoever shall during parturition of the mother destroy the vitality or life in a child in a state of being born and before actual birth, which child would otherwise have been born alive, shall be confined in the penitentiary for life or for not less than five years.

Art. 1196. By medical advice
Nothing in this chapter applies to an abortion procured or attempted by medical advice for the purpose of saving the life of the mother.

Plaintiffs in the Texas case have not challenged the constitutionality of Article 1195.

2. The appeal was brought under 28 U.S.C. § 1253. The District Attorney purported to bring a cross-appeal, also under 28 U.S.C. § 1253. Both sides also took protective appeals to the U.S. Court of Appeals for the Fifth Circuit, which held them in abeyance pending our decision. We postponed a decision on jurisdiction to a hearing on the merits. 402 U.S. 941 (1971).

3. See Ga. Criminal Code § 26-1202(a). Georgia's criminal code provides in relevant part:

26-1201. Criminal Abortion. Except as otherwise provided in section 26-1202, a person commits criminal abortion when he administers any medicine, drug or other substance whatever to any woman or when he uses any instrument or other means whatever upon any woman with intent to produce a miscarriage or abortion.

26-1202. Exception.
(a) Section 26-1201 shall not apply to an abortion performed by a physician duly licensed to practice medicine and surgery pursuant to Chapter 84-9 or 84-12 of the Code of Georgia of 1933, as amended, based upon his best clinical judgment that an abortion is necessary because:
  (1) A continuation of the pregnancy would endanger the life of the pregnant woman or would seriously and permanently injure her health; or
  (2) The fetus would very likely be born with a grave, permanent, and irremediable mental or physical defect; or
  (3) The pregnancy resulted from forcible or statutory rape.
(b) No abortion is authorized or shall be performed under this section unless each of the following conditions is met:
  (1) The pregnant woman requesting the abortion certifies in writing under oath and subject to the penalties of false swearing to the physician who proposes to perform the abortion that she is a bona fide legal resident of the State of Georgia.
  (2) The physician certifies that he believes the woman is a bona fide resident of this State and that he has no information which should lead him to believe otherwise.
  (3) Such physician's judgment is reduced to writing and concurred in by at least two other physicians duly licensed to practice medicine and surgery pursuant to Chapter 84-9 of the Code of Georgia of 1933, as amended, who certify in writing that based upon their separate personal medical examinations of the pregnant woman, the abortion is, in

their judgment, necessary because of one or more of the reasons enumerated above.

(4) Such abortion is performed in a hospital licensed by the State Board of Health and accredited by the Joint Commission on Accreditation of Hospitals.

(5) The performance of the abortion has been approved in advance by a committee of the medical staff of the hospital in which the operation is to be performed. This committee must be one established and maintained in accordance with the standards promulgated by the Joint Commission on the Accreditation of Hospitals, and its approval must be by a majority vote of a membership of not less than three members of the hospital's staff; the physician proposing to perform the operation may not be counted as a member of the committee for this purpose.

(6) If the proposed abortion is considered necessary because the woman has been raped, the woman makes a written statement under oath, and subject to the penalties of false swearing, of the date, time and place of the rape and the name of the rapist, if known. There must be attached to this statement a certified copy of any report of the rape made by any law enforcement officer or agency and a statement by the solicitor general of the judicial circuit where the rape occurred or allegedly occurred that, according to his best information, there is probable cause to believe that the rape did occur.

(7) Such written opinions, statements, certificates, and concurrences are maintained in the permanent files of such hospital and are available at all reasonable times to the solicitor general of the judicial circuit in which the hospital is located.

(8) A copy of such written opinions, statements, certificates, and concurrences is filed with the Director of the State Department of Public Health within 10 days after such operation is performed.

(9) All written opinions, statements, certificates, and concurrences filed and maintained pursuant to paragraphs (7) and (8) of this subsection shall be confidential records and shall not be made available for public inspection at any time.

(c) Any solicitor general of the judicial circuit in which an abortion is to be performed under this section, or any person who would be a relative of the child within the second degree of consanguinity, may petition the superior court of the county in which the abortion is to be performed for a declaratory judgment whether the performance of such abortion would violate any constitutional or other legal rights of the fetus. Such solicitor general may also petition such court for the purpose of taking issue with compliance with the requirements of this section. The physician who proposes to perform the abortion and the pregnant woman shall be respondents. The petition shall be heard expeditiously and if the court adjudges that such abortion would violate the constitutional or other legal rights of the fetus, the court shall so declare and shall restrain the physician from performing the abortion.

(d) If an abortion is performed in compliance with this section, the death of the fetus shall not give rise to any claim for wrongful death.

(e) Nothing in this section shall require a hospital to admit any patient under the provisions hereof for the purpose of performing an abortion, nor shall any hospital be required to appoint a committee such as contemplated under subsection (b)(5). A physician, or any other person who is a member of or associated with the staff of a hospital, or any employee of a hospital in which an abortion has been authorized, who shall state in writing an objection to such abortion on moral or religious grounds shall not be required to participate in the medical procedures which will result in the abortion, and the refusal of any such person to participate therein shall not form the basis of any claim for damages on account of such refusal or for any disciplinary or recriminatory action against such person.

26-1203. Punishment. A person convicted of criminal abortion shall be punished by imprisonment for not less than one nor more than 10 years.

4. In particular, the District Court struck down portions of §§ 26-1202(a) and (b)(3) that permit abortions only where the life of the woman would be endangered, the fetus would be born with severe birth defects, or the pregnancy resulted from rape. The District Court also struck down § 26-1202(b)(6), which requires certification in situations involving pregnancies caused by rape; and § 26-1202(c), which authorized state officials or relatives to petition the court for injunctions against abortions.

5. We postponed a decision on jurisdiction to the hearing on the merits. 402 U.S. 941 (1971). We dismissed the defendants' attempt to cross-appeal the District Court's decision for want of jurisdiction. 402 U.S. 936 (1971). An alternative appeal of that decision is currently pending in the United States Court of Appeals for the Fifth Circuit. The constitutionality of those provisions of Georgia's statute struck down by the District Court is not technically before us, *Swarb v. Lennox*, 405 U.S. 191 (1972), but our decision today obviously affects the resolution of those issues before the Fifth Circuit.

6. Dr. Hallford, a physician who performs abortions, sought and was granted leave to intervene in Roe's class action. He alleged that he had been arrested for violating Texas abortion statutes and that two prosecutions are still pending against him. We have held that state criminal defendants may not challenge pending criminal prosecutions in federal court if they could raise their federal constitutional claims adequately in state proceedings. *Younger v. Harris*, 401 U.S. 37 (1971). However, *Younger* may not properly apply if, as Dr. Hallford asserts, under Texas

law, he cannot, in the pending state criminal proceedings, seek temporary injunctive relief that would allow him to perform new abortions. We need not decide if this assessment of Texas state law is correct, or whether *Younger* would apply if it is correct. If Roe is able to obtain a declaration that the Texas statute is unconstitutional, this will resolve the constitutional issues in Dr. Hallford's criminal prosecution. Such a holding would also resolve the constitutional claims made by the married couple, who are proceeding under the pseudonyms John and Mary Doe (not to be confused with the Mary Doe in the Georgia case, *Doe v. Bolton*). The Does stated that Mrs. Doe, on the advice of her doctor, had given up the use of birth control pills for health reasons. They argued that this inhibited their present conjugal relations. Because of possible contraceptive failure, Mrs. Doe might someday become pregnant. Because her doctor had advised her to avoid pregnancy, she wanted the ability to terminate her pregnancy by an abortion performed by a competent, licensed physician under safe, clinical conditions.

7. The Court was also informed at oral argument that physicians had been prosecuted under the predecessor to Georgia's recent 1968 abortion statute. Tr. of Oral Arg. 21–22.

8. In his famous dissent in *Lochner,* Justice Holmes famously insisted that courts should not impose a particular view of economic liberty, leaving controversial questions of economic policy to legislatures. But even Justice Holmes agreed that the liberty protected by the Due Process Clause should extend to "fundamental principles as they have been understood by the traditions of our people and our law." 198 U.S. at 76 (Holmes, J., dissenting), and he repeatedly asserted the duty of this Court to protect freedom of speech and association against infringement. See, e.g., *Abrams v. United States*, 250 U.S. 616, 624 (1919) (Holmes, J., dissenting); *Gitlow v. New York*, 268 U.S. 652, 672 (1925) (Holmes, J., dissenting). We think that his opinion in *Buck v. Bell*, 274 U.S. 200 (1927), shows the limitations of a full-scale abdication of judicial review. There the Court upheld a compulsory sterilization law for mental incompetents that applied only to those persons confined in state institutions and not to the much greater number of mentally incompetent persons living outside. Justice Holmes summarily dismissed the claim that this policy failed to provide equal protection of the laws, arguing that it was "the usual last resort of constitutional arguments to point out shortcomings of this sort," 274 U.S. at 208. Upholding the law against a due process challenge, he stated brusquely that "three generations of imbeciles are enough." Id. at 207. Although we distinguished *Buck v. Bell* rather than directly overruling it in *Skinner v. Oklahoma,* we have refused to extend Justice Holmes's reasoning in our subsequent jurisprudence, and it is hard to regard the decision as one of this Court's shining moments.

9. Texas Laws 1854, c. 49 § 1, set forth in 3 Gammel, Laws of Texas, 1502 (1898). The statute was modified into what is essentially the present statute in 1857. See Texas Penal Code of 1857, Arts. 531–536; Paschal's Laws of Texas, Arts. 2192–2197

(1866); Texas Rev. Stat. Arts. 536–541 (1879); Texas Rev. Crim. Stat., Arts. 1071–1076 (1911).

10. Even Texas's exemption for abortions necessary to save the life of the mother might raise constitutional problems under this theory. We do not assume that there is any constitutional problem with a state's allowing a defense of self-defense to a charge of murder, perhaps even when the self-defense is against an innocent attacker who does not understand the danger he poses. Nevertheless, the defense of self-defense usually requires a reasonable fear of imminent danger to the defendant. A threat to a woman's health might be discovered long before it becomes necessary to abort, and doctors might well be tempted to exaggerate the danger in order to permit the abortion. Hence, if the fetus is a person, it is not clear why the fetus should not be entitled to a judicial hearing (with appropriate representation by counsel appointed by the court, cf. *Gideon v. Wainwright,* 372 U.S. 335 (1963) (holding that the Constitution requires appointment of counsel for criminal defendant who cannot afford one) before the mother and her doctor would be entitled by law to end the fetus's life. However, Texas's abortion law does not provide for such hearings to protect the rights of the fetus.

Moreover, as we discuss infra, Texas does not make it a crime for women to perform abortions on themselves. If a fetus is a person under the meaning of the Fourteenth Amendment, it is not clear how the exemption for self-abortions would withstand scrutiny under the Due Process or Equal Protection Clauses.

11. At oral argument, counsel for the State of Texas conceded that there was an unofficial practice of not prosecuting doctors for performing early abortions in cases of rape where the woman had reported the rape promptly. If so, then Texas's balancing of interests is more like Georgia's than is apparent from the statutory language.

12. See *Thompson v. State,* 493 S.W. 2d 913, 918 (1971), in which the court declared that "the State of Texas has a compelling interest to protect fetal life" and that Art. 1191 "is designed to protect fetal life."

13. We note that in a separate provision, Art. 1195, Texas makes it a crime to kill a child "in a state of being born" during "parturition of the mother." The penalties for this offense are more severe than for ordinary abortion. Appellants do not challenge its constitutionality.

SIEGEL, J., concurring.

I concur in the opinion of the Chief Justice holding the Texas and Georgia abortion statutes unconstitutional. I write separately to state what I understand to be the principal constitutional basis for that judgment.

Government has long regulated women's lives on the assumption that their family role made them different kinds of citizens from men. But what is customary is not always constitutional. Too often, laws that single women out for special treatment in virtue of their maternal role have excluded women from participating as equals with men in core activities of citizenship. As we have now come to understand it, the equal citizenship principle embodied in the Fourteenth and Nineteenth Amendments prohibits state action premised on traditional assumptions about the sexes that perpetuates second-class citizenship for women. For this reason, laws that regulate women's conduct as mothers warrant careful constitutional scrutiny. The criminal abortion statutes here in issue, which coerce pregnant women to perform the work of motherhood, do not survive such scrutiny. The statutes reflect and enforce traditional assumptions about the sexes, and can no longer be reconciled with the understanding that women are equal citizens with men.

Understandings of the equal citizenship principle evolve in history. In this opinion I demonstrate, first, that an emerging understanding of the equal citizenship principle warrants careful scrutiny of traditional modes of regulating women's conduct, and, second, that the criminal abortion statutes in issue violate this emergent understanding of the equal citizenship principle.

I.

Americans have long defined themselves as a people committed to values of liberty and equality. But the nation's understanding of those values has shifted, quite substantially, over the centuries. At times these shifts in understanding occur incrementally and imperceptibly; at others, such changes have grown out of extended periods of national self-examination.

Debates over the meaning of the equal citizenship principle are the pride—the very life—of our constitutional tradition. Such debates can bring the community to question customs and traditions that seem to define it. For, as the nation has forged new understandings of its constitutional commitments, it has, from time to time, come to change institutions and practices that have long defined the community, in order to bring its ways of life in line with evolving understandings of its core constitutional values.

It was by reason of our willingness to wrestle with the meaning of our constitutional commitments and to reconsider entrenched practices in light of new understandings that we fought the great civil war that transformed this nation from a nation of slavery to a nation of freedom. It was by reason of our willingness to reconsider the meaning of our founding commitments that, after seventy-five years of debate, the nation amended its constitution to give half the adult population the right to vote.

We can see this practice of debate, reflection, and revision of constitutional understandings in our own day. One hundred years after the nation abolished slavery, the nation is still revising its understanding of how the equal citizenship principle governs state regulation of race. See *Harper v. Virginia Board of Elections*, 383 U.S. 663, 669–70 (1966) (striking down Virginia's poll tax under the Equal Protection Clause):

> [T]he Equal Protection Clause is not shackled to the political theory of a particular era. In determining what lines are unconstitutionally discriminatory, we have never been confined to historic notions of equality. . . . Notions of what constitutes equal treatment for purposes of the Equal Protection Clause *do* change. This Court in 1896 held that laws providing for separate public facilities for white and Negro citizens did not deprive the latter of the equal protection and treatment that the Fourteenth Amendment commands. *Plessy v. Ferguson*, 163 U.S. 537. Seven of the eight Justices then sitting subscribed to the Court's opinion, thus joining in expressions of what constituted unequal and discriminatory treatment that sound strange to a contemporary ear. When, in 1954—more than a half-century later—we repudiated the "separate-but-equal" doctrine of *Plessy* as respects public education, we stated: "In approaching this problem, we cannot turn the clock back to 1868 when the Amendment was adopted, or even to 1896

when *Plessy v. Ferguson* was written." *Brown v. Board of Education,* 347 U.S. 483, 492.

Moved by an evolving understanding of equal citizenship in matters of race, in the past several decades, this Court has interpreted the Fifth and Fourteenth Amendments to require governments to change traditional ways of regulating education, politics—even the family.[1] These same evolving understandings of equal citizenship prompted the President to order a reorganization of the military[2] and moved Congress to prohibit certain customary practices in the world of work, politics, housing, and public accommodations.[3]

We are now in just such a period of national struggle and reassessment about the meaning of equal citizenship values, not only as they bear on the great question of race in American life but also as they illuminate fundamental questions concerning relations between the sexes. Cf. *White v. Crook,* 251 F. Supp. 401, 406–7, 408 (M.D. Ala. 1966) (holding Alabama's exclusion of Negroes and of women from jury service unconstitutional) ("The argument that the Fourteenth Amendment was not historically intended to require the states to make women eligible for jury service reflects a misconception of the function of the Constitution and this Court's obligation in interpreting it. The Constitution of the United States must be read as embodying general principles meant to govern society and the institutions of government as they evolve through time. It is therefore this Court's function to apply the Constitution as a living document to the legal cases and controversies of contemporary society."). These changes in the nation's understanding of the equal citizenship principle call into question practices long thought constitutional.

II.

At birth, this nation declared itself committed to values of liberty and equality, but its founders understood those commitments to apply variously to different adult members of the community. The founding generations tolerated or practiced slavery and understood marriage to vest men with near-total control over women's lives.

Public and private institutions of the early republic presumed that women were men's inferiors and dependents. Constitutional and common law rested on the assumption that dependency was a free woman's lifelong estate, and that, as a young woman matured, she would move from the jurisdiction of her father to that of her husband. Thus, in all states, men barred women from voting, on the theory that male relatives would or should represent them.[4] The common law organized the institution of marriage to give husbands authority over their wives—authority to represent, to subject, and to discipline; the law secured this authority by giving husbands rights in their wives' real and personal property and in the value of their wives' labor. In nominal exchange, the common law gave wives the rights of a dependent: a right to support from their husbands that had no direct means of enforcement at law. 1 Blackstone, *Commentaries on the Laws of England,* 430–33 (1765) (describing the wife's loss of personal rights, the husband's right to discipline his wife, and his duty to support her) ("By marriage, the husband and wife are one person in law: that is, the very being or legal existence of the woman is suspended during the marriage, or at least is incorporated and consolidated into that of the husband: under whose wing, protection, and cover, she performs every thing."); 2 Blackstone, *Commentaries on the Laws of England,* 433–36 (1765) (describing the husband's acquisition of rights in his wife's property). Social practice buttressed this order of legally coerced dependency. Over the centuries, women were barred, first by custom and then by law, from serving in a variety of trades and occupations reserved to men; even today, women receive little more than half the pay of men who have equal educational attainment and perform similar work.[5] These constitutionally sanctioned laws and customs denied women the opportunity to support themselves and so only amplified the intense pressure on women to marry —a pressure only women of independent means might resist. See generally Leo Kanowitz, *Women and the Law: The Unfinished Revolution* (1969); John D. Johnson & Charles L. Knapp, "Sex Discrimination by Law: A Study in Judicial Perspective," 46 *N.Y.U. L. Rev.* 675 (1971).

Systems of dominion are neither total nor stable, especially in a society as skeptical of aristocracy and status as is ours. See U.S. Const., art. I, § 9, cl. 8 (prohibiting titles of nobility). By the Civil War era, a nascent women's movement had begun to challenge this order of male privilege, invoking the magisterial cadences of the Declaration of Independence to do so. See 1 *History of Woman Suffrage* 70 (Elizabeth Cady Stanton, Susan B. Anthony, & Matilda Joslyn Gage, eds.) (1881) (reproducing the Declaration of Sentiments first delivered at the suffrage movement's inaugural Seneca Falls convention in 1848) ("We hold these truths to be self-evident: that all men and women are created equal; that they are endowed by their

Creator with certain inalienable rights; that among these are life, liberty, and the pursuit of happiness; that to secure these rights governments are instituted, deriving their just powers from the consent of the governed."). The nineteenth-century woman's rights movement protested both the common law of marital status and the constitutional order of male suffrage; by the war's end, the movement had claimed for women the right to vote and to practice law under the newly ratified Fourteenth Amendment. See 2 *History of Woman Suffrage* 407 (Elizabeth Cady Stanton, Susan B. Anthony, & Matilda Joslyn Gage, eds.) (1882) (account of the suffrage movement's "New Departure" in which women attempted to vote and enter professions under the Fourteenth Amendment). See also id. at 407– 520 (reproducing constitutional argumentation before Congress); id. at 586–755 (reporting trials of women who attempted to vote under the Fourteenth Amendment).

These protests were successful initially in producing modest state law reform of marriage and, from this Court, an energetic defense of the status quo. In the immediate aftermath of the Civil War, this Court ruled that the exclusion of all women from the franchise was consistent with the basic principles organizing our constitutional order. *Minor v. Happersett*, 88 U.S. (21 Wall) 162, 177 (1874). Similarly, it upheld sex-based legislation restricting women's market opportunities as premised on the reasonable understanding that "[t]he paramount destiny and mission of woman are to fulfill the noble and benign offices of wife and mother. This is the law of the Creator." *Bradwell v. Illinois*, 83 U.S. (16 Wall) 130, 141 (1873) (Bradley, J., concurring). See also *Muller v. Oregon*, 208 U.S. 412, 422 (1908) ("Her physical structure and a proper discharge of her maternal functions— having in view not merely her own health, but the well-being of the race —justify legislation to protect her from the greed as well as the passion of man.").

In time, however, the woman suffrage movement prevailed. Women persuaded those with power voluntarily to cede some of it, by emphasizing the principles of liberty and equality at the heart of our constitutional tradition, by appeal to the principle of self-representation for which the Revolution had been fought, and by appeal to the anticaste principle animating the nation's searing struggles over slavery. Nearly three-quarters of a century after the Seneca Falls convention, at which the movement first invoked the Declaration of Independence to protest male suffrage, We the People responded by amending the Constitution to provide that "The right of the citizens of the United States to vote shall not be denied or abridged by the United States or by any State on account of sex." U.S. Const., amend. XIX, § 1. The suffrage amendment transformed constitutional assumptions about family and federalism that had endured since the founding. It broke with the premise of male household headship that had long justified women's disfranchisement and for the first time in constitutional history applied to women as a group the principles of self-representation and anticaste for which the Revolution and Civil War had been fought.

Yet, enfranchising women 150 years after the founding of the republic has not sufficed to confer upon them equality of citizenship in fact. Women may vote, but if we look to those spheres where citizens commonly participate in collective life—to the realms of politics, work, and education—we find that women do not hold positions of authority and often do not even participate, at times still by reason of express prohibition. More than half the nation's citizens are women, but there has never been a female president; no woman presently sits in the Senate, only fourteen sit in the House, and scarcely any have ever been appointed as judges. See Sassower, "Women in the Law: The Second Hundred Years," 57 A.B.A. J. 329, 330–31 (1971) (observing that there are three women serving as federal district judges and one woman who is a federal court of appeals judge). It is only ten years since Congress barred the practice of openly paying men and women different amounts for the same work (Equal Pay Act of 1963, 77 Stat. 56, 56–57, as amended, 29 U.S.C.S. § 206(d)). Sex lines in education and employment are common, and it is only in the past several years that we as a nation have begun to judge them wrongful. See Title IX of the Education Amendments of 1972, 86 Stat. 235, 373–75, 20 U.S.C.S. §§ 1681 et seq. (prohibiting sex discrimination in all education programs that receive federal funds); *Mengelkoch v. Industrial Welfare Commission,* 442 F.2d 1119 (9th Cir. 1971) (holding that the question of whether a California statute limiting the number of hours women could work violated equal protection posed a substantial constitutional question, thereby justifying a three-judge panel); *Sail'er Inn, Inc. v. Kirby,* 5 Cal.3d 1, 20 (Cal. 1971) (invalidating under the Equal Protection Clause a California law prohibiting women from working as bartenders) ("Laws which disable women from full participation in the political, business and economic arenas are often characterized as 'protective' and beneficial. Those same laws applied to racial or ethnic minorities would readily be recognized as invidious and impermissible. The pedestal upon which women have been placed has all too often, upon closer inspection, been revealed as a cage."); Equal

Employment Opportunities Commission Guidelines, 29 C.F.R. § 1604, 2(b) (amended in 1969 to declare states' protective labor legislation in conflict with Title VII) ("The commission has found that such laws ... do not take into account the capacities, preferences, and abilities of individual females and tend to discriminate rather than protect"). As this society begins to question long-standing traditions, stereotypical assumptions about the roles of men and women that for centuries justified women's disfranchisement and subordination in marriage continue to shape institutions and practices in the public and private spheres.

It was with the understanding that the vote was but the first step toward true equality of citizenship that women across the nation joined in a strike for equality on August 26, 1970, the half-century anniversary of the Nineteenth Amendment's ratification. The strike emphasized that an equal right to vote has not sufficed to make women equal citizens with men. See Linda Charlton, "Women March Down Fifth Avenue in Equality Drive," *New York Times,* Aug. 27, 1970, p. 1. To realize the Nineteenth Amendment's promise, the nation would have to extend the principles of liberty and equality on which the Amendment was based and repudiate understandings and practices that had developed during the long period when the nation thought it reasonable to treat women as dependent, disenfranchised citizens. The strike memorialized ratification of the suffrage amendment with the message that women will not have an equal opportunity to participate in the core activities of citizenship—education, employment and politics—until the nation transforms the conditions in which women bear and rear children. With this understanding, the strike sought ratification of the Equal Rights Amendment now before the states, and three interlocking reforms: equal opportunity in education and work, as well as rights to child care and rights to abortion that would enable women to avail themselves of these new opportunities. Id. at 1, 30; see also 116 Cong. Rec. S22,216–17 (June 30, 1970) (printing Margaret Crimmins, "Drum-Beating for Women's Strike," *Wash. Post,* June 30, 1970, at D3).

The President responded by establishing the President's Task Force on Women's Rights and Responsibilities, a committee charged with "review-[ing] the present status of women in our society and recommend[ing] what might be done in the future to further advance their opportunities." 117 *Cong. Rec.* S30,158, (1971) (recommending the enactment of antidiscrimination legislation and reform of child care, including "[a]doption of the liberalized provisions for child care in the family assistance plan and authorization of Federal aid for child care for families not covered by the family assistance plan"). As the President recently observed on the anniversary of the Nineteenth Amendment's ratification: "As significant as the ratification of the Nineteenth Amendment was, it was not cause for ending women's efforts to achieve their full rights in our society. Rather, it brought an increased awareness of other rights not yet realized." Presidential Proclamation No. 4147, reprinted in 8 *Weekly Comp. Pres. Doc.* 1286, 1286–87 (Aug. 26, 1972).

Congress, too, has responded. It has reaffirmed the nation's commitment to the equal citizenship principle and signaled the nation's determination to ensure that women are equal participants in all spheres of civic life. A decade ago, it passed the Equal Pay Act of 1963, which provides that no employer covered by the Act "shall discriminate . . . between employees on the basis of sex." 77 Stat. 56, as amended, 29 U.S.C.S. § 206 (d). See generally Thomas E. Murphy, "Female Wage Discrimination: A Study of the Equal Pay Act 1963–1970," 39 *U. Cin. L. Rev.* 615 (1970). And, in enacting Title VII of the Civil Rights Act of 1964, Congress expressly declared that no employer, labor union, or other organization subject to the provisions of the Act shall discriminate against any individual on the basis of "race, color, religion, sex, or national origin." 78 Stat. 253, 42 U.S.C.S. § 2000e et seq.

Congress is now acting steadily to extend these commitments. The Equal Rights Amendment, passed by Congress on March 22, 1972, and submitted to the legislatures of the States for ratification, declares that "(e)quality of rights under the law shall not be denied or abridged by the United States or by any State on account of sex." H.R.J.Res. No. 92-208 (1972). And when Congress used its power to enforce the Fourteenth Amendment to apply the employment discrimination provisions of the Civil Rights Act of 1964 to the states, it took special care to emphasize the urgency of combating sex discrimination. Equal Employment Opportunity Act of 1972, 86 Stat. 103, 103; H.R. Rep. No. 92-238, at 5 (1971), reprinted in 1972 U.S.C.C.A.N. 2137, 2141 ("Discrimination against women is no less serious than other forms of prohibited employment practices and is to be accorded the same degree of social concern given to any type of unlawful discrimination."); see also S. Rep. No. 92-415, at 7–8 (1971). This same Congress prohibited sex discrimination in all educational programs that receive federal funds, Title IX of the Education Amendments of 1972, 86 Stat. 235, 373–75, 20 U.S.C.S. §§ 1681 et seq., and enacted a wide variety of statutes that prohibit sex discrimination in public- and private-sector transactions.[6] In this same session, Congress embarked upon the project of alleviating conflicts between work and family by enacting a tax credit for child care expenses. Revenue Act of 1971, 85 Stat. 497, 518–20, (allowing working parents with combined incomes of up to $18,000 a year to take tax deductions for child care of up to $400 a month and those with combined incomes above $18,000 to take a more modest deduction). Thus, Congress itself has concluded that the equal citizenship principle requires the nation to change customary ways of organizing relations between the sexes, and this conclusion of a coequal branch of Government is not without significance to the question presently under consideration. Cf. *Oregon v. Mitchell*, 400 U.S. 112, 248–49 (1970) (Brennan, White, and Marshall, JJ., concurring in part and dissenting in part); *Katzenbach v. Morgan*, 384 U.S. 641, 648–49 (1966).

As an evolving understanding of the equal citizenship principle has moved Congress to review and to prohibit certain practices that have long organized relations between the sexes, so, too, has this Court recognized that the nation's conception of equal citizenship requires scrutiny of traditional practices rooted in stereotypical assumptions about the roles of men and women. In *Reed v. Reed*, 404 U.S. 71 (1971), we held that an Idaho statute that preferred males over similarly situated females as administrators of a family member's estate violated the Fourteenth Amendment. Because the state statute "provides that different treatment be accorded to the applicants on the basis of their sex," we held, "it thus establishes a classification subject to scrutiny under the Equal Protection Clause." Id. at 75. As our decision in *Reed* and the recent actions of Congress show, the nation's commitment to the principle of equal citizenship embodied in the Fourteenth and Nineteenth Amendments requires careful scrutiny of practices that enforce traditional assumptions about the sexes or that perpetuate second-class citizenship for women.

III.

Accordingly, legislation that criminalizes abortion requires careful scrutiny to determine whether it conforms to principles of equal citizenship under the Fourteenth and Nineteenth Amendments.

Laws that regulate the conduct of pregnant women warrant careful scrutiny because they distribute benefits and burdens on the basis of sex. This is so, even if the regulation concerns a condition that affects some, but not all, women. Cf. *Phillips v. Martin Marietta Corp.*, 400 U.S. 542

(1971) (holding that a policy prohibiting employment of women, but not men, with pre-school-age children discriminates on the basis of sex in violation of Title VII). We scrutinize state action that regulates pregnancy as sex-based because most women, and no men, have the capacity to bear children, and so regulation of pregnancy is prone to bias, in impetus and impact. See *Cohen v. Chesterfield County School Bd.,* 4 Fair Empl. Prac. Cas. (BNA) (4th Cir. 1972) (holding that mandatory maternity leave policy is sex-based discrimination subject to equal protection scrutiny) ("Is this sex-related? To the simple query the answer is just as simple: Nobody—and this includes Judges, Solomonic or life tenured—has yet seen a male mother. A mother, to oversimplify the simplest biology, must then be a woman.") (quoting *Phillips v. Martin Marietta Corp.,* 416 F.2d 1257, 1259 (5th Cir. 1969) (dissenting from denial of motion for rehearing en banc)). The fact that a law concerns a real physical difference between the sexes does not save it from searching review; physical differences between the sexes, in particular a women's unique capacity to gestate life, occasion some of the most persistent and deep-rooted assumptions about the different roles and worth of men and women. See *Heath v. Westerville Bd. of Educ.,* 345 F. Supp. 501, 505 n.1 (S.D. Ohio 1972) (relying on *Reed* to invalidate regulations requiring termination of employment at a fixed stage of pregnancy) ("[D]efendant Board's treatment of pregnancy . . . is more a manifestation of cultural sex role conditioning than a response to medical fact and necessity. The fact that [the plaintiff] does not fit neatly into the stereotyped vision . . . of the 'correct' female response to pregnancy should not redound to her economic or professional detriment."); *Williams v. San Francisco Unified School District,* 340 F. Supp. 438 (N.D. Cal. 1972) (relying on *Reed* to hold that mandatory maternity leave policy violated equal protection); cf. *Sprogis v. United AirLines,* 444 F.2d. 1194, 1198 (7th Cir. 1971) (interpreting sex-discrimination provisions of Title VII) ("Discrimination is not to be tolerated under the guise of physical properties possessed by one sex.").

Because state regulation of pregnant women is sex-based state action, when the state distributes benefits and burdens on the basis of pregnancy, it must act in ways that are consistent with the equal citizenship principle: wives and mothers are entitled to participate in education, work, and politics on the same terms as husbands and fathers. Thus, regulation aimed at pregnant women may not be premised on stereotypical assumptions about the sexes or perpetuate second-class citizenship for women, and the state may no longer regulate pregnant women on the assumption that mothers participate in the activities of citizenship on different terms than do men.[7] See *LaFleur v. Cleveland Board of Education*, 465 F.2d 1184 (6th Cir. 1972) (holding invalid under the Equal Protection Clause a school board rule that required pregnant teachers to take an unpaid leave of absence that would begin five months before birth and end at the beginning of the first school term after the child was three months old). Justifications this Court once held to be reasonable grounds for restricting the life opportunities of women are no longer constitutionally sufficient.

Once, members of this Court asserted that "the paramount destiny and mission of woman are to fulfill the noble and benign offices of wife and mother." *Bradwell v. Illinois*, 83 U.S. (16 Wall) 130, 141 (Bradley, J., concurring.) Interpreting our constitutional commitments on the assumption that a woman's family role unsuited her for the pursuits of citizenship in which men engaged, this Court concluded that the Fourteenth Amendment provided no protection against state laws that singled out women for restrictions on their employment. *Muller v. Oregon*, 208 U.S. 412, 422–23 (1908) (ruling that such legislation was warranted in view of a woman's "physical structure and a proper discharge of her maternal functions") ("The two sexes differ in structure of body, in the functions to be performed by each, in the amount of physical strength, in the capacity for long continued labor, . . . the influence of vigorous health upon the future well-being of the race, the self-reliance which enables one to assert full rights, and in the capacity to maintain the struggle for subsistence. This difference justifies a difference in legislation, and upholds that which is designed to compensate for some of the burdens which rest upon her."). Consistent with this understanding of family roles, the nation excluded women from equal participation in education, in work, and in politics, and organized the realms of work, education, and politics on the premise that those who participate in the core pursuits of citizenship are unburdened by obligations of family care.

Americans continue to value and to esteem the labor women perform as wives and mothers; yet, as the recent actions of all branches of government testify, Americans no longer deem it acceptable to define and to limit women's life opportunities on the assumption that a woman's family role makes her a different kind of citizen from a man. This change in the understanding of women's role requires us to reconsider traditional restrictions on women's conduct to determine whether they are consistent with prevailing understandings of the equal citizenship principle. Justifications for restricting access to abortion thought reasonable in a world that viewed men and women as citizens who live in separate spheres may not satisfy constitutional requirements today.

Today, as we have seen, the state cannot regulate pregnant women on the assumption that women's role as mothers unfits them for education, employment, or politics or requires them to participate in the activities of citizenship on terms different from those that apply to men. Yet, criminal abortion statutes were enacted on just this assumption: the assumption that women were obliged to devote themselves to the work of raising children in a way that men were not.

At common law, abortion was legal until quickening, a pregnant woman's first perception of fetal movement, and the practice of contraception was wholly unregulated.[8] All this changed in the mid-nineteenth century, when doctors of the newly formed American Medical Association advocated the passage of legislation that would criminalize contraception and abortion.

Doctors invoked a set of interlocking arguments about human reproduction to justify these new legal controls on contraception and abortion —claims about women and the unborn life they might bear. The leader of the criminalization campaign invoked the authority of medical science to argue that life begins at conception: "The first impregnation of the egg, whether in man or in kangaroo, is the birth of the offspring to life; its emergence into the outside world for a wholly separate existence is, for one as for the other, but an accident in time." Horatio Robinson Storer, *Why Not? A Book for Every Woman* 31 (1866) (hereinafter *Why Not?*). He also invoked the authority of medical science when he asserted that a woman had a duty to procreate that was dictated by her anatomy:

> Were woman intended as a mere plaything, or for the gratification of her own or her husband's desires, there would have been need for her of neither uterus nor ovaries, nor would the prevention of their being used for their clearly legitimate purpose have been attended by such tremendous penalties as is in reality the case.

Id. at. 80–81.

It was because the medical profession acted from beliefs about women as well as the future generations they might bear that doctors opposed contraception, as well as abortion. Physicians who advocated the criminalization of abortion and contraception argued that a woman who shirked her duty to bear children committed "physiological sin." H. S. Pomeroy, *The Ethics of Marriage* 97 (New York, Funk & Wagnalls 1888). The only way that a wife could ensure her health was to bear children, pregnancy being "a normal physiological condition, and often absolutely necessary to the physical and moral health of woman." Edwin M. Hale, *The Great Crime of the Nineteenth Century* 6n (Chicago, C. S. Halsey 1867). As Storer explained:

> Is there then no alternative but for women, when married and prone to conception, to occasionally bear children? This, as we have seen is the end for which they are physiologically constituted and for which they are destined by nature. . . . [The prevention and termination of pregnancy] are alike disastrous to a woman's mental, moral, and physical wellbeing.

Horatio Robinson Storer, *Why Not?* 74–76; see also Horatio Robinson Storer, *Is It I? A Book for Every Man* 115–16 (Boston, Lee & Shepard 1868) ("Every married woman, save in very exceptional cases, which should only be allowed to be such by the decision of a competent physician, every married woman, until the so-called turn in life, should occasionally bear a child; not as a duty to the community merely . . . but as the best means of insuring her own permanent good health.")

Thus, physicians arguing for the criminalization of abortion reasoned that life begins at conception, but their judgments about abortion were equally and explicitly premised on the view that a woman's anatomy was her destiny, that a woman's highest and best use was in bearing children. The doctors viewed all of women's reasons for seeking an abortion as equally and unnaturally egoistic because all were derogations of maternal duty, as Augustus Gardner explained: "Is it not arrant laziness, sheer, craven, culpable cowardice, which is at the bottom of this base act? . . . Have you the right to choose an indolent, selfish life, neglecting the work God has appointed you to perform?" Augustus K. Gardner, Physical Decline of American Women, reprinted in Augustus K. Gardner, *Conjugal Sins Against the Laws of Life and Health* 225 (New York, J. S. Redfield 1870). The AMA's 1871 *Report on Criminal Abortion* denounced the woman who aborted a pregnancy: "She becomes unmindful of the course marked out for her by Providence, she overlooks the duties imposed on her by the marriage contract. She yields to the pleasures—but shrinks from the pains and responsibilities of maternity." D. A. O'Donnell and W. L. Atlee, Report on Criminal Abortion, 22 *Transactions of the AMA* 239, 241 (1871). Thus, the same doctors who invoked medical science to condemn abortion as "foeticide" at one and the same time condemned the practice as violating women's roles:

> Woman's rights and woman's sphere are, as understood by the American public, quite different from that understood by us as Physicians, or as Anatomists, or Physiologists.
>
> "Woman's rights" now are understood to be, that she should be a man, and that her physical organism, which is constituted by Nature to bear and rear offspring, should be left in abeyance, and that her ministrations in the formation of character as mother should be abandoned for the sterner rights of voting and law making.
>
> The whole country is in an abnormal state, and the tendency to force women into men's places, creates new ideas of women's duties, and therefore . . . the marriage state is frequently childless. . . . These influences act and react on public sentiment, until the public conscience becomes blunted, and duties necessary to women's physical organization are shirked, neglected, or criminally prevented.

Montrose A. Pallen, "Foeticide, or Criminal Abortion," 3 *Medical Archives* 193, 205–6 (1869) (paper read before the Missouri State Medical Association, April 1868).

The nation no longer credits the belief that men and women occupy separate spheres and roles, and yet the role concepts the separate-spheres tradition fostered continue to play an implicit and sometimes explicit part in judgments about abortion. As a nation, we still expect men and women differently to comport themselves in matters concerning sex and parenting, and these judgments play a large part in determining whether and when abortion is acceptable. Today, it is commonly assumed that the question of abortion depends on judgments about unborn life; yet, views about the acceptability of the practice in fact vary with judgments about the sexual relations in which unborn life was conceived and the reasons and activities that might lead women to avoid motherhood. Thus, instead of demonstrating a consistent valuation of unborn life across contexts, societal judgments about abortion depend on views about the women at whom regulation is aimed. This is all the more evident in more recent therapeutic abortion statutes that make the permissibility of abortion explicitly dependent on medical evaluation of women's reasons for avoiding motherhood.

For example, the liberalized criminal abortion statute proposed by the Model Penal Code authorizes a physician to perform an abortion "if he believes there is substantial risk that continuance of the pregnancy would gravely impair the physical or mental health of the mother or that the child would be born with gave physical or mental defect, or that the pregnancy resulted from rape, incest, or other felonious intercourse." Model Penal Code § 230.3(2). (Georgia's statute follows this model; it allows abortions where a physician determines "based upon his best clinical judgment that an abortion is necessary because" "[a] continuation of the pregnancy would endanger the life of the pregnant woman or would seriously and permanently injure her health" or "[t]he fetus would very likely be born with a grave, permanent, and irremediable mental or physical defect" or "[t]he pregnancy resulted from forcible or statutory rape." Ga. Code § 26-1202(1)–(3)).

The statutory exception allowing women to have abortions if they conceive by rape indicates that the state's decision to prohibit abortion rests on unarticulated assumptions about how women are to comport themselves sexually—a code the state enforces by selectively allowing women access to abortion. What are the terms of this code? By long-standing common law tradition, states do not apply the law of rape between husband and wife.[9] And so, by law, a husband may rape his wife, and after he has forced her to have sex, the state will force her to bear the child. When criminal abortion statutes with rape exceptions incorporate these traditions, they enforce judgments about married women like those expressed in the nineteenth-century record. The rape exception carries forward norms of sexual comportment in other ways. Rape exceptions of this kind express and perpetuate a sexual double standard. States will punish pregnant women who have "voluntarily" engaged in sex by making them bear children, even though the state has imposed no similar duties, burdens, or sanctions on the men who were coparticipants in the act of conception. The state does not hold the pregnant woman's partner accountable for sharing the work of parenting, nor does it alter the sex-based citizenship consequences of performing the work: during pregnancy and then for some two decades after, a woman will face severe restrictions on her ability to participate in education, employment, or politics—restrictions the society is only now beginning to ameliorate.

Traditional sex-role assumptions also shape the exception that allows abortions to save the pregnant woman's life or to prevent serious and permanent injury to her health. As we have seen, criminal abortion statutes enforce the sex-role understanding that a pregnant woman is a mother, one who is expected to devote her life to rearing children in ways men are not. The therapeutic exception extends this tradition. While criminal abortion statutes compel a pregnant woman to subordinate her welfare to that of the unborn, the therapeutic exception indicates that the state will subordinate the welfare of the unborn to that of the pregnant woman when the state judges the woman's reasons for avoiding motherhood sufficiently weighty. The state will allow a pregnant woman to avoid motherhood only when she is at risk of losing her mind or health. The therapeutic standard for abortions thus defines women as childbearers just as thoroughly and completely as the nineteenth-century medical profession did. Cf. Eugene Quay, "Justifiable Abortion," 49 *Geo. L.J.* 173, 234 (1961) (criticizing therapeutic exception to criminal abortion laws) ("A mother who would sacrifice the life of her unborn child for her own health is lacking in something. If there could be any authority to destroy an innocent life for social considerations, it would still be in the interests of society to sacrifice such a mother rather than the child who might otherwise prove to be normal and decent and an asset."); Elizabeth Truninger, "Abortion: The New Civil Right," 56 *Wom. Lawyer's J.* 99, 99–100 (1970) ("But under even the Therapeutic Abortion Law, a woman often must be determined crazy if she does not wish to bear the child she carries. Much of this thinking can be traced to society's limited perception of women's role solely as a mother.").

In other words, today, no less than in the nineteenth century, regulation of abortion reflects judgments about women, as well as the unborn life they bear. As we have seen, the statutes' design reflects sex-role assumptions about conception and parenting and is surely not dictated by the physiology of reproduction. To illustrate this in yet a different way: A state that criminalizes abortion to protect the unborn could nonetheless compensate or assist the pregnant woman on whom it would impose motherhood. Why, then, is it that no abortion law enacted in the United States has ever offered assistance to pregnant women in coping with the consequences of gestating and raising the children that the state has forced them to bear? That no state has attempted to ameliorate the effects of two decades of life-transforming labor that a criminal abortion statute exacts from women demonstrates that criminal prohibitions on abortion still embody judgments about the women whose conduct the statutes regulate —judgments that can be understood by considering the views expressed by the statutes' original proponents, who viewed motherhood as "the end for which [women] are physiologically constituted and for which they are destined by nature." Horatio Robinson Storer, *Why Not?* 76.

Abortion statutes like those in Texas and Georgia not only reflect status-role judgments about women; they inflict status-role harms on women. As we have seen, such statutes do not compensate or assist the pregnant woman on whom they would impose motherhood but instead compel women to assume the role of motherhood in a society that penalizes women if they do not perform the work of motherhood as a legal and social dependent of a man. As amici observe:

> A woman who has a child is subject to a whole range of *de jure* and *de facto* punishments, disabilities and limitations to her freedom from the earliest stages of pregnancy. She may be suspended or expelled from school and thus robbed of her opportunity for education and self-development. She may be fired or suspended from her employment and thereby denied the right to earn a living and, if single and without independent income, forced into the degrading position of living on welfare.
>
> In Texas, a father of an out-of-wedlock child has neither the common law nor the statutory duty to support his child. *Home of Holy Infancy v. Kaska*, 397 S.W. 2d 208 (Tex. 1965). See also *Lane v. Phillips*, 6 S.W. 610 (Tex. 1887), *Beaver v. State*, 256 S.W. 929 (Cr. App. Tex., 1923). Having been forced to give birth to a child she did not want, a woman may be subject to criminal sanctions for child neglect, e.g., D.C. Code §22-902, if she does not care for the child to the satisfaction of the state. In some states even here the disabilities for the woman are greater than for the man. Of course, again, if the woman is unmarried and paternity was never legally established, the woman bears these legal burdens alone. Even where the father is present, social mores and expectations dictate that, in the overwhelming majority of cases, the mother rather than father will be primarily responsible for raising the children.

Brief of Amici Curiae New Women Lawyers et al. at 24, 29, *Roe v. Wade*, 410 U.S. 113 (1973) (No. 70-18). These practices are mutually reinforcing, long-standing, and widespread. Women who by choice or circumstance do not conform to these sex-role assumptions experience pregnancy and motherhood as a profound threat that will expose them to unending sanction and to denigration and deprivation, with untold injury to themselves and to children they have or might bear. For this reason, there are "[a]n estimated 1,000,000 illegal abortions [that] take place in the country annually, usually at the hands of unqualified practitioners. Thousands of the women so aborted suffer permanent injury and some death." Lorry Plagenz, "States Legislate Abortion Reform, But Hospitals Are Reluctant to Comply," *Modern Hospital* 82, 85, July 1969.[10]

Abortion statutes such as Texas's and Georgia are sex-biased in impetus and impact, and these constitutional debilities of the statutes do not dissipate by emphasizing that the statutes vindicate an interest in protecting unborn life. There might come a day in which this society consistently expressed its concern about the welfare of future generations in a way that is not dependent on and entangled with judgments about the citizens who conceive and raise them. We do not now live in such a society. Rather than valuing unborn life consistently, states instead condemn abortion selectively, in ways that vary with judgments about the women at whom the prohibition is aimed. Rather than assist or compensate women whom they would compel to bear children, states with criminal abortion statutes treat women who gestate and raise future generations as dependents and second-class citizens, persons who can be expected (or forced) to devote their lives to others, and penalized if they endeavor to live autonomously. States may so act, but if they do so, they cannot expect their laws to be judged as if they simply expressed respect for the value of unborn life. The criminal abortion laws here in issue do much more; they reflect and enforce traditional, status-based judgments about women of a sort once openly voiced when the statutes were first enacted but now no longer acceptable to express because inconsistent with the nation's evolving understanding of equal citizenship.

We base judgments about the statutes' constitutionality on the structure of abortion laws as they have been enacted and enforced, not on some idealization of the regulation that omits constitutionally salient features of its actual practice. For this reason, it does not advance the case for constitutional justification to call abortion murder. Criminal abortion statutes enacted in the past century have *not* regulated abortion as murder. Whatever respect for unborn life abortion laws express, state criminal laws have never valued unborn life in the way they value born life. States have never treated women who seek to abort a pregnancy as they would a woman who was seeking to murder a born person. States have not used the criminal law to incarcerate women who obtain or attempt to obtain an illegal abortion. Instead, they have used the criminal law to coerce and intimidate women into performing the work of motherhood. In judging the constitutionality of such laws, we examine the social understandings the laws reflect and enforce. Abortion laws do not treat women as murderers, but as *mothers*[11]—citizens who exist for the purpose of rearing children, citizens who are expected to perform the work of parenting as dependents and nonparticipants in the citizenship activities in which men are engaged. States that wish to protect unborn life must do so in ways that do not use the power of the state to enforce sex-differentiated roles and responsibilities in matters of sex and parenting.

For these reasons, abortion restrictions of the sort contained in the Texas and Georgia statutes violate equal citizenship guarantees of the Fourteenth and Nineteenth Amendments. "Restrictive laws governing abortion such as those of Texas and Georgia are a manifestation of the fact that men are unable to see women in any role other than that of mother and wife." Brief of Amici Curiae New Women Lawyers et al. at 24, 32, *Roe v. Wade*, 410 U.S. 113 (1973) (No. 70-18).[12] The history and structure of such laws "reflect[] arbitrary notions of a woman's place wholly at odds with contemporary legislative and judicial recognition that individual potential must not be restrained, nor equal opportunity limited, by law-sanctioned stereotypical prejudgments." Brief for Petitioner at 7, *Struck v. Sec'y of Def.*, 409 U.S. 1071 (1972) (No. 72-178). "[T]he Nineteenth Amendment sought to reverse the previous inferior social and political position of women: denial of the vote represented maintenance of the dividing line between women as part of the family organization only and women as independent and equal citizens in American life. [But] abortion laws, in their real practical effects, deny the liberty, and equality of women to participate in the wider world, an equality which is demanded by the Nineteenth Amendment." First Amended Complaint at 6–7, *Women of Rhode Island v. Israel* (D.R.I. June 22, 1971) (No. 4605).[13] Such statutes violate the equal citizenship principle because they compel pregnant women to assume the role and to perform the work of motherhood, without acknowledgment or recompense, in a society still organized on the understanding that those who do the primary work of bearing and rearing children are a dependent class, not full participants in those activities that the society most highly values and centrally associates with citizenship. And, "as long as women are unable to control their reproductive lives they will be forced to disrupt their education, forgo their career, and will never be a totally functioning part of the government which determines [their] rights." Brief of Amici Curiae New Women Lawyers et al. at 24, 32, *Roe v. Wade*, 410 U.S. 113 (1973) (No. 70-18).

Now as before, individuals may form their own judgments about the morality of abortion and determine when, if ever, they believe recourse to the practice appropriate. But they may not invoke the power of the state to make such choices for others. The community may not invoke the power of the state to appropriate the life of one of its citizens for the purpose of making another, all the more so when such coercion perpetuates a network of understandings and practices that treats those who rear children as second-class citizens.

Freely undertaken, motherhood remains a profound source of fulfillment and pride for women, despite its many burdens. Women may choose to perform the work in reliance on the support of another, or they may struggle to support themselves and their children in a world that penalizes those who do the work of gestating and raising children. But these are choices that the Constitution protects as the woman's alone. Given the way this nation has historically treated citizens who bear and rear children—a history that still powerfully shapes attitudes and practices in America today—government may give support to pregnant women, but it may not coerce them to give birth.

For these reasons, government may not deny women effective access to abortion, and all regulation of the practice must be consistent with principles of equal citizenship.

NOTES

1. See, e.g., *Brown v. Board of Education*, 347 U.S. 483 (1954) (holding that state policies maintaining segregation in public education violate the Fourteenth Amendment's Equal Protection Clause); *Bolling v. Sharpe*, 347 U.S. 497 (1954) (ruling that segregation in public schools is unconstitutional under the Fifth Amendment's Due Process Clause); *Anderson v. Martin*, 375 U.S. 399 (1964) (holding that a Louisiana statute that mandated the designation of a candidate's race on election ballots violated equal protection because it enlisted the power of the state to enforce private racial prejudices); *Loving v. Virginia*, 388 U.S. 1 (1967) (striking down criminal prohibitions on interracial marriage).

2. See Exec. Order No. 9981 (1948), 3 C.F.R. 722 (1941–1948) (ordering desegregation of the military and requiring equality of opportunity regardless of race or national origin).

3. See Title II and Title VII of the Civil Rights Act of 1964, 78 Stat. 253, (1964), 42 U.S.C.S. §§ 2000a et seq. (prohibiting discrimination on the basis of race in public accommodations and employment); Voting Rights Act of 1965, 79 Stat. 437, 42 U.S.C.S. § 1973 (barring abridgement of the right to vote on the basis of race);

Civil Rights Act of 1968, 82 Stat. 81, 42 U.S.C.S. §§ 3601–3631 (banning discrimination on the basis of race in the sale and rental of real estate).

4. Women were not allowed to vote anywhere except in New Jersey, which adopted qualified suffrage for women at the nation's founding and retained it for several decades. While the state constitution referred to property ownership and not to sex, married women's limited property rights effectively limited the franchise to single women with some property. This unique period of woman suffrage lasted until 1807, when it was ended by an act of the legislature. See generally Richard P. McCormick, *The History of Voting in New Jersey: A Study in the Development of Election Machinery, 1664–1911* (1953); J. R. Pole, "Suffrage Reform and the American Revolution in New Jersey," 74 *Proceedings of the N.J. Hist. Scty.* 173 (July 1956).

5. See *Bradwell v. Illinois,* 83 U.S. (16 Wall) 130, 139 (1872) (upholding the constitutionality of a state's exclusion of women from the practice of law); *Muller v. Oregon,* 208 U.S. 412, 422–23 (1908) (upholding the constitutionality of state laws imposing sex-based restrictions on the terms and conditions of employment); Eliot A. Landau & Kermit L. Dunahoo, "Sex Discrimination in Employment: A Survey of State and Federal Remedies," 20 *Drake L. Rev.* 417, 420 (1971).

6. See, e.g., Comprehensive Health Manpower Training Act of 1971, Pub. L. No. 92-157, sec. 110, § 799a, 85 Stat. 431, 461, and the Nurses Training Act of 1971, Pub. L. No. 92-158, sec. 11, § 845, 85 Stat. 465, 479–80 (amending Titles VII and VIII of the Public Health Services Act to prohibit sex discrimination in admissions to all training programs for health professionals receiving funds under these Titles); Act of Oct. 14, 1972, Pub. L. No. 92-496, § 3, 86 Stat. 813, 813–14 (expanding the mandate of the U.S. Commission on Civil Rights, a study group on minority problems established by Congress in 1957, to include sex discrimination); Act of Dec. 15, 1971, Pub. L. No. 92-187, §§ 1–3, 85 Stat. 644, 644 (amending §§ 2108, 5924, and 7152 of Title 5 of the United States Code so as to equalize employment benefits for married female federal employees); Revenue Sharing Act of 1972, Pub. L. No. 92-512, § 122, 86 Stat. 919, 932 (prohibiting discrimination on the basis of sex in the disbursement of federal funds for fiscal assistance to state and local governments); Act of Aug. 5, 1971, Pub. L. No. 92-65, §§ 112, 214, 85 Stat. 166, 168, 173 (prohibiting sex discrimination in access to all programs or activities funded under the Public Works and Economic Development Act of 1965 and the Appalachian Regional Development Act of 1965); Federal Water Pollution Control Act Amendments of 1972, Pub. L. No. 92-500, § 13, 86 Stat. 816, 913 (prohibiting sex discrimination in any program or activity receiving federal funds under the Federal Water Pollution Control Act or the Environmental Financing Act).

7. It is for this reason that the EEOC has recently issued regulations protecting pregnant employees against discrimination on the job. See E.E.O.C. Guidelines on Sex Discrimination, 29 C.F.R. 1604.10 (1972) ("A written or unwritten employment policy or practice which excludes from employment applicants or employees

because of pregnancy is in prima facie violation of Title VII."); see also Office of Federal Contract Compliance Sex Discrimination Guidelines, 41 C.F.R. 60-20.3 (g) (applicable to employers performing federal contracts) ("Women shall not be penalized in their conditions of employment because they require time away from work because of childbearing"); Department of Health, Education, and Welfare Higher Education Guidelines 12–13 (October 1972) (prohibiting discrimination against pregnant women); see generally Comment, "Love's Labors Lost: New Conceptions of Maternity Leaves," 7 *Harv. Civ. Rts. Civ. Libs. L. Rev.* 260 (1972); Walter J. Curran, "Equal Protection of the Law: Pregnant School Teachers," 285 *New England J. Med.* 336 (1971).

8. E. Coke, Institutes III 50 (1644); 1 W. Hawkins, *Pleas of the Crown,* c. 31, § 16 (4th ed. 1762); 1 W. Blackstone, *Commentaries on the Laws of England* 129–30 (1765); M. Hale, *Pleas of the Crown* 433 (1st Amer. ed. 1847). For discussions of the role of the quickening concept in English common law, see L. Lader, *Abortion* 78 (1966); J. Noonan, "An Almost Absolute Value in History," in *The Morality of Abortion* 223–26 (J. Noonan ed. 1970); Cyril C. Means, "The Law of New York Concerning Abortion and the Status of the Foetus, 1664–1968: A Case of Cessation of Constitutionality (pt. 1)," 14 *N.Y.L.F.* 411, 418–28 (1968); Loren G. Stern, "Abortion: Reform and the Law," 59 *J. Crim. L.C. & P.S.* 84 (1968); Eugene Quay, "Justifiable Abortion—Medical and Legal Foundations, (pt. 2)," 49 *Geo. L.J.* 395, 430–32 (1961); G. Williams, *The Sanctity of Life and the Criminal Law* 152 (1957).

9. American jurisdictions recognize a marital rape exemption, whether in express statutory or implied terms; see Comment, "Rape and Battery between Husband and Wife," 6 *Stan. L. Rev.* 719 (1954); Annot., 84 A.L.R.2d 1017 (1962) (discussing continuing adherence to marital rape exemption)—a centuries-old tradition recently reaffirmed by the Model Penal Code. See Model Penal Code. § 213.1 ("A male who has sexual intercourse with a female not his wife is guilty of rape if; . . .").

10. The social judgments that shape attitudes about pregnant women and the practice of abortion lead this society to discriminate among women, even in determining whom it will protect from the trauma and risk of illegal abortion. Women of means have far greater access to legal abortion, with recent studies demonstrating that the average number of hospital abortions done for private patients was 7.1 per year, while the average for nonprivate patients was 1.7 a year. Id. For these reasons, of the nonhospital abortion deaths that occurred in Georgia between 1950 and 1969, 69 percent occurred among black women. Roger W. Rochat, Carl W. Tyler, Jr., & Albert K. Schoenbucher, "An Epidemiological Analysis of Abortion in Georgia," 61 *AJPH* 542, 542, 543 (1971). ("Abortion mortality from nonhospital abortions in Georgia is becoming increasingly a black health problem; presumably, this reflects the lower socio-economic status of blacks in Georgia.") Even with liberalization of abortion in Georgia, before and after its codification in law, this problem persists; mortality "has declined among whites

and married black women, [it] has remained high for unmarried black women." Id. at 549. These public health statistics illustrate, yet again, how judgments about women determine access to abortion.

11. For example, until Georgia's recent overhaul of its criminal laws in light of the Model Penal Code, the Georgia code grouped, and distinguished, abortion and infanticide. See Ga. Code § 26-11 ("Abortion, Foeticide and Infanticide"), repealed, Ga. Laws 1968, p. 1338. In addition, the Model Penal Code, which has revolutionized criminal laws across the nation, groups abortion among "crimes against the family," distinguishing it from the companion crimes of bigamy, incest, child endangerment, and persistent nonsupport of a child. Model Penal Code, Article 230 "Offenses against the Family," §§ 230.1–230.5.

12. Elizabeth Truninger, "Abortion: The New Civil Right," 56 *Wom. Lawyer's J.* 99, 99–100, 101 (1970) ("Much of this thinking [about abortion] can be traced to society's limited perception of women's role solely as a mother.") ("It is not surprising then that the legal arguments being made are that the abortion law denies equal protection and abridges the women's constitutional right to life and to decide whether to bear children. Actions have been filed in many places throughout the country challenging the constitutionality of abortion statutes . . . on these grounds.")

13. See William Hodes, "Women and the Constitution: Some Legal History and a New Approach to the Nineteenth Amendment," 25 *Rutgers L. Rev.* 26, 51 (1970) (arguing "that the 19th amendment really had very little to do with the vote, but instead established the total equality of women and men . . . under such an interpretation, one need only demonstrate that a certain practice discriminates against women as a class, or that it is a badge and an indicia of the pre-1920 status of second-class citizen, in order to find primary corrective power in the national government") ("Since the binding of women to the home is the real basis for the inferior position of women in our society, and since it is where the traits of slavery are still most visible, it is not surprising to find that many of [the feminist movement's] demands center on ways to deal with the problems which women face as a result of their unavoidable childbearing function. A prime example is the question of abortion.").

TUSHNET, J., concurring.

The questions presented in the present cases go far beyond the issues of vagueness, which we considered in *United States v. Vuitch,* 402 U.S. 62. They involve the right of privacy, one aspect of which we considered in *Griswold v. Connecticut,* 381 U.S. 479, 484, when we held that various guarantees in the Bill of Rights create zones of privacy.[1] The Griswold case involved a law forbidding the use of contraceptives. We held that law as applied to married people unconstitutional.

The Ninth Amendment obviously does not create federally enforceable rights. It merely says, "The enumeration in the Constitution, of certain rights, shall not be construed to deny or disparage others retained by the people." But a catalogue of these rights includes customary, traditional, and time-honored rights, amenities, privileges, and immunities that come within the sweep of "the Blessings of Liberty" mentioned in the preamble to the Constitution. Many of them, in my view, come within the meaning of the term "liberty" as used in the Fourteenth Amendment.

First is the autonomous control over the development and expression of one's intellect, interests, tastes, and personality. These are rights protected by the First Amendment and, in my view, they are absolute, permitting of no exceptions. All of these aspects of the right of privacy are rights "retained by the people" in the meaning of the Ninth Amendment.

Second is freedom of choice in the basic decisions of one's life respecting marriage, divorce, procreation, contraception, and the education and upbringing of children. These rights, unlike those protected by the First Amendment, are subject to some control by the police power. Thus, the Fourth Amendment speaks only of "unreasonable searches and seizures" and of "probable cause." These rights are "fundamental," and we have held that in order to support legislative action the statute must be narrowly and precisely drawn and that a "compelling state interest" must be shown in support of the limitation. The liberty to marry a person of one's own choosing, *Loving v. Virginia,* 388 U.S. 1; the right of procreation, *Skinner v. Oklahoma,* 316 U.S. 535; the liberty to direct the education of one's children, *Pierce v. Society of Sisters,* 268 U.S. 510, and the privacy of the marital relation, *Griswold v. Connecticut,* supra, are in this category.[2]

This right of privacy was called by Mr. Justice Brandeis the right "to be let alone." *Olmstead v. United States,* 277 U.S. 438, 478 (dissenting opinion). That right includes the privilege of an individual to plan his own affairs, for, "outside areas of plainly harmful conduct, every American is left to shape his own life as he thinks best, do what he pleases, go where he pleases." *Kent v. Dulles,* 357 U.S. 116, 126.

Third is the freedom to care for one's health and person, freedom from bodily restraint or compulsion, freedom to walk, stroll, or loaf. These rights, though fundamental, are likewise subject to regulation on a showing of "compelling state interest."

The Georgia statute is at war with the clear message of these cases—that a woman is free to make the basic decision whether to bear an unwanted child. Elaborate argument is hardly necessary to demonstrate that childbirth may deprive a woman of her preferred lifestyle and force upon her a radically different and undesired future. For example, rejected applicants under the Georgia statute are required to endure the discomforts of pregnancy; to incur the pain, higher mortality rate, and aftereffects of childbirth; to abandon educational plans; to sustain loss of income; to forgo the satisfactions of careers; to tax further mental and physical health in providing child care; and, in some cases, to bear the lifelong stigma of unwed motherhood, a badge which may haunt, if not deter, later legitimate family relationships.

Such reasoning is, however, only the beginning of the problem. The State has interests to protect. Vaccinations to prevent epidemics are one example, as *Jacobson v. Massachusetts,* 197 U.S. 11, holds. The Court held that compulsory sterilization of imbeciles afflicted with hereditary forms of insanity or imbecility is another. *Buck v. Bell,* 274 U.S. 200. Abortion affects another. While childbirth endangers the lives of some women, voluntary abortion at any time and place regardless of medical standards would impinge on a rightful concern of society. The woman's health is part of that concern, as is the life of the fetus after quickening. These concerns justify the State in treating the procedure as a medical one.

Georgia's enactment has a constitutional infirmity because, as stated by the District Court, it "limits the number of reasons for which an abortion may be sought." I agree with the holding of the District Court, "This the

State may not do, because such action unduly restricts a decision sheltered by the Constitutional right to privacy."

The vicissitudes of life produce pregnancies which may be unwanted, or which may impair "health" in the broad *Vuitch* sense of the term, or which may imperil the life of the mother, or which in the full setting of the case may create such suffering, dislocations, misery, or tragedy as to make an early abortion the only civilized step to take. These hardships may be properly embraced in the "health" factor of the mother as appraised by a person of insight. Or they may be part of a broader medical judgment based on what is "appropriate" in a given case, though perhaps not "necessary" in a strict sense.

The "liberty" of the mother, though rooted as it is in the Constitution, may be qualified by the State for the reasons we have stated. But where fundamental personal rights and liberties are involved, the corrective legislation must be "narrowly drawn to prevent the supposed evil," *Cantwell v. Connecticut,* 310 U.S. 296, 307, and not be dealt with in an "unlimited and indiscriminate" manner. *Shelton v. Tucker,* 364 U.S. 479, 490. And see *Talley v. California,* 362 U.S. 60. Unless regulatory measures are so confined and are addressed to the specific areas of compelling legislative concern, the police power would become the great leveler of constitutional rights and liberties.

There is no doubt that the State may require abortions to be performed by qualified medical personnel. The legitimate objective of preserving the mother's health clearly supports such laws. Their impact upon the woman's privacy is minimal. But the Georgia statute outlaws virtually all such operations—even in the earliest stages of pregnancy. In light of modern medical evidence suggesting that an early abortion is safer healthwise than childbirth itself, it cannot be seriously urged that so comprehensive a ban is aimed at protecting the woman's health. Rather, this expansive proscription of all abortions along the temporal spectrum can rest only on a public goal of preserving both embryonic and fetal life.

The present statute has struck the balance between the woman's and the State's interests wholly in favor of the latter. I am not prepared to hold that a State may equate, as Georgia has done, all phases of maturation preceding birth. We held in *Griswold* that the States may not preclude spouses from attempting to avoid the joinder of sperm and egg. If this is true, it is difficult to perceive any overriding public necessity which might attach precisely at the moment of conception. As Mr. Justice Clark has said:

> To say that life is present at conception is to give recognition to the potential, rather than the actual. The unfertilized egg has life, and if fertilized, it takes on human proportions. But the law deals in reality, not obscurity—the known rather than the unknown. When sperm meets egg life may eventually form, but quite often it does not. The law does not deal in speculation. The phenomenon of life takes time to develop, and until it is actually present, it cannot be destroyed. Its interruption prior to formation would hardly be homicide, and as we have seen, society does not regard it as such. The rites of Baptism are not performed and death certificates are not required when a miscarriage occurs. No prosecutor has ever returned a murder indictment charging the taking of the life of a fetus. This would not be the case if the fetus constituted human life.

"Religion, Morality, and Abortion: A Constitutional Appraisal," 2 *Loyola U. (L.A.) L. Rev.* 1, 9–10 (1969).

In summary, the enactment is overbroad. It is not closely correlated to the aim of preserving prenatal life. In fact, it permits its destruction in several cases, including pregnancies resulting from sex acts in which unmarried females are below the statutory age of consent. At the same time, however, the measure broadly proscribes aborting other pregnancies which may cause severe mental disorders. Additionally, the statute is overbroad because it equates the value of embryonic life immediately after conception with the worth of life immediately before birth.

The right of privacy has no more conspicuous place than in the physician-patient relationship, unless it be in the priest-penitent relationship. It is one thing for a patient to agree that her physician may consult with another physician about her case. It is quite a different matter for the State compulsorily to impose on that physician-patient relationship another layer or, as in this case, still a third layer of physicians. The right of privacy —the right to care for one's health and person and to seek out a physician of one's own choice protected by the Fourteenth Amendment—becomes only a matter of theory, not a reality, when a multiple-physician-approval system is mandated by the State.

Crucial here, however, is state-imposed control over the medical decision whether pregnancy should be interrupted. The good-faith decision of the patient's chosen physician is overridden and the final decision passed on to others in whose selection the patient has no part. This is a total destruction of the right of privacy between physician and patient and the intimacy of relation which that entails.

The right to seek advice on one's health and the right to place reliance on the physician of one's choice are basic to Fourteenth Amendment values. We deal with fundamental rights and liberties, which, as already noted, can be contained or controlled only by discretely drawn legislation that preserves the "liberty" and regulates only those phases of the problem of compelling legislative concern. The imposition by the State of group controls over the physician-patient relationship is not made on any medical procedure apart from abortion, no matter how dangerous the medical step may be. The oversight imposed on the physician and patient in abortion cases denies them their "liberty," viz., their right of privacy, without any compelling, discernible state interest.

Georgia has constitutional warrant in treating abortion as a medical problem. To protect the woman's right of privacy, however, the control must be through the physician of her choice and the standards set for his performance.

The protection of the fetus when it has acquired life is a legitimate concern of the State. Georgia's law makes no rational, discernible decision on that score. For, under the Code, the developmental stage of the fetus is irrelevant when pregnancy is the result of rape, when the fetus will very likely be born with a permanent defect, or when a continuation of the pregnancy will endanger the life of the mother or permanently injure her health. When life is present is a question we do not try to resolve. While basically a question for medical experts, as stated by Mr. Justice Clark, it is, of course, caught up in matters of religion and morality.

NOTES

1. There is no mention of privacy in our Bill of Rights, but our decisions have recognized it as one of the fundamental values those amendments were designed to protect.

2. *Griswold* involved legislation touching on the marital relation and involving the conviction of a licensed physician for giving married people information concerning contraception. There is nothing specific in the Bill of Rights that covers that item. Nor is there anything in the Bill of Rights that in terms protects the right of association or the privacy in one's association. Yet we found those rights

in the periphery of the First Amendment. *NAACP v. Alabama,* 357 U.S. 449, 462. Other peripheral rights are the right to educate one's children as one chooses, *Pierce v. Society of Sisters,* 268 U.S. 510, and the right to study the German language, *Meyer v. Nebraska,* 262 U.S. 390. These decisions, with all respect, have nothing to do with substantive due process. One may think they are not peripheral to other rights that are expressed in the Bill of Rights. But that is not enough to bring into play the protection of substantive due process.

ALLEN, J., concurring in the judgment.

We are asked to decide the constitutionality of Texas and Georgia criminal statutes that restrict abortions. Our decision will have broad and historic implications. This Court cannot afford to minimize the significance of its appointed task. At the heart of these proceedings is the question of the capacity of women—daughters, wives, and mothers—to make responsible family planning choices. No one understands the intimate demands of pregnancy better than the pregnant woman herself. No one's body or life is more greatly affected than hers. Sadly, there are those who view abortion restrictions as necessary safeguards against the imagined immorality or helpless vulnerability of a weaker, and ideally self-sacrificing, sex. Yet women, no less than men, have moral sense and moral capacity. As free and equal citizens, women, too, are entitled to act on informed, autonomous judgments about what is best. I concur in the opinion of Chief Justice Balkin that women have a constitutional right to "choose the conditions under which they will take on the responsibilities of motherhood so as to facilitate and secure their equal citizenship."

I write separately, first, to underscore paramount equalities and privacies at stake in what we do. It is these far-reaching privacies and long-awaited equalities that make the woman's ability to choose abortion much more than an ordinary liberty calling for heavy deference to state legislators. It is time to acknowledge that thorough-going procreative autonomy, embracing decisions regarding sterilization, contraception, abortion, and child rearing, is "implicit in the concept of ordered liberty," *Palko v. Connecticut*, 302, U.S. 319, 325, 326 (1937), overruled on other grounds, 395 U.S. 784 (1969). The ability to choose abortion is so fundamental that government abortion restrictions call into play the strictest judicial scrutiny. Texas and Georgia have enacted statutes that prohibit, restrict, and severely impede access to medically safe abortions. Neither state has advanced a compelling state interest that justifies erecting prohibitive barriers to abortion; we cannot let stand their statutes or similar statutes. While states surely have a legitimate interest in the protection of human life that is, was, or will be, this interest cannot justify roadblocks to equality and decisional privacy for pregnant women.

I write separately, second, to raise concerns about the Court's conclusion that the constitutional right to abortion amounts to a right to a reasonable time for deciding whether or not to abort. Abortion, like other medical matters, may be regulated by the state. However, the power to regulate in the name of public health and safety, women's health, or the welfare of the unborn is subject to constitutional limitation. According to Chief Justice Balkin, the practical standard that flows from the Fourteenth Amendment's guarantees "is whether the state's regulatory scheme gives the woman the ability to protect her health and safety, and offers her a fair and realistic chance to decide whether to become a parent, through a safe and realistically available method of abortion." However, the fundamental nature of the right to terminate pregnancy must mean that access to medically safe abortion cannot be cut off absolutely after a legislated "reasonable time."

Notwithstanding the states' interest in the unborn, access to abortion must not be entirely cut off to a woman who seeks to end pregnancy at any stage for legitimate reasons, including the woman's safety or her physical or emotional health. The Constitution requires that state law afford women what might be termed a "judicial by-pass" mechanism to seek the right to otherwise prohibited abortions. Under such a mechanism, women for whom abortion is disallowed by statute would have a realistic opportunity to establish before a competent court that they are in need of a medically safe abortion under the unique circumstances of their cases.

I.

The United States is undergoing a transformation as profound as any it has known. Women of all races and minorities of every hue and sad history are gaining overdue recognition as the equals of white men. This transformation is no happenstance. It is a product of more than a century of deliberate efforts to end pernicious discrimination and inequality. Those efforts have concentrated on several key fronts, including Congress, the state legislatures, and the courts.

A century ago, this Court was asked to strike down an Illinois decision that refused Myra Bradwell the right to obtain a license to practice law. See *Bradwell v. Illinois*, 83 U.S. 130 (1873). The Court declined. In refusing Mrs. Bradwell, the Court effectively sided with traditions that imposed domestic roles on women, however well qualified they might be by reason of inclination, intelligence, or training for less customary callings. Three Justices concurred in the memorable opinion that "[t]he paramount destiny and mission of woman are to fulfil the noble and benign offices of wife and mother. This is the law of the Creator." See 83 U.S. at 141 (Bradley, J., concurring).

The Creator is no longer presumed to be a bigot and an oppressor. The civil rights and women's rights movements of our era promise success. Thirty years from today, the roster of lawyers newly admitted to the bar is likely to contain approximately equal numbers of women and men of diverse races. Fifty years from today, it will be difficult for our grandchildren to comprehend why sex and color differences were considered relevant to the capacity to work in a chosen profession. In the meantime, female gender, pregnancy, and maternity are still perceived by some to stand in "natural" opposition to the demands of physically and mentally challenging occupations. Too many a husband, father, brother, or lover set on male domination is still persuaded of the moral error of women's liberty and equality. Some women, too, understandably balk at the new social order that suddenly expects them to do that which a few short years ago was unthinkable for their kind. In 1965, poor black girls were led to expect to end their schooling with high school and to become wives, mothers, and professional housemaids. In 1970, those same girls were offered the birth control pill and full scholarships to elite universities.

II.

Although radical transformation in societal attitudes and laws is occurring before our eyes, women are not yet the equals of men. We must take judicial notice of the glaring disparities readily apparent to any observer of the American scene. Men and women pervasively inhabit separate spheres. The greatest concentrations of women are found in care-taking roles and in the low-paid, low-prestige occupations. Women are less well educated and less well employed than men of similar ability. Federal government data, including census data collected by the U.S. Census Bureau in 1970, quantifies the stark educational and economic differences.

Whereas the median number of years spent in school for white men is 12.1 years, for minority women the number drops to 10.2 years, and for black women, in particular, the number drops to 10 years. The data show that, whereas about 7 million of the 51.8 million men over twenty-five years of age have spent four years or more in college, only 4.7 million of the 58 million women over twenty-five have done so.

Overall, female-headed households are about 20 percent poorer than men and male-headed households. Women who live apart from men are more likely to be poor. More than half of the female-headed families with young children live below the poverty line. The causes of women's depressed economic status are well understood. Women have been relegated to important but economically and socially inferior employment. Women outnumber men only in occupations traditionally deemed unsuitable for the male sex. Women lead men in the numbers of cleaning service workers, health service workers, child care workers, housemaids, clerical workers, and nurses. In 1970, there were 644,178 female housemaids and only 22,686 male housemaids; 122,062 female child care workers and only 9,196 male child care workers; 891,831 female nurses, dieticians, and therapists and only 53,152 men in those fields.

Men seeking the more prestigious and better paid occupations have had to face little competition from women. In 1970, there were 247,841 male lawyers and only 12,311 female lawyers; 255,105 male physicians, and only 25,824 female physicians; 87,691 male dentists, and only 3,110 female dentists; 211,830 male clergy and only 6,237 female clergy; 348,158 male college and university professors and 138,063 female professors. Women are excluded from the board rooms of major corporations. The disparities found in business and private employment exist in public employment, as well. In 1970, there were 362,396 male police officers and detectives, 13,098 female police officers and detectives; 174,922 male firefighters, compared to only 23,919 female firefighters.

Because women lag behind men educationally and economically, they are cut off from many of the common rewards of talent, achievement, and influence. Women are also at a political disadvantage. Woman can vote but do not lead. There has been no woman president or vice president. Women do not occupy seats in the president's cabinet. A woman in either house of Congress is a rare novelty. Women do not head major public agencies. The federal judiciary remains heavily male. The picture on the state level is similar. State assemblies, gubernatorial offices, and mayoral positions are male preserves.

III.

Sex and race inequality will not magically disappear once women have the right to seek the abortions that justice demands. Actual maternity has never been the sole detriment. Sex and color, as hard as they are to separate from connotations of sexuality and maternity, are themselves points of resistance. Husbands, boyfriends, and parents may stand in the way of effective choice. A woman forced to stay home by the threat of censure or fisticuffs is not capable of seeking medical abortion. Some women will have trouble exercising their rights to choose, even where there is no threat of external sanction. Brought up to view pregnancy as a punishment for sex, some women may be reluctant to escape maternal duties seemingly demanded by their personal moral codes. In addition, some women and supportive families will lack the money for abortion.

Liberties do not come automatically with the means to pay for their exercise. Fundamental freedom to travel does not come with a train ticket. Fundamental freedom to marry does not come with a guarantee that the state will provide a spouse. We do not reach the question here of whether government programs that pay for women's health and prenatal care can refuse to pay for medical abortions. Yet, the abortion right paired with a ban on government subsidy for abortions is as meaningless for the poorest women as the right to vote paired with a poll tax was for the poorest Alabama sharecroppers. It is doubtful that the government may use its funding powers selectively to fund only its favored reproductive choices.

Procreative liberty is not a panacea for what ails gender relations in this country. However, women who can reliably control their reproductive capacities are able to better plan their lives and take advantage of the new educational and employment opportunities. Medical science finally has placed the capacity to safely and reliably control when and whether to have children within women's reach. Contraception and abortion are tools women can use to take charge of their lives, subject, of course, to men's loosening their—at times violent and oppressive—grip on women's minds and bodies. The availability of contraception and abortion reduces the number of women who become pregnant or, if pregnant, give birth.

Thousands of abortions are already being performed every year on American women. Most are technically illegal, self-induced, or obtained at a great expense and inconvenience. Women are made to dissimulate, to penetrate layers of required approvals, to travel outside their home states, and even to leave the United States. All of this for procedures simple enough to be performed in half an hour's time in a physician's office. As a result of prohibitions and restrictions on abortion, women victimized by rape or incest routinely have their victimization compounded by pregnancy. Women whose mental and physical health are endangered by pregnancy are forced to assume unreasonable risks. Women whose children and elderly parents suffer material want and inattention with each new pregnancy press on or perish.

IV.

The Texas statutes before us are Articles 1191–1194 and 1196 of the state's Penal Code. These provisions make it a crime to "procure an abortion" or even to attempt abortion, except "an abortion procured or attempted by medical advice for the purpose of saving the life of the mother." The Texas statute and comparable statutes in other states sweepingly criminalize virtually all of the abortions routinely sought by thousands of women who face social or economic difficulties each year. The Texas law and similar laws require that the pregnant woman abandoned by her husband nevertheless assume the duties of motherhood, alongside the teenager impregnated by her uncle and the college coed whose contraception failed. For reasons set forth by Chief Justice Balkin, blanket abortion prohibitions like those enacted in Texas fall outside the bounds of rational state interest and legitimate authority. They are unconstitutionally restrictive of Fourteenth Amendment reproductive liberty. They certainly do not pass strict scrutiny.

Since the earliest beginnings of Western thought, matters relating to childbearing and child rearing have belonged more to the *oikos* (household) than to the *polis* (state). See Hannah Arendt, The Human Condition 38–78 (1959). The founding fathers of the United States presumed that choices relating to the course of pregnancy would be made by families, not by the state. However, state and federal restrictions on contraception and abortion had become a part of the American legal landscape even before the Comstock Laws of 1873 and 1876 outlawed trafficking in "every article or thing designed or intended for the prevention of conception or procuring of abortion," Act of July 12, 1876, 19 Stat. 90, amending 17 Stat. 598–99. Still, reproductive liberty is no mere innovation of today's discontent, experimental culture.

Indeed, in *Meyer v. Nebraska,* 262 U.S. 390, 399 (1923), the Court found that the Fourteenth Amendment protects a "right of the individual . . . to marry, establish a home and bring up children . . . and generally to enjoy those privileges long recognized at common law as essential to the orderly pursuit of happiness by free men." A parent is even free to educate offspring in the language of a foreign culture, notwithstanding the state interest in fostering "a homogeneous people with American ideals." Id. at 401. For nurture, and never domination, the existence, hearts, and minds of young children belong to their parents. In *Skinner v. Oklahoma,* 316 U.S. 535 (1942), the court rejected Oklahoma's effort to reduce crime through a discriminatory plan to sterilize certain recidivist thieves and not others. The right to procreate is "one of the basic civil rights of man," id. at 541; therefore, under the holding of *Skinner,* laws that touch on reproductive freedoms must burden or protect all citizens equally.

A. The Right to Privacy

In *Griswold v. Connecticut,* 381 U.S. 479 (1965) (opinion of Douglas, J.), we subsumed the right to choose whether or not to bear a child under the general heading of the "right to privacy." This way of framing the Court's understanding of the limits of state authority over procreation has been widely criticized. See, for example, Paul C. Kauper, "Penumbras, Peripheries, Emanations, Things Fundamental and Things Forgotten: The Griswold Case," 64 *Mich. L. Review* 235, 253 (1965). *Griswold*'s poetic derivation of the privacy right from the shadows and emanations of the Bill of Rights is indeed obscurantist. Talk of the "penumbras" of the Bill of Rights as the source of a privacy protection was unfortunate. It is true that various provisions of the Bill of Rights embody respect for privacy of thought, association, home, and property. However, the right to privacy in question, the right to choose whether or not to bear a child, is an incident of the Fourteenth Amendment. The Court in *Griswold* itself recognized as much. See 381 U.S. at 482 ("we are met with a wide range of questions that implicate the Due Process Clause of the Fourteenth Amendment. . . . We do not sit as a super-legislature to determine the wisdom, need, or propriety of laws that touch economic problems, business affairs, or social conditions. This law, however, operates directly on an intimate relation of husband and wife and their physician's role in one aspect of that relation."). The problem with Justice Douglas's opinion for the court in *Griswold* was not his assertion that procreative liberty connects in some important way with privacy, because it surely does, but his characterization of the *source* of the right to procreative privacy as the "penumbra" of the Bill of Rights rather than the Fourteenth Amendment.

The explicit recognition of privacy as an implicit constitutional value has been greeted with futile resistance. The evidence is ample that the life of privacy as an explicit value in all domains of law is just beginning. The language of privacy rights has become increasingly explicit in tort doctrines, see William L. Prosser, "Privacy," 48 *Calif. L. Rev.* 383 (1960). It is now explicit in constitutional law related to procreation, *Griswold v. Connecticut,* supra, and also unrelated to procreation, see, e.g., *Katz v. United States,* 389 U.S. 347 (1967) and *Loving v. Virginia,* 388 U.S. 1 (1967). The explicit language of privacy will surely soon work its way into state and federal statutes enacted to forestall the reach of the "dossier society" created by computer data banks in private industry and government. See Arthur R. Miller, "Computers, Data Banks and Individual Privacy: An Overview," 4 *Colum. Human Rights L. Rev.* 1 (1972) ("Concern over privacy is hardly irrational. . . . Few people seem to appreciate the fact that modern technology is capable of monitoring, centralizing and evaluating.").

New technologies and a new, egalitarian political order are calling attention to the lines drawn between citizen and government, self and other. "[T]o mark off the limits of the public and the private realms is an activity that began with man himself and is one that will never end; for it is an activity that touches the very nature of man," Milton Konvitz, "Privacy and the Law: A Philosophical Prelude," 31 *Law & Contemporary Problems* 272–76 (1966). Privacy, in its decisional, informational, physical, and proprietary senses, is a core value of civilized society, see *Olmstead v. United States,* 277 U.S. 438 (1928) (Brandeis, J., dissenting). Privacy protection is a requirement both of "inviolate personality," see Warren and Brandeis, "The Right to Privacy," 4 *Harv. L. Rev.* 193, 194 (1890), and human dignity, see Bloustein, "Privacy as an Aspect of Human Dignity," 39 *N.Y.U. L. Rev.* 962 (1964).

B. Privacy and Procreative Liberty

Three common meanings of privacy were in bold enough relief in *Griswold*: decisional privacy, physical privacy, and informational privacy. A fourth common meaning, proprietary privacy, was absent from *Griswold*. Each of the first three connects vitally to reproductive liberty. A married couple must be free to decide whether to use birth control; the partners must have "decisional privacy." A married couple must be free to live secluded from the watchful eye of agents of government seeking to know what the partners decided; they must have "physical privacy" and "informational privacy."

The only one of four extant conceptions of privacy not at play in *Griswold* was proprietary privacy. It is worth noting that in the decades after Samuel Warren and Louis Brandeis urged legal protection for privacy, see "The Right to Privacy," 4 *Harv. L. Rev.* 193 (1890), it was proprietary privacy claims to the exclusive use of photographs that first presented themselves to the state courts. See *Roberson v. Rochester Folding Box Co.*, 171 N.Y. 538, 64 N.E. 442 (1902). The right to "privacy" in that sense was the first right to privacy explicitly recognized as such in American law, see *Pavesich v. New England Life Ins. Co.*, 122 Ga. 190, 50 S.E. 68 (1905). The plaintiff in *Pavesich* complained that his photograph had been used without his permission for commercial advertising.

We need not enmesh ourselves in the history of privacy in U.S. law or in an arcane philosophical debate about whether all of the varied uses of the term "privacy" or "right to privacy" are well considered. The terms have varied meanings and connotations. This much is clear and bears emphasis. The core privacy concern in *Griswold*, and now in *Roe* and *Doe*, is concern about decisional privacy, that is, about the limits of public, government interference in the liberty to make decisions about procreation. Because serious efforts to regulate and restrict family planning would entail surveillance and information gathering concerning intimacies, physical and informational privacy are secondarily implicated.

As yet unacknowledged by any federal or state court are the deeper, more pervasive physical and informational privacy concerns implicated in the decision to use contraception or abortion. Solitude and seclusion are two paradigmatic forms of privacy. To be blunt, having children initiates a form of life in which the experience of solitude and seclusion is difficult to achieve, especially for women charged with the care of young children. See Charlotte Perkins Gilman, Women and Economics (1898) ("The home is the one place on earth where no one of the component individuals can have any privacy. . . . At present any tendency to withdraw and live one's own life on any plane of separate interest or industry is naturally resented, or at least regretted by the other members of the family. This affects women more than men, because men live very little in the family and very much in the world.). A woman's decision to prevent the birth of a child can also be motivated by her desire for healthy solitude and seclusion for herself and other members of her family, including other children.

We recently made plain that the right to privacy implicit in Fourteenth Amendment liberty belongs to unmarried no less than married individuals seeking contraception, *Eisenstadt v. Baird,* 405 U.S. 438 (1972). In *Eisenstadt,* we overturned the criminal conviction of a Massachusetts man whose only offense was lecturing to a college audience about family planning and giving an unmarried female member of his audience a sample package of a common contraceptive foam found in most drug stores. The right of privacy means, if anything, the right of the individual, "married or single, to be free from unwarranted governmental intrusion into matters so fundamentally affecting a person as the decision whether to bear or beget a child." 405 U.S. at 453 (opinion of Brennan, J.). Constitutional liberty does not allow Texas to make a woman's decision "whether to bear and beget a child" for her. Women must be recognized as free to choose whether to go through with a pregnancy, much as they are free to abstain from sex and to marry.

This Court would readily strike down a regime of laws that compelled women to abort their pregnancies. Only a catastrophic famine and world-historic disaster as improbable as the War of the Worlds could even tempt us to do it. In *Skinner v. Oklahoma,* this Court struck down a eugenics statute that allowed states to sterilize men classified as morally deficient recidivist felons. The court characterized procreation, along with marriage, as "one of the basic civil rights of man." Abortion cannot be prescribed for the unwilling, nor prohibited to the willing.

Like the right to prevent pregnancy, the right to terminate pregnancy is a fundamental right. It is fundamental because having primary say over the capacity to procreate goes to the very core of what it means to be a free person. Tyrants and dictators will insist that some people have children and that others not have children. In a free society governed by a just rule of law, persons cannot be required as a matter of course to bear or rear children. To be sure, in some nations of Europe blessed with political economies similar to our own, strict bans on contraception and abortion are tolerated as just. But the argument that ordered liberty requires procreative autonomy is not dented by the observation that Ireland, Italy, Germany, and France may prefer to continue subjugating their long-suffering female citizens. We have more than once before in this century been in the forefront of liberty and equality when compared to sister nations across the Atlantic.

V.

The Georgia statutes before us are Georgia Criminal Law §§ 26-1201 through 26-1203. These statutes offer a more liberal scheme than the Texas law. Realistic and humane, they allow a licensed physician to perform an abortion where "(1) a continuation of the pregnancy would endanger the life of the pregnant woman or would seriously and permanently injure her health," or "(2) the fetus would very likely be born with a grave, permanent, and irremediable mental or physical defect," or "(3) the pregnancy resulted from forcible or statutory rape." Yet, the Georgia law impairs freedom to decide by compelling women seeking abortions and their physicians to traverse a discouraging gauntlet of accountability unrelated to the woman's health or urgent public health concerns. In addition to a requirement that the patient be a Georgia resident and other requirements, the statutes impose three procedural conditions: (1) that the abortion be performed in a hospital accredited by the Joint Committee on Accreditation of Hospitals (JCAH); (2) that the procedure be approved by the hospital staff abortion committee; and (3) that the performing physician's judgment be confirmed by independent examinations of the patient by two other licensed physicians.

But these requirements amount to little more than the state meddling in the appropriately private choices of women and in the confidential physician-patient relationship. The accredited hospital requirement is not called for by the health needs of abortion patients or anyone else. Typical abortions are performed within the first dozen weeks of pregnancy and do not require a hospital for health or hygienic purposes. Condition (1) only serves to make abortions more expensive and to limit the right to perform them to physicians with privileges at accredited hospitals. The requirement of a hospital committee invades the informational privacy of the abortion patient and adds time and expense to abortion procedures not justified by reference to the medical needs of the patient or public health. Condition (2) only serves to make abortion less private, more expensive, and more time consuming. Women's health is hardly advanced by inviting a committee of strangers to participate in the family planning decisions of someone who may be of a dissimilar moral, religious, and cultural outlook. Condition (3) adds a layer of accountability to the work of physicians that is rarely imposed for medical procedures. A physician who wishes to perform a hysterectomy or appendectomy, more complex and invasive procedures than typical abortions, need not seek the concurrence of other colleagues, let alone two other licensed physicians. This condition is imposed to discourage physicians from performing abortions and to thereby make it more difficult and expensive for women to obtain abortions. These restrictions recreate the regime of prohibition that are suppose to liberalize.

The states are not free, under the guise of protecting maternal health or potential life, to intimidate women and physicians into continuing pregnancies. The Georgia statute and any similar statutes erecting a restrictive regime of abortion permissions are unconstitutional indirect constraints on Fourteenth Amendment liberty. It might be argued that certain restrictions constrain abortions but not unduly. However, it is incumbent upon this Court today to insist that strict scrutiny not be suspended on the grounds that a restriction could be characterized as only a wee bit burdensome—as not "unduly" burdensome.

The requirement of spousal or parental consent might be thought to properly involve families in women's decision making. The requirement of a waiting period or counseling might be thought to properly encourage reflection about options and alternatives. But such requirements presuppose that others know better than women the intimate circumstances that lead women to seek abortion in the first place. They also presuppose that women will not involve supportive family members, will not reflect, and will not seek the opinions of moral advisers and social service providers unless the state compels them to. Prejudice only supports these presuppositions.

Reporting the names and addresses of abortion patients to state officials would also serve as an unwarranted restriction on abortion. The goal of statistical record-keeping could clearly be accomplished by means of anonymous reporting standards, designed to protect the confidentiality and informational privacy of abortion patients. It might be argued that states are surely justified in placing time limits on abortion. But restrictions of this sort are also suspect. The specter of a woman obtaining an abortion for frivolous, nonmedical reasons when she is in her eighth month of pregnancy would argue for state-imposed time limits were it other than a chimera. Society does not needs laws that forbid what no sane clinician would do and no sane woman would seek to have done.

To uphold the challenged statutes against the background of *Skinner v. Oklahoma* and *Loving v. Virginia* would be hard enough. To do so on the heels of *Griswold v. Connecticut* and *Eisenstadt v. Baird* is impossible. The Constitution does not permit the state to impose pregnancy or parenthood on its citizens through direct or indirect constraints prompted by illiberal moralism and paternalism.

VI.

Minimal state intrusion in reproductive matters was the rule at the inception of our nation and remained so for many years. Women made use of folk remedies to control their fertility, and the government made no effort to step in. The main impetus for regulating abortion and birth control came from sources of little relevance and no continuing validity today. First, fears about the health of women motivated restrictions in the nineteenth century, when medical options for contraception and abortion were hazardous. Today, contraception is safe and abortion safer than pregnancy for women's health. Second, in the past century, moralistic fears about the spread of pornography and obscenity led to laws that suppressed birth control and abortion. In 1832, Charles Knowlton was sent to jail by Massachusetts authorities for publishing a best-seller that was probably the first comprehensive medical book on contraception. The useful life of paternalism and moralism has expired. We have recently held under the First Amendment that moralistic laws cannot criminalize a man's use of obscene material in the privacy of his own home, *Stanley v. Georgia,* 394 U.S. 557 (1969). We must now hold under the Fourteenth Amendment that moralistic laws cannot criminalize the relationship between a medical professional who provides abortion and his or her patient.

VII.

Our decision is as weighty and politically charged as any we have ever confronted. The right of privacy of which we speak is the right to decide upon the "private use of . . . intimacy." *Poe v. Ullman,* 367 U.S. 497 (1961) (Harlan, J., dissenting). Much is at stake in our decision for the future of women, weighed down in the past by societal norms and expectations of self-sacrificing maternalism. Also at stake is the legal status, if not of the unborn, then of moral and religious sentiments about the first beginnings of human life.

Because the right to terminate pregnancy is fundamental, the states may not abridge the right in the absence of a compelling interest. The state has an interest in protecting human life. It also has an interest in cultivating respect for humanity. That interest has never been interpreted to mean that the state is authorized to do anything it pleases in the name of the sanctity of human life. It cannot require that all fertile persons produce children; it cannot require the affluent to adopt malnourished children as their own. It need not eschew capital punishment. It may not artificially extend the life spans of the ill and dying or mandate specific rituals of respect for the deceased. But, out of respect for humanity, present-day state laws honor the living and the dead in countless many ways. The dead are honored through the enforcement of wills and by the requirement that corpses be handled with dignity. The state shows regard for future generations by requiring the conservation of natural resources and by funding public works projects that will benefit our unborn grandchildren more than us ourselves. Viewed in this light, the recognition of a state interest in respect for the earliest beginnings of human life *in utero* is nothing extraordinary. Providing healthy food, medicine, and prenatal care for pregnant women is one way the state might legitimately express respect for the earliest beginnings of life.

The state interest in the unborn and in cultivating respect for the earliest beginnings of human life cannot properly extend to victimization of the fully born who seek to shape the vital contours of their own futures. The embryo or fetus is biologically and socially located in a domain of autonomy that limits the ability of the state to ascribe to it an overriding "right to life." The state interest in the unborn cannot mean that an unwilling citizen can be forced to carry a fetus to term in her abdomen and then to assume the identity as mother of a child she rears or places for adoption. The state interest in respecting the dead has not meant that an unwilling citizen can be forced to spend hours a day paying ritual homage to ashes in an urn. There are limits on what the state can force a person to do for others.

Chief Justice Balkin proposes to test the constitutionality of state laws by reference to whether such laws burden the fundamental constitutional right to end pregnancy by denying women a reasonable period of time within which to make a choice and exercise it:

> We hold today that the constitutional right to abortion requires that legislatures must specify a period of time during pregnancy in which women may obtain medically safe abortions. During this period legislatures may require that abortions be performed by a licensed physician. Legislatures

may restrict or even completely prohibit abortions performed after the end of the statutorily defined period, except where an abortion is necessary, in the judgment of medical professionals, to preserve the life or health of the mother. This formulation recognizes the two aspects of the right to reproductive freedom. A woman's right to choose whether or not to become a parent requires that she be given a reasonable time to decide, but a woman's right to protect her life and health continues throughout the pregnancy. In deciding upon the appropriate length of the statutory period, legislatures must choose a date that vindicates the woman's fundamental rights under the Fourteenth Amendment, and this choice is subject to judicial review.

The Court's formula improves upon any that would seek to limit the right by appeal either to unavoidably philosophical and religious conceptions of when human life begins or to medically variable notions of fetal viability. Soon after fertilization of an egg, a developmentally human entity exists; some fetuses that women may wish to abortion could survive outside the womb with or without medical assistance. Yet, recognizing humanity and viability in the unborn does not undercut the constitutional case for abortion grounded on equality and privacy. The Court's formula also improves upon patently irrational standards that purport to promote the state interest in the unborn uniformly but premise the right to abort on the circumstances of maternal health or the circumstances of pregnancy (i.e., rape and incest).

The Court's "reasonable time to decide" standard is an improvement that can be improved upon. The unimproved standard seems to presuppose that typical pregnant women and their doctors need state laws to prevent them from aborting pregnancies after the woman has had a realistic and reasonable opportunity to make and effectuate a choice to obtain a medically safe abortion. However, this Court has no basis for believing that typical women delay aborting beyond a "reasonable" period. Nor does this Court have any basis for believing that typical licensed physicians are willing to perform abortions on patients long after a realistic and reasonable period for choice. The state laws that will be constitutionally permissible under the Court's formula may be like laws that prohibit riding hippopotamuses through the streets of St. Louis—constitutional, but wholly unnecessary.

If there were no laws limiting the time after which abortions could take place, the vast majority of abortions would continue to be performed, as the legal ones currently are, in the first trimester of pregnancy. A percentage would take place in the early second trimester, and the rare abortion would take place in the third trimester. Early abortion will be always be preferred because it is least costly, least medically complex, and least morally and emotionally complicated for women and families. In exceedingly difficult and tragic cases, abortions are at times sought by women who are well along in their pregnancies. (The circus occasionally brings hippos into town.) These women include teenagers unfamiliar with the symptoms of pregnancy and women of any age whose health or economic or social circumstances result in understandable delays or changes of heart. The argument of liberty and equality advanced by the Court points to the need for flexibility in state abortion law. Yet, the Court offers a bright-line-based standard with no flexibility for individual cases.

Chief Justice Balkin recognizes that any state legislated time limit is going to be, to some extent, arbitrary: "A line must be drawn at some point to enable the state to express its sincere and legitimate interest in the human potential of the fetus. But the line must not be drawn so early as to effectively extinguish the constitutional right to choose. There is no magical formula for demarcating such a line with mathematical precision." Because "the balance between the competing factors is essentially legislative, and must be drawn by legislatures themselves," the right to end pregnancy is subject to a degree of burdensome political whimsy, checked by cumbersome powers of judicial review.

States are permitted to set limits on abortion that are not burdensome to the fundamental right to choose or that further compelling state interests. Certain schemes of time-limited abortion rights pass constitutional muster. If a state chooses to erect otherwise constitutionally permitted general time limits, I believe it must simultaneously legislate a judicial bypass mechanism that will allow court-approved abortions to take place after the time limits have passed. Women's liberty and equality are implicated in "late" as well as in "early" abortion.

It is worth noting that other state limits on abortion not at issue in this proceeding would similarly require a judicial by-pass mechanism. States may seek, for example, to ban abortions for minors or to require parental notification or approval for minors' abortions. Age limits on abortion are arguably constitutional. We do not face these questions here but undoubtedly will in good time. Were the Court to someday hold that age limits on access to abortion are constitutional, I believe it would also need to hold that a judicial by-pass mechanism is a constitutional requirement. Through such a mechanism, a young woman could establish to a judge that she is mature enough to obtain an abortion without parental involvement or that she is at risk of physical or emotional violence that countermands parental involvement.

VIII.

It is tempting, but short-sighted, to depict pregnant women as in conflict with their fetuses. Yet, some fetuses—about half of them—are destined also to be women. As such, they, too, will confront lives of considerable denial and inequality. It is for the benefit of unborn and born women, present and future women, that we grant constitutional abortion liberty today.

Consider the collective life of Man and the collective life of Woman. Man takes on productive labors. Man makes progress in those labors, improving the lot of humankind and ensuring that subsequent generations of Man can build on the accomplishments of the preceding. Woman takes on the traditional labors of women, including the labor of motherhood. But, she is like Sisyphus in the Greek myth. She perpetually rolls her prescribed stone uphill, only to have it always roll down again. There is an element of futility in what she does. Her daughters and granddaughters must repeat her exact labors. Woman does not progress. The sacrifices mothers make for their daughters enable the daughters to make the same sacrifices for their daughters, and they for theirs, and so on. Man labors for the son who will invent the radio, the grandson who will create a life-saving vaccine, and the great grandson who will win the Nobel Prize for literature. The world still awaits its first woman astronaut, president, and chief justice. It is time that Woman held firm her stone and took in life from the hilltop.

RUBENFELD, J., concurring in *Roe v. Wade* and concluding that the writ of certiorari should be dismissed as improvidently granted in *Doe v. Bolton*.

The question before us is clear. Can the law force women to bear children against their will? The answer is no, and we ought to say so today without equivocation.

From time out of mind, societies have found ways to keep women from deciding freely whether or when they will bear children. One way to effect this result is by prohibiting contraception and abortion. We have already held that states can no longer ban contraception. *Eisenstadt v. Baird*, 405 U.S. 438 (1972); *Griswold v. Connecticut*, 381 U.S. 479 (1965). It is time we held the same of abortion.

I.

Petitioners Roe and Doe filed these suits years ago, challenging abortion laws in Texas and Georgia, respectively. Because their pregnancies have long since ended, respondents argue that their claims must be dismissed as moot. If so, no woman could ever have the judiciary finally determine whether an abortion law violated her constitutional rights. She would either lack standing at filing or lose it along the way. The law is not quite so perverse, *Moore v. Ogilvie*, 394 U.S. 814, 816 (1969) ("capable of repetition, yet evading review"), and judicial review not quite so easily evaded.

II.

Texas makes abortion a crime from conception, unless "for the purpose of saving the life of the mother." Tex. Pen. Code arts. 1191, 1194. There are no exceptions. A man who rapes and impregnates a thirteen-year-old Texas girl can count on that state's officers to force her, under threat of prison, to carry his seed for nine months and then to mother his offspring. This barbarism has no place under our Constitution.

Exactly 100 years ago, this Court upheld a state statute that excluded women from the legal profession. *Bradwell v. Illinois,* 83 U.S. (16 Wall.) 130 (1873). At that time, members of this Court could still call "repugnant" the "idea of a woman adopting a distinct and independent career." Id. at 141 (concurring opinion). "The paramount destiny and mission of woman," it was said, "are to fulfil the . . . offices of wife and mother. This is the law of the Creator." Id.

The Texas statutes before us today belong to this era. Their effect is to compel women to "fulfil the . . . offices of wife and mother," even when they do not wish to. Under such laws, women today are still forced into motherhood against their will.

It is astounding that members of this Court today can describe a woman's interest in terminating an unwanted pregnancy as mere "convenience, whim, or caprice." Post at 243 (dissenting opinion). Laws that prohibit abortion differ categorically from virtually every other law on our books. They do not merely prohibit a particular act. They oblige an unwilling individual to carry out a specific, sustained, long-term, life-altering, and life-occupying course of conduct. A woman forbidden to abort an unwanted pregnancy is forced to bear a child. She is made to accept significant health risks. She will undergo radical bodily change. She may die.

Nor is it only nine months of a woman's life that may be occupied with the task that Texas seeks to force on her. It can be years and years. For, though a particular woman may choose, when given a choice, to end an unwanted pregnancy, she will in all likelihood not choose to abandon a delivered child. On the contrary, she will probably raise the child, one of the more demanding jobs a person can be asked to undertake.

Texas will not be heard to say that its abortion laws "merely" force pregnant women to bear children, not to raise them. Once a woman gives birth to a child, Texas has other laws that (quite properly) require her to fulfill long-term parental obligations. "The parent is under a legal obligation to educate and maintain the child, and it has no legal claim upon others to perform that duty." *Gulley v. Gulley,* 111 Tex. 233, 237–38 (1921). In any event, having forced an unwilling woman to carry and bear, Texas cannot disclaim responsibility if, as a natural and foreseeable consequence, the woman ends up feeling bound, by the deep sentiments of love or duty that characteristically arise, to keep and raise her child. A woman who has given birth can be expected to feel bound to her baby by ties that defy description; if Texas has forced an unwilling woman into this position, it is responsible for the consequences.

Hence, we deal here with a state law that, as a real-life matter, not metaphorically but practically and concretely, can force on an individual who did not intend or want it what is tantamount to a full-time, years-long occupation. The Constitution does not permit this.

A slave can be assigned an occupation. So can a prison inmate. But no law can impose an occupation on a free citizen. A statute that tells a man he will be a farm hand for the next ten years—or even the next nine months—would be struck before the ink was dry. In *Bailey v. Alabama*, 219 U.S. 219 (1911), we held that a state could not constitutionally force a man, under threat of prison, to work for a year on a farm even though he had expressly promised to perform this work and had accepted money for doing so. How, then, can a state force an unwilling woman into the labors of motherhood?

A woman's right not to be impressed into unwanted labor is no less than a man's. Bearing and raising children is no less onerous than the farm work at issue in *Bailey*. If a state cannot force a man to till a field, it cannot force a woman to mother a child.

There is nothing "extra-constitutional" or "extra-textual" about this right. After the Thirteenth Amendment abolished slavery, the Fourteenth was enacted to prevent states from using other legal devices, overt or covert, to deny any American the fundamental "privileges or immunities of citizens" that distinguish free men from slaves. It is unsurprising, therefore, that this Court has recognized under the Fourteenth Amendment "the right of every citizen of the United States to follow any lawful calling, business, or profession he may choose." *Dent v. West Virginia*, 129 U.S. 114, 121 (1889); see *Greene v. McElroy*, 360 U.S. 474, 492 (1959). This right should not be overstated. Some occupations, such as prostitution, can be banned outright. Others, such as the practice of medicine, can be made dependent on qualifications difficult to attain. See *Dent*, 129 U.S. at 122. The freedom to choose one's occupation does not guarantee that every occupation must be within every individual's reach.

But there can be no doubt about the core meaning of this freedom. It is the right not to have an occupation forcibly or legally imposed on one. It is the right not to be forced into labor against one's will, for it is that right which chiefly distinguishes the free from the slave. And no law could more plainly violate this right than a law forcing a woman to bear a child.

Slave women were regularly forced to procreate whether or not they wished to. Indeed, subjection to forced mating may be the chief defining feature of female enslavement. The Fourteenth Amendment had one over-riding purpose: to prevent states from replicating through law the distinctive forms of dominion and subjugation exercised over this nation's slaves. "The amendment was an attempt to give voice to the strong National yearning for that time and that condition of things, in which . . . every citizen of the United States might stand erect on every portion of its soil, in the full enjoyment of every right and privilege belonging to a freeman, without fear of violence or molestation." *Slaughter-House Cases*, 83 U.S. 36, 123 (1872) (dissenting opinion). A fundamental right of a free woman is the right not to be forced into childbearing against her will.

True, a woman who never had sexual intercourse would never face the strictures of an abortion law, and on this ground Texas says it does not force any woman to bear a child. The argument is specious—and would remain specious even were it not undermined by the state's failure to make an exception to its abortion laws in cases of rape. If a pregnant woman does not want to be a mother, Texas's prohibition of abortion will overrule her decision. It will force her, under threat of imprisonment, to carry and bear the child. No casuistry can alter this fact.

Perhaps Texas means to argue that women somehow "consent" to child-bearing whenever they voluntarily engage in sexual intercourse. But we do not consent to an event just because we knowingly engage in conduct that risks it. I do not consent to a car accident by driving on the highway. Nor can a woman be said to have "waived" her constitutional rights by engaging in sex. Constitutional rights are not waived absent actual consent. *Johnson v. Zerbst*, 304 U.S. 458, 464 (1938); *Ohio Bell Tel. Co. v. Public Utilities Com.*, 301 U.S. 292, 307 (1937). Petitioner in *Bailey* did not waive his rights against forced labor even though he had contracted to do the work and had accepted money for doing it. How, then, can a woman be said to have waived her rights against forced labor merely by engaging in sexual intercourse?

Texas, in essence, tells a woman to remain abstinent or accept the state's power to force childbearing upon her should pregnancy ensue. No one would defend a law that left men with a comparable choice—either abstain from sexual intercourse or accept the state's power to force labor upon you—on the ground that the state had left men "free to choose." States have no constitutional power to put a man to a choice between, say, celibacy and farm work. So, too, they have no power to put a woman to a choice between celibacy and motherhood. That is the essential principle established by *Griswold* and *Eisenstadt,* and it applies a fortiori here.

III.

The answer to all this, according to counsel for Texas, is that states have a compelling interest in protecting "unborn life" from the moment of conception. Citing cases in which we have suggested that constitutional rights may be curtailed when a law is narrowly tailored to further a compelling state interest, e.g., *Grayned v. Rockford,* 408 U.S. 104, 119 (1972), Texas argues that a single-celled human zygote—the fertilized ovum—is a person, or independent human being, from the moment of conception, or at any rate that state legislatures may so conclude and, on this basis, ban abortion no matter how early it occurs in a woman's pregnancy.

This argument is not a good one, but it deserves a careful and respectful reply. Many conscientious Americans believe that human life begins at conception. They may rightly ask why a state cannot enact this position into its law.

The idea that a fertilized ovum is an independent human being from the moment of conception is a relatively new one—medically, morally, and legally. In the Anglo-American tradition, and indeed in most other Western traditions, it was well understood that a fetus had to be considerably developed before abortion became an offense. Thus, at common law, abortion was not a crime until "quickening," which occurred around the fifth gestational month. See, e.g., *Commonwealth v. Bangs,* 9 Mass. 387, 388 (1812); *State v. Cooper,* 22 N.J.L. 52, 58 (1849); 1 W. Blackstone, Commentaries at *125–26. Even after quickening, a charge of murder did not lie for abortion unless there had been a live birth. *Dietrich v. Northampton,* 138 Mass. 14, 17 (1886) (Holmes, J.). In general, as Holmes put it, the rule was that there could be no "person recognized by the law" without a live birth. Id.; see *Steadfast v. Nicoll,* 3 Johns. Cas. 18, 25 (N.Y. 1802) (Radcliffe, J.) (child "not *in esse*" at common law while still "*en ventre sa mere*").

But ideas change, and states have never been required to adhere in every respect to the common law. Nevertheless, under our Constitution, there are views that individuals may adopt but that states cannot. For example, individuals whose faith tells them that God infuses a soul into each of us upon conception are of course entitled to hold, express, and act on this belief, provided they do not transgress the rights of others in doing so. But no state could enact this postulate into law, because it is plainly religious in nature.

Acknowledging this point, as it must, Texas argues that its abortion statute does not enact any distinctively religious articles of faith. Rather, the state argues, "advances in medical science" support the position that an independent human being, or person, comes into existence at the moment of conception. Texas bases this claim on three asserted facts: the fertilized egg is "genetically complete"; its natural development into a child has begun; and there is no other, non-arbitrary point in the course of gestation at which personhood could be said to begin.

By this logic, a planted acorn is an oak tree. The acorn is genetically complete, its natural development into a tree has begun, and there is no non-arbitrary line that divides a planted acorn from a fully grown tree. Texas's position seems to be that, where no bright line interrupts a gradual process of change, the two end points may be deemed equivalent. It would follow that night is day, and winter spring—or at least that legislators may make it so.

Stripped, as it must be, of religious backing, Texas's argument rests on a fallacy. It confounds the potential with the actual. It conflates the seed with what the seed may one day become.

Any sensible person must see how painful, how difficult to accept, the Court's decision today will be to those who oppose abortion. For someone who believes that a single-celled zygote is an independent human being, all abortion is murder: women who obtain abortions are heinous criminals, doctors who perform abortions are killers, and, we are told, those who respect women's right to make this decision for themselves are "cowards and collaborators." I do not doubt the sincerity and passion of those who hold this view. One can only hope that they will in turn respect the good faith of those who disagree, rather than succumbing to the hysteria and righteous unreason so visible, regrettably, in one of today's dissenting opinions.

The author of that opinion says, for example, "The full genetic makeup of a unique living being of the species *homo sapien* [*sic*] is present at conception, and that makeup constitutes a human life." This is the heart of the dissenting justice's opinion; it is the proposition on the basis of which he launches his extraordinary rhetoric of "mass murder" and "atrocity." But the "full genetic makeup of a unique living being of the species *homo sapien*" obviously does not and cannot "constitute a human life." The same "full genetic makeup" is equally present in almost every cell of one's body.

I doubt that even my dissenting colleague believes he commits murder every time he has blood drawn—a procedure that extracts and kills numerous white blood cells, each of which bears "the full genetic makeup of a unique living being."

Justice Paulsen also writes, "The living human embryo is already *alive,* and it is a *human* life. Abortion does not destroy potential life. Abortion kills a living human being." Italics are not arguments. One could as well write, "The living human blood cell is already *alive,* and it is a *human* blood cell. Thus, blood tests kill living human beings." Cells may be alive, and human, but that does not make them human beings.

To be sure, unlike an ordinary blood cell, the zygote is part of a human being's life cycle. This is a very important difference, but, again, it does not make the zygote a human being. A caterpillar is part of a butterfly's life cycle. It is not, however, a butterfly—any more than an acorn is an oak.

Trying to avoid these simple truths, Justice Paulsen writes, "I would note that a planted acorn *is* an oak tree seed and thus *is* an oak tree, just one at an early stage." Yes, and night *is* day, just at an early stage. And babies *are* teenagers, teenagers old codgers, and all men dust—just at an early stage.

Mankind has not yet identified with precision—perhaps it never will—the exact moment at which human beings come into existence or pass away, and therefore states have considerable latitude in deciding these things for themselves. Some states, for example, accept the concept of "brain death," e.g., Kan. Stat. Ann. 1972 Supp. 77-202, while others do not. More states will probably do so as our knowledge of the brain increases. Perhaps one day science will provide an understanding of "brain birth" that may forge a consensus about life's beginning. But until that day, or even after it, states are free to differ on the legal status of human embryos and, specifically, on the question of when, during the course of gestation, an independent human being comes into existence. The judgment is a moral one, and, generally speaking, states are free to arrive at their own conclusions on moral matters. *Carpenters & Joiners Union v. Ritter's Cafe,* 315 U.S. 722, 726 (1942).

But a state's prerogative to legislate morality is not unlimited. The prerogative ends when legislating morality would deprive an individual of a constitutional right. There are four-letter words whose public use is immoral, yet a state may not deny an individual the right to express his dissenting political opinion on that basis. *Cohen v. California,* 403 U.S. 15 (1971). Interracial marriage was long considered immoral, but states cannot enact that morality into law when doing so would result in a denial of equal protection. *Loving,* supra. Fundamental liberties would be meaningless drivel if states could take them away on the basis of moral judgments.

It follows that even though private individuals are free to adopt the moral judgment that human life begins at conception, Texas is not free to ban abortion outright upon that ground. For then Texas would be able to force women to bear children against their will—and thus extinguish their constitutional right of privacy—on the basis of a putative moral judgment, which the Constitution does not allow.[1]

There is no occasion here to decide when, at the earliest, a state may ban abortion, but the constitutional principle is clear enough. The right at stake is a woman's right not to be forced by the state to bear a child. Hence, so long as a state gives pregnant women sufficient time to decide whether to bear, the state does not violate this right. In other words, while a state cannot ban abortion from the moment of conception, it may prohibit abortion at a time late enough in the woman's term that she has had a reasonable amount of time to discover her pregnancy and to make her own choice about whether to bear. If, for example, a woman has the legal right to choose abortion until the twentieth week of pregnancy, see, e.g., proposed Uniform Abortion Act § 2(b)(2), Conference of Commissioners on Uniform State Laws, 58 *A.B.A. J.* 380 (1972), she cannot reasonably complain afterward that the state forced motherhood upon her. This is the principle adopted by the Court, I believe, and I concur in that portion of the Chief Justice's opinion that makes this clear (although I do not reach, as he does, a question that is not presented here—whether a state that prohibits late-term abortions must make an exception where the woman's life is endangered).

IV.

Given the views just expressed, I cannot agree with the Court's disposition of *Doe v. Bolton.* Georgia prohibits abortion from conception except in cases of rape, grave threat to the woman's health, or "irremediable" birth "defect." Ga. Crim. Code §§ 26-1201, 26-1202(a). The statute requires that the operating physician attest that the abortion is "necessary because" of one of these three conditions, that at least two other physicians concur in this "clinical judgment," that the abortion be approved yet again by a medical committee of the hospital in which it is to be performed, and that a host of further regulations be complied with, many of which are procedural in nature. Id. at § 26-1202(b).

What we ought to say is that this statute is unconstitutional because it does not respect a woman's right to choose for herself whether to bear a child—a decision that can no more be made to depend on special reasons or justifications than can an individual's decision to speak his mind on some matter of political opinion. But the Court does not say this. Instead, the Court strikes down some of Georgia's procedural regulations while declining to rule on the substantive heart of the statute: the provisions that prohibit abortion except in the three specified circumstances. The reason is jurisdictional. The district court below already invalidated those provisions, and that holding is currently on appeal in the Fifth Circuit. As a result, in the Chief Justice's view, those provisions are not before us. The difficulty is that the statute's other provisions, which the Court strikes down, make little or no sense on their own.

Georgia has essentially banned abortion in the absence of rape or what is deemed to be medical necessity. The bulk of its statute seeks to create procedural rules and safeguards to ensure that these exceptional circumstances exist. If for jurisdictional reasons we cannot reach the heart of Georgia's abortion law, it makes little sense to rule on the state's further, procedural regulations.

If this case genuinely required us to decide the appropriate standards of review applicable to time, place, and manner regulations of abortion, I might have supposed it logical to employ the standards we apply to content-neutral time, place, and manner regulations of speech. In general, such restrictions must be narrowly tailored to serve the legitimate interests they putatively serve. *Grayned,* 408 U.S. at 116–17. Although we sometimes describe such narrow-tailoring review in terms of "balancing" benefits and burdens, the principle in all such cases is that the constitutional right "must not, in the guise of regulation, be abridged or denied." Id. at 117 (quoting *Hague v. CIO,* 307 U.S. 496, 516 (1939)). In other words, the state's legitimate regulatory authority cannot be used as a pretext for what is really an attempt to penalize or obstruct the exercise of the constitutional right; narrow-tailoring review serves to smoke out such impermissible purposes. Where states impose time, place, and manner regulations on abortion, the constitutional analysis should be the same.

But this narrow-tailoring test does not apply to Georgia's abortion regulations, which seek to prohibit abortion except when "necessary," any more than our First Amendment time, place, and manner test would apply to a law that prohibited people from expressing their political opinions except when "necessary." Such a law would be unconstitutional in its entirety. If it contained provisions setting forth for the procedures through which the requisite "necessity" had to be shown, those provisions would not get the benefit of our relatively lenient time, place, and manner test. The same is true of Georgia's abortion statute; it is unconstitutional in its entirety. Because, however, a majority of the Court considers the statute as a whole not before us, I would dismiss the writ as improvidently granted.

V.

The right we protect today is now known as the right of privacy. That term can be misleading. The right of privacy is not a right to engage in that "purely private conduct" which affects no one but oneself. There is no such conduct, or, if there is, decisions about reproduction are not instances of it. Nor does this right protect those "purely private domains" of life which must remain free from all state regulation. There are no such domains, or, if there are, sexuality and reproduction are not among them. Nor, finally, is the Fourteenth Amendment's privacy the same as the Fourth Amendment's, which guards against unreasonable state intrusions into the home and other private places. The privacy we protect today is even more fundamental than this.

Public life could not exist if government lacked the power to prohibit all sorts of actions that majorities want suppressed. But private life could not exist if the state could affirmatively dictate the course of an individual's future.

Plato, in his *Republic*, envisioned "guardians" exercising near-total control over individuals' lives, assigning them to particular jobs, dictating their family situations. In feudal societies, individuals' occupations were often determined at birth, and their marriages were often chosen for them. In our own time, we have seen totalitarian governments "relocate" individuals, assigning them to lives and jobs of the state's choosing. But as this Court said fifty years ago: "Although such measures have been deliberately approved by men of great genius, their ideas touching the relation between individual and State were wholly different from those upon which our institutions rest." *Meyer v. Nebraska,* 262 U.S. 390, 402 (1923).

If our governments had unchecked power to force men to work at particular occupations, or women to bear children against their will, our lives would in a real sense no longer be our own. Instead of citizens having authority over their state, the state could write the scripts of its citizens' lives. Under our Constitution, an individual is not the "creature of the state." *Pierce v. Society of Sisters,* 268 U.S. 510, 535 (1925). The right of privacy is the right to a private life—a life of one's own—and it is implicated whenever government attempts, going beyond mere prohibitions of activity deemed harmful, to take over an individual's future, forcing him to carry out a specific, long-term, life-occupying course of conduct he does not choose for himself.[2]

Some have called the right of privacy unenumerated and, on this ground, have denied or disparaged it. Their solicitude for the Constitution's text would be more plausible if they were not themselves violating it: "The enumeration of certain rights, in the Constitution, shall not be construed to deny or disparage others retained by the people." U.S. Const. amend. IX. To be sure, hyper-technical readings can always be found to rob the Ninth Amendment of its plain meaning, but it is indisputably reasonable, at the very least, to take the Ninth Amendment to mean what its words seem plainly to suggest: that the enumerated constitutional rights are not exhaustive. In my view, the right of privacy is not unwritten; it is, as I have said, one of the "privileges or immunities of citizenship" protected by the Fourteenth Amendment. But even if I thought otherwise, the Ninth Amendment would be a clear and sufficient answer to those who say this Court acts without a reasonable basis in the Constitution's text when it enforces unenumerated rights.

As there are privileges of citizenship, so too there are duties, such as jury or military service, that government may undoubtedly compel all to perform at appropriate times within appropriate limits. *Selective Draft Law Cases,* 245 U.S. 366, 390 (1918); *Butler v. Perry,* 240 U.S. 328, 333 (1916); *Robertson v. Baldwin,* 165 U.S. 275, 298 (1897) (Harlan, J., dissenting). But we do not deal here with such public duties of citizenship. Rather, we deal with a law that would force a particular private life on particular private individuals; a law that would force on an unwilling woman what is likely to be a full-time, years-long occupation; a law whose purpose and effect is to make women bear children against their will. This the right of privacy does not allow.

NOTES

1. As to the separate claim, advanced by Texas without any support or evidence, that the word "person" as used in the Fourteenth Amendment was intended to include "unborn life," the Chief Justice's opinion contains a fully adequate response.

2. Accordingly, I see no reason in this case to call into question, as the Chief Justice does, Justice Holmes's opinion for the Court in *Buck v. Bell,* 274 U.S. 200 (1925).

WEST, J., concurring in the judgment.

I concur in the judgment of the Chief Justice. I agree that the Texas and Georgia abortion statutes are unconstitutional under the Fourteenth Amendment. I write separately on the question of the laws' constitutionality because my reasons for believing these laws to be constitutionally problematic are somewhat different from those offered by the Chief Justice, and by Justices Allen, Siegel, Sunstein, Rubenfeld, Amar, and Tushnet, as well.

I disagree, however, with the breadth and sweep of reasoning suggested by the Chief Justice's opinion. It is Congress, not this Court, that is explicitly directed by Section 5 of the Fourteenth Amendment to respond to states that engage in practices or laws that are unconstitutional under Section 1 of the Fourteenth Amendment. Congress must be given the opportunity to exercise its responsibility, and its right, to evaluate the scope of the unconstitutionality of the Texas and Georgia laws and to take whatever remedial steps it deems necessary to address the problem. While it is fully appropriate for the courts and for this Court to render our opinion regarding the constitutionality of these particular laws, and while we must decline to enforce laws that we find unconstitutional, it is for Congress to assess the full magnitude of the constitutional mandate and hence the full scope of the violation under the Fourteenth Amendment, and to determine appropriate remedial measures.

I first discuss the reasons I find the Georgia and Texas statutes unconstitutional and then address what I regard to be the remedial path we ought to follow.

I. Equal Protection

Our case law under the Fourteenth Amendment has established that state legislation may violate the Equal Protection Clause if the law in question penalizes or targets or in some way treats one group more harshly than another where, for all reasons that should matter to the state, those groups are similarly situated. *Royster Guano Co. v. Virginia,* 253 U.S. 412 (1920) ("The classification must be reasonable, not arbitrary and must rest upon some ground of difference having a fair and substantial relation to the object of the legislation, so that all persons similarly circumstanced shall be treated alike."). We recently held as much in a case involving a classificatory scheme that distinguished between potential executors of an estate on the basis of sex. *Reed v. Reed,* 404 U.S. 71 (1971). If the group adversely impacted by the law has historically borne the brunt of legal, political, and social subordination, then this Court may find that the offending statute is unconstitutional and accordingly refuse to enforce it if the classification does not serve an important or compelling state purpose. The Equal Protection Clause, as we have interpreted it, basically requires state legislation to be fair and rational and requires of courts vigilance when irrational legislation seems targeted at groups that have been grossly subordinated, vilified, or ill treated. This may not be the most natural reading of the Equal Protection Clause of the Fourteenth Amendment, or the most morally ambitious, or even the reading most supported by the Amendment's history, as I discuss later. It is nevertheless the principle that clearly emerges from our case law.

The legislative "rationality" required by this "antidiscriminatory" understanding of the Equal Protection Clause in turn rests on an understanding of the minimal moral requirements of decent government, and that is that the various groups or classes of people defined by legislation must be treated fairly and rationally by legislators—no less than the "Rule of Law" requires that individuals must be treated fairly and rationally by courts. Legislators and judges alike must treat all persons with equal dignity and respect—legislators, when deciding what the law *shall be,* and judges, when deciding what the law *is*—and what this requires of both is that distinctions drawn between persons or groups of persons, whether by judges in our decisions or by legislators in proposed laws, not be invidious, or maliciously motivated. Likes must be treated alike by Congress, by state legislatures, and by courts. When a group is defined by and then burdened by legislation, it must be for a good and morally justified reason, and not because that group is viewed as inherently less worthy or deserving of respect than others. Our Fourteenth Amendment jurisprudence as developed by this Court, as well as our commitment to the Rule of Law, reflects that central commitment of a liberal, free, and equal people.

The question, then, under the Equal Protection Clause, is whether these laws criminalizing abortion irrationally burden a subordinated group and, if so, whether there is any justifiable reason for imposing the burden. In my view, the laws regulating and criminalizing abortion that are under review today fail to meet this test, and for a couple of reasons touched on but not fully explored in the Chief Justice's opinion.

The problem with the Georgia statute in this regard is brought into sharp relief by the circumstances of the unnamed plaintiff, Mary Doe. At the time she filed her complaint, Mary Doe was twenty-two years old, married, and pregnant and had already given birth to three children. Her husband abandoned her during the course of this pregnancy, although he has since that time returned to the marriage. She has spent time in a state mental hospital. She has lost custody of all of her children at some point during their young lives, the youngest to adoption, and the two older to social services. She states that she has neither the economic nor the emotional resources to raise another child, and, given the fate of her existing three children, there is no reason to disbelieve her. She sought out an abortion. She was told, however, that her reasons for wishing to end her pregnancy were not sufficient under Georgia law, which permits abortion only if the pregnancy is the result of rape, if the pregnancy carries a serious risk of injury or death to the mother, or if the fetus has a grave mental or physical abnormality.

What the record does not explain, however, is how it came to be that this mentally unwell, emotionally unstable, economically impoverished, noncustodial mother and abandoned wife became pregnant, yet again, at only twenty-two years of age. In a moment of unwarranted but joyous optimism, did this ill woman seek out intercourse with her loving husband because she wanted a fourth child? Or, did she seek out, welcome, or at least consent to intercourse because she wanted the sexual pleasure, or the physical companionship, or to express or receive the love of her husband, knowingly accepting the risk that an unwanted pregnancy might ensue? Or, did she consent to intercourse with the husband who would abandon her some months later because the consequences of not submitting to intercourse—his ill temper, or his threats, or his needling abuse—would be too heavy? Or, did she never even think of "consenting" or "not consenting"—did it never even occur to her that she might say no to intercourse in the face of her husband's desire? Or, did she in fact willfully withhold consent, and was her will overridden? Was the intercourse not only unwanted but nonconsensual, as well? Was she raped?

The Georgia statute that Mary Doe is challenging provides that a woman who is pregnant because of a rape may procure an abortion if certain conditions are met. Ga. Criminal Code Sec. 26-1202(a)(3). What, though, constitutes "rape"? If the Georgia law of rape is read in conjunction with long-standing and unchallenged common law traditions, as statutory criminal law typically is, then "rape" is forced intercourse with a female, *so long as* the female is not the perpetrator's *wife*. This universally accepted common law rule—the so-called marital rape exemption—has recently been codified in the Model Penal Code's modern model rape statute. (Model Penal Code Sec 213.1(1): "rape" consists of sexual intercourse between a male and a "female not his wife," and "sexual assault" is sexual contact between one person and another "not his spouse.") Therefore, reading Georgia's rape law, this modern abortion law, and their common law background jointly, it is apparently the will of the Georgia legislature that pregnancies caused by nonconsensual forced intercourse *outside* marriage may be terminated by lawful abortions, but pregnancies caused by nonconsensual, forced, and even violent intercourse *inside* marriage may not. Women "raped" by their husbands who become pregnant as a result must endure the pregnancy and birth of the eventual child. Women raped outside marriage by a nonspouse need not, again assuming certain conditions are met. Women such as Mary Doe, consequently, may or may not have become pregnant as a result of forcible intercourse; the state's refusal to criminalize forced intercourse within marriage renders the very distinction between consensual and nonconsensual marital intercourse somewhat illusory. Either way, however, if the intercourse leads to pregnancy, the pregnancy will go to term, and the woman who was first penetrated and then impregnated without her consent will also give birth to a child, and most likely mother the child, as well.

For married women such as Mary Doe, these laws, taken together, do much more than impose a "burden"; they effectuate a profound alienation of the affected woman from her own body and hence from her very identity. Maybe Mary Doe consented to the intercourse that resulted in this unwanted pregnancy and maybe she did not—we will never know. Possibly, and more important, *neither will she.* As a married woman, Mary Doe has no authority, no autonomy, and no control over her sexual body; penetration of her body by her husband is not conditioned on her consent. Her body is penetrable at *his* will, not hers. From *her* perspective, her consent to intercourse is not so much "assumed"—although the state may view it as such—it is just *irrelevant.* The lack of it has no consequences.

And, given the effect of Section 26-1202 of the Criminal Code under review today, nor does she have any control over her reproductive body, should a pregnancy follow from the rape. Again, from her perspective, her consent or nonconsent to the invasion and possession of her body by the growing fetus inside her is simply irrelevant. It is not a factor either way. Her consent is not a condition of her womb being used to nurture and support the life of another. Thus, her body is penetrable by a penis, and habitable by a fetus, with or without her consent. Precisely because she is married, Mary Doe can refuse neither the intercourse nor the pregnancy when both are forcibly imposed upon her.

Why must married women, but not unmarried women and no men, bear and then birth the children conceived in forced, nonconsensual, violent intercourse? What is the basis for this classificatory distinction? One reason might lie in the historical understanding of the nature, function, and destiny of married women. Throughout most of the nineteenth century, and as the Chief Justice ably records in his decision in this case, married women lacked almost all aspects of legal, political, and civil identity. By virtue of the laws and practices of coverture, they could not own property, sue in their own name, or enforce valid contracts. See, for example, Louisiana Code, Article 2404, which provided that "The husband is the head and master of the partnership or community of gains; he administers its effects, disposes of the revenues which they produce, and may alienate them by an onerous title, without the consent and permission of his wife." By virtue of political compromises during the Reconstruction era, women could not vote, and by virtue of custom and law both, they could not work in most of the organized crafts or professions. See *Bradwell v. Illinois,* 83 U.S. 130 (1873) ("It is true that many women are unmarried and not affected by any of the duties complications, and incapacities arising out of the married state, but these are exceptions to the general rule. The paramount destiny and mission of woman are to fulfill the noble and benign offices of wife and mother. This is the law of the Creator. And the rules of civil society must be adapted to the general constitution of things, and cannot be based upon exceptional cases."). Just as important, although not so frequently noted as the absence of civic and political authority, married women also, distinctively, lacked sovereignty, or authority, over their physical bodies. By virtue first of chastisement laws, then custom, and then the exercise of prosecutorial discretion, they could not call upon the state's police power in fending off their husband's physical attacks. See, e.g., *Bradley v. State,* 1 Miss. 156 (1824) ("The only question submitted for the consideration of the court, is, whether a husband can commit an assault and battery upon the body of his wife. This, as an abstract proposition, will not admit of doubt. . . . [E]very principle of public policy and expediency, in reference to the domestic relations, would seem to require the establishment of the rule we have laid down, in order to prevent the deplorable spectacle of the exhibition of similar cases in our courts of justice. Family broils and dissentions cannot be investigated before the tribunals of the country, without casting a shade over the character of those who are unfortunately engaged in the controversy."). By virtue of tort immunity doctrines, nor could women sue for intentional torts, including assault and battery, committed by their husbands upon their bodies. See, e.g., *Rogers v. Rogers,* 265 Mo. 200 (1915). By virtue of the common law's marital rape exemption, coupled with custom, they could neither consent to nor withhold consent from intercourse with their husbands. See Sir Matthew Hale, 1 The History of the Pleas of the Crown 629 (London, Sollom Emlyn, 1778) ("The husband cannot be guilty of a rape committed by himself upon his lawful wife, for by their mutual matrimonial consent and contract the wife hath given up herself in this kind unto her husband, which she cannot retract."). Further, they had no legal entitlement to the fruits of their reproductive or productive labor; neither the children nor the income they produced with the labor of their bodies during the marriage were theirs. See generally 2 Joel Pretiss Bishop, Commentaries on the Law of Marriage and Divorce Secs. 525–51 (5th ed. 1873). And, by force of the first wave of mid-nineteenth-century abortion laws, they could not terminate their pregnancies, even if brought on by the violent, forced nonconsensual intercourse with their husbands.

What married women of the time *were* apparently supposed to do—given their lack of civil rights, the exemption of forced marital sex from the criminalization of rape, women's exclusion from professional and craft labor, the law's refusal first to criminalize violent assault within marriage and then to actually police against it, the paternal right to the children in the event of a dissolution of the marriage, and the ban on abortion—was to produce the children of the men to whom they were married, with no more regard to their own volition, desire, or needs than one would seek from a machine or from a farm animal. Under this statutory scheme, a married woman, somewhat like a mental incompetent, was by definition someone who neither consents nor withholds consent to the use of her body by others, including her husband and offspring. This identifying trait —having a body that is for the sexual and reproductive use of others, coupled with absence of entitlement to the fruits of one's labor—provided the married woman a function and a demarcation from others, including other women. In retrospect, this trait, function, and demarcation strikes us as profoundly unfree, unequal, and illiberal. *All remnants* of it should *also* strike us, today, as profoundly unconstitutional.

Some of this regime has been dismantled—although no thanks to this Court. By virtue of various nineteenth-century "Married Women's Property Acts," married women attained the right to hold property in their own name. By constitutional amendment, married as well as unmarried women won the right to vote, in 1920. (Amendment XIX, U.S. Constitution: "The Right of citizens of the United States to vote shall not be denied or abridged by the United States or by any State on account of sex.") By virtue of the twentieth-century Civil Rights Acts, all women now have a panoply of civil and employment-related rights long denied them (e.g., Title VII, Civil Rights Act of 1964, 42 U.S.C. Sec. 2000e). Nevertheless, *much of this regime still exists,* including that which is, at least arguably, its rock-solid core: for most purposes, married woman still lack the sovereignty that others take for granted over their physical, sexual, and reproductive bodies. A married woman still has no reasonable expectation that the state will protect her against violent assault by her husband—violence that would unquestionably trigger a state response, were it to occur outside the home and perpetrated by one stranger or nonintimate upon another. Domestic violence inside a marriage is for the most part still not criminal to the same degree as violence outside the marriage, and to the extent that it is criminal, the laws are not enforced. Likewise, forced intercourse inside marriage still is not rape. A married woman still has no right to consent to or withhold consent from the sexual penetration of her body by her husband, just as she still has no reasonable expectation that she can invoke the state's aid to help fend off his violent assaults. Again, this is in contrast to the expectation of both nonmarried women and all men that they will be protected by the state against violent sexual assaults that occur outside marriage, that the assault will be regarded by police and community as criminal, that perpetrators will be punished and potential wrongdoers deterred. And, pursuant to this modern abortion statute, in the state of Georgia and in its sister states that (at least nominally) allow nonmarried women the right to obtain an abortion of a pregnancy that results from a rape, a married woman has no right to terminate a pregnancy that might result from intercourse, whether or not that intercourse, no less than the pregnancy that followed from it, was forced upon her. Again, this is in contrast to the right that women in those same states retain, if raped by a perpetrator other than their husband, to abort the pregnancy that might result as a consequence of the intercourse.

Thesis

For this reason, I believe that the distinction implicitly drawn by the Georgia legislature between forced intercourse and pregnancy in marriage and rape followed by legal abortion outside of marriage, to be an unconstitutional violation of the Equal Protection Clause, under the now well-established understanding of equal protection spelled out earlier. It treats one group of persons—women impregnated as a result of rapes by their husbands—in a profoundly different and deeply injurious way, from groups similarly situated—women impregnated as a result of rapes by nonspouses. And, it is a distinction—married versus unmarried—that seems to owe more to the historical subordination of married women to their husband's identity, will, and volition than to any legitimately rational or public-regarding purpose. It is in a quite literal sense a refusal to grant equal protection of the law to a group—married women—historically subordinated in law and culture both. Even assuming that this contemporary law banning abortion was passed so as to protect fetal life, nevertheless, it is hard to make any other sense of the distinction drawn by the State, pursuant to these two bodies of law taken jointly, between a woman's right to terminate the pregnancy caused by rape *outside* marriage, and a wife's lack of such a right to terminate pregnancies caused by forced intercourse *inside* marriage. Are the children of married rapists of greater intrinsic value to the state than the children of nonmarried rapists? Perhaps. As likely, however, the distinction between married women and all others rests on the habits of mind, traditions, and centuries of practices, in Georgia and elsewhere: children born of marriage are the property of the husband and are of value for that reason, and his wife is there to dedicate her body to the cause of their conception and nurturance. This obliteration of a married woman's chosen identity, the voidance of her capacity for consent or choice, and the violence to which this legal regime relegates her is unconstitutional to the core. The state is not providing her equal protection of the law against these criminal assaults; in fact, it is providing her with virtually no protection. It then aggravates the harm by denying her redress to the self-help necessitated by its own willful abdication of its duty to protect her, equally with all other citizens, against the violence that caused her pregnancy.

The problems posed by the Texas statute are different, but just as serious. Texas has not created an unjustifiable distinction between married women and all other persons with respect to the consequences of pregnancy brought on by rape. Rather, Texas allows for legal abortion *only* to save the life of the mother. Penal Code, Art. 1191 and 1196. There is no exception for pregnancies brought on by rape outside marriage or forced intercourse within it, just as there are no exceptions for pregnancies that carry with them the risk of serious harm to the mother. Under the Texas law, *any* raped woman, or any raped child—married or unmarried, adult or minor—who becomes pregnant must carry the pregnancy to term unless the pregnancy threatens her life.

In my view, this refusal to permit women and girls who are pregnant by virtue of rape to obtain an abortion violates the Fourteenth Amendment's guarantee of equal protection of the law. This law, and hence the state, treats women and girls impregnated by rape drastically differently from the way it treats all other crime victims, and, indeed, all other citizens. Women and girls pregnant by rape are required by law to physically bear, nurture, and sustain the life of another human being, and at considerable cost to their own physical well-being. Minimally, if the pregnancy is a relatively easy one, they will suffer fatigue, dizziness, extreme discomfort, nausea, sleeplessness, disfigurement, a high risk of serious harm and injury, a substantial risk of death, and the certainty of extreme and extended pain during the childbirth itself. The pregnancy resulting from rape will also, almost undoubtedly, aggravate the extreme mental and emotional distress caused by the trauma of the rape, will badly interfere with or curtail the victim's education, should she be in grade school or college, and severely compromise her employment prospects. It may interrupt or end her advancement in most jobs, careers, professions, or trades. The rape victim must endure this, furthermore, without the assistance and loving support of the father of the child—assistance and support that in typical pregnancies render the burdens of pregnancy and child raising bearable, and even enjoyable—or, at least, possible. Raped women and girls who become pregnant are forced to provide this physically dangerous, emotionally traumatizing, and economically and educationally disastrous service, and to endure these risks, injuries, and harms, where they not only do not desire to do so, and have at no point *consented* to do so, but also have at no point consented to any act that carries with it even a *risk* of pregnancy. They are forced to provide this service not only in spite of, but because of, the bare and brutal fact that they have been the victim of a violent crime.

This forced "good samaritanism" required of these victims of criminal violence is an utter anomaly in our law. At no other point in our

Unif
legal
Proposition
good"serve"

jurisprudence do we require of any citizen who has been the victim of a violent crime that, precisely because he has been so victimized, he must therefore devote his material, physical body to sustain the life of another, against his will or without his consent. In fact, as is often remarked, our state laws require virtually *nothing* of strangers, vis-à-vis other strangers in need; the states do not prosecute or even hold civilly liable anyone, ever, for failing to come to the aid of others, even where the costs or risks of doing so would have been negligible or nonexistent. More striking, though, outside this context of criminalized abortion, never do states hold a crime victim himself criminally liable for trying to avoid the physical consequences of a crime or for seeking to resist having his physical body used, against his will, so as to sustain the life or well-being of another, where the threat to the life or well-being of the other is a direct result of the crime itself. In fact, we would prosecute and severely punish whatever agency would force such an immense involuntary sacrifice upon an individual. Thus, regardless of whether or not we characterize the fetus as a "human being," a "potential life," a "human life," a "human fetus," or a "collection of cells," there is a dramatic disparity between the law's treatment of a woman who is pregnant as a result of rape and the law's treatment of virtually all other victims of violent crime. The law requires the pregnant woman to donate her body, risk serious injury and sickness, endure fatigue, nausea, dizziness, disfigurement, and somewhere between ten and thirty hours, on average, of excruciating pain, compromise her economic independence during the pregnancy, and severely limit her options following it, all so as to sustain the life of a human being she never consented to aid or create. Again, no other victim of any other sort of crime imaginable has these consequences visited upon him.

Whether or not a woman who doesn't wish to do any of this, and who consented to neither the intercourse, the pregnancy, nor the risk of the pregnancy, *ought* to bear this sacrifice is a deep moral question we need not touch upon; of course the fetus is innocent of the rape and did nothing to cause the violent nature of his conception. Perhaps, because of the innocent life within her, the raped woman *ought to* endure the pregnancy. Perhaps she should be viewed as morally heroic if she does so. But that is not the question posed by these statutes. The question posed is whether or not the state may constitutionally require this level of physical sacrifice of raped pregnant women, but of virtually no other crime victims, to the physical needs of others. I believe that the Equal Protection Clause does not permit this drastically different treatment.

Of course, women and men are differently situated. Women can be raped and impregnated as a result of the rape. Men can be raped, although it is rare, but they cannot be impregnated as a result. But it does not follow from that difference that the law can justifiably impose extreme burdens of sacrifice and physical risk and severe economic limitations on women that are not imposed upon men in other situations that demand physical sacrifice. And we simply do not require of men who are victims of crime this degree of physical sacrifice. Although we might admire the man who donates blood, or a kidney, to save the life of a stranger, we do not require him to do so or hold him criminally liable if he attempts to resist those who would force this sacrifice upon him, even if his means of escape brought on the death of an innocent, dependent, and needy stranger. Would we force a man who had first been forced to donate sperm to then risk his health and to relinquish further body parts, as well as his future economic and educational opportunities, to save or nurture the life of a fetus created from his involuntarily donated sperm? The hypothetical may be fantastic, but the conclusion is perfectly ordinary: of course we wouldn't. Nor, more generally, do we deny the victims of violent crime whatever medical procedure might aid them in their attempt to return to the full physical health that may have been compromised by the violence done upon them. To disallow raped women the option of abortion requires of her a sacrifice of self—physical and economic—utterly at odds with the individualistic ethos of our constitutional scheme quite generally, and, more to the point here, far beyond anything required of men or women in other circumstances in which the sacrifice of their physical bodies might save or protect the lives of others.

Why do we treat raped women so differently from other victims of violent crime? Raped women, unlike other victims of violent crime, are subjected to a range of diminished police, prosecutorial, and adjudicative responses to their violation. Unlike those of other victims of criminal assault, their claims and allegations will not be prosecuted if there is no "corroborating evidence." See, e.g., *State v. Madrid,* 259 P.2d 1044 (Idaho 1953); *Bradshaw v. State,* 199 S.W.2d 747 (Ark. 1947). Unlike those of other victims of criminal assault, a victim's claim or allegation that she was raped will not be heard as credible and will certainly not be acted upon if she had the misfortune to be acquainted with her assailant. See, e.g., *Packineau v. U.S.,* 202 F.2d 681 (8th Cir. 1953); *Lewis v. State,* 64 So.2d 634 (Miss. 1953). Unlike other victims of criminal assault, a rape victim, to have any hope that her claim will be believed, must demonstrate that she physically "resisted" a rapist to demonstrate her lack of consent, even if, as may often be the case, that act of resistance might have threatened her life. See, e.g., *Prokop v. State*, 28 N.W.2d 200 (Neb. 1947). Unlike those of other victims of criminal assault, a rape victim's prior sexual history is deemed relevant to the adjudication of the defendant's guilt or innocence and will accordingly be subjected to examination, should there be a trial, and will likely somehow exonerate her assailant if she has been sexually active. See, e.g., *Seals v. State*, 40 S.E. 731 (Ga. 1902). Unlike those of other victims of criminal assault, a rape victim's allegations are made, and heard, against a centuries-old presumption that claims of rape are frequently, and perhaps usually, and certainly easily, fabricated. Most important, perhaps, unlike its treatment of other victims of criminal assault, the state's impulse to criminalize the conduct of which the rape victim complains has its origin not in an attempt to protect citizens from this form of violence but in an attempt to protect the man, clan, family, tribe, or race that "owns" her from the theft of her virginity or its rights to exclusive control of her sexuality. And, pursuant to this law, unlike other victims of criminal assault, a victim of rape may not seek medical assistance to minimize or avoid the injury to her body and future brought on by the crime she has suffered. This pervasive distinction between victims of rape and victims of other crimes of violence, of which this abortion law is a piece, seemingly rests on an invidious distinction between women, and their need to be protected against sexual assault and its aftermath, and the needs of all citizens to be protected against violence. Texas's insistence in its abortion law that victims of rape may not avail themselves of the medical procedures necessary to restore their health is part of that pattern. As such, it is a clear denial of the Fourteenth Amendment's guarantee that no state shall be permitted to deny a citizen or group of citizens the equal protection of the laws.

The hardest question posed by these state laws, I believe, is whether the same result follows with respect to unwanted pregnancies that follow consensual intercourse. Again, the question under our jurisprudence is whether or not the law treats pregnant women differently from others similarly situated and, if so, whether that different treatment is without justification. On first blush, there is an undeniable difference between the law's treatment of the pregnant woman and the human life within her on one hand and the able adult and the needy *stranger* on the other; as noted earlier, a fully able adult is not even required to call for help, should he observe a baby drowning in a puddle of water, much less remove the child from danger. The distinguishing feature here, presumably, is that the pregnant woman, if pregnant as a result of consensual intercourse, in some sense created the fetus, or at least contributed to the risk that the fetus would come into being, while the adult walking by the drowning stranger presumably did not cause the emergency facing the child in the puddle or contribute to the risk that that child would come to harm. Her relationship to the fetus is in that respect arguably more like the relationship of parent to child than that of adult to drowning stranger. And parents, of course, of both sexes, are indeed legally required to care for their children regardless of whether they consciously chose to accept the risk of their conception.

Nevertheless, there is a difference between the sacrifice demanded of parents and the sacrifice demanded of pregnant women: the requirement that parents care for their born children notably does not extend to a requirement that the parent sacrifice any part of his physical body to do so. A parent is not required to donate even a milliliter of blood, much less a kidney, or bone marrow, even to save the life of his born child, and even though the parent of the born child quite willfully and consensually brought the child into the world. Such a parent would be neither criminally nor civilly liable for his refusal to do so. It would matter not one whit that the parent consciously and perhaps joyously conceived and raised the child; regardless, the parent is not legally obligated to provide materials extracted from his own body even to save the child's life. Furthermore, should the born child—perhaps a grown born child—attempt to extract the blood or the kidney from the parent by force, without the consent of the unwilling parent, perhaps by drugging him and strapping him to a gurney, the state would step in when called upon to help the parent ward off the child's attack. The child, not the parent, would be charged with a crime. And, again, the state would take this action, even were the child fully morally innocent, the parent morally culpable, the child brought into the world by the parent's willful decision to conceive and raise her, the child's life at stake, and the burden on the parent negligible.

Why do we expect so much more of pregnant women than of all other parents? It is easy enough to see why we require so little in the way of bodily sacrifice of parents: citizens generally—and that certainly includes parents of born children—are sovereign over their bodies. They need *never* donate their bodies or parts of their bodies to serve the physical needs of others. If they do, they are admirable, or courageous. But they are not required to do so. *Pregnant women alone* must, by law, give their bodies over to the survival needs of others. Pregnant women alone lack the power to withhold consent to the use of their bodies and their bodies' parts by others. Perhaps our acceptance of this striking difference between pregnant women and all other citizens is that we have grown accustomed to viewing pregnancy, childbirth, and motherhood as a part of the story of fate, and nature, rather than a part of the story of choice, or of liberal citizenship, or even of free society; reproduction is an aspect of life that is thrust upon us, not an aspect of life, like the choice of occupation, that we opt for or against. Surely, for many, when an unexpected or unplanned pregnancy is welcome, its fated naturalism is a part of its charm, its mystique, its magic, and its power to inspire awe; it is, for many, perhaps, even a welcome limit to, or relief from, the "empire of choice." But when a pregnancy is unwelcome, and nonconsensual, and must be endured, its unchosen, thrust-upon-her nature is not a part of its charm; it is a part of its horror, and even its terror. That the states of Georgia and Texas demand of women that they simply endure these nonconsensual pregnancies is a sign, I believe, that it is women's bodies themselves, and not just joyous and welcome pregnancies, that have been delegated to the world of "fate," rather than the world of choice—where "fate," stripped of mystery, means the choices and wishes of stronger people and the needs and demands of fetal life. Although Justice Rosen is right to complain that pregnancy is not slavery, and motherhood is not wage labor, it is this delegation of women's bodies to the unthinking, unwilled realm of fate—this quite literal objectification of pregnant women—that invites comparison of the rigors of forced pregnancy occasioned by the criminalization of abortion—even when done so as to protect the innocent unborn child—to legal slavery, and of the pregnant woman's body to the status of chattel. And because this is a difference in treatment that cuts so deeply, I believe it is a difference that is unconstitutional under the Fourteenth Amendment.

The question is not, however, free from doubt. Men, and perhaps in the future women as well, must from time to time respond to a military draft and thereby sacrifice their bodily safety and integrity for the safety and freedom of others. (It is worth noting, however, that, unlike pregnant women, they are compensated for doing so, not only with an income but also with a generous packet of educational and financial benefits.) And our law of "good samaritanism" may change and require more of parents of both sexes by way of their children, born and unborn, in which case the disparity between the law's treatment of pregnant women and others may lessen, as well (although the law would have to change a good deal). Better state support for pregnant women and for young mothers, or, alternatively, some sort of mandated contribution to the welfare of the pregnant woman or the young mother by fathers, might also change the constitutional balance somewhat. Nor is the right, as I have described or defended it, absolute. I agree with Justice Rubenfeld that at some point in a pregnancy, a woman's consent to the pregnancy can be assumed because of her failure to obtain an abortion in a timely manner. She might, for that very reason, be precluded from a late-term abortion. Therefore, while I believe the current restrictions on abortion to be unconstitutional, even as applied to women who became pregnant through consensual intercourse, I do not believe the right is absolute, and I do not agree that the states are absolutely forbidden to regulate abortion to protect fetal life. The regulation, however, must proceed in a way that respects pregnant women's rights to equal protection of the laws. The Texas and Georgia statutes, and particularly their refusal to grant exceptions in the case of pregnancies caused by forced intercourse, do not do so.

II. Due Process

Does the criminalization of abortion constitute a state-sponsored deprivation of liberty without due process of law? Classically, and paradigmatically, deprivations of liberty without due process of law occur when the state restricts someone's freedom without providing "due legal process": a citizen is jailed without a fair and public trial or is jailed without having been permitted to retain a lawyer. On its face, such a constitutional mandate is as far as can possibly be imagined from the concerns of privacy, or the Millian understanding of liberty, or the delicate deference to individual and marital life styles, that seemingly underlie this Court's recent "privacy" jurisprudence, beginning with Justice Harlan's dissent in *Poe v. Ullman* and continuing through to the Chief Justice's opinion in this case. See *Poe v. Ullman,* 367 U.S. 497 (1961); *Griswold v. Connecticut,* 381 U.S. 479 (1965); and *Eisenstadt v. Baird,* 405 U.S. 438 (1972). With Justices Amar and Paulsen, I believe these cases and their holdings cannot be so justified— the Constitution does not enact John Stuart Mill's *On Liberty* anymore than it enacts Herbert Spencer's social statics—although they may be justified on other grounds. I do not support the continual erosion of this Court's credibility, as well as its own sense of responsibility to law and the Rule of Law, by needlessly extending either the "privacy" or "substantive due process" rationales those cases articulate. Nor do I see the connection between the right to use contraception involved in *Griswold* and *Eisenstadt* and the right to abortion sought in this case that strikes most of this Court as compelling and obvious—indeed, strikes Justice Sunstein as so obvious as to require no justification.

That the stated rationales of *Griswold* and *Eisenstadt* decisions are seemingly dubious, or that the rights to contraception they articulated are in no obvious way analogous to a right to an abortion, or that the phrase "substantive due process" is oxymoronic, does not, however, imply that the Fourteenth Amendment's guarantee that no state shall deprive individual citizens of their liberty without due process of law is not in some other way implicated, and possibly violated, by these laws. By its plain meaning and language, although we have never held as much, the clause arguably reaches a class of case not adequately described by either the "pure process" or the "substantive process" lines of cases this Court has thus far developed. That no state shall deprive a citizen of liberty without legal process, once we take out the double negative, suggests that a state must recognize some measure of liberty, which can then be taken away only *with* legal process. A person might then be deprived of liberty without "due process of law" when her freedom of movement or self-sovereignty is unduly restricted by someone or something other than the state and the state then does nothing to prevent it—such a deprivation would indeed be without due process of law. A master's domination of a slave, coupled with the state's refusal to criminalize the master's use of the violence requisite to perpetuate that domination, might be regarded as a paradigm instance. Surely the lynchings of free black citizens by whites, with no state prosecutions of those murders and no threat of legal reprisals, likewise deprives those murdered individuals of their lives and liberties without "due process of law" and violates their right to "equal protection of the law." *No* legal process, due or otherwise, adjudged the victims of these lynchings to have been guilty of capital crimes; rather, they were deprived of life and liberty without due process of law. Vigilante justice to which the state turns a willfully blind eye is another clear example: private punitive action, followed by state inaction, constitutes such a violation of the right not to be deprived of liberty without due process *of law*. Likewise, if one group of citizens decided unilaterally to immobilize and then re-educate a recalcitrant group by capturing its members and then putting them into mandatory boot camps, and the state permitted this to occur, that, too, would be a deprivation of liberty without due process of law. Should the state then pass laws criminalizing conduct taken by the bur-

dened group that might alleviate the private immobilization or deprivation of liberty that would surely exacerbate the constitutional violation: in
that event, the state, by criminalizing the defensive actions the burdened
group might undertake so as to ward off the curtailment of their liberty,
would have actively, rather than passively, abided the deprivation of liberty
without due process of law.

The issue under the "due process-liberty" clause of the Fourteenth
Amendment, I believe, is whether a forced nonconsensual pregnancy is a
deprivation of liberty without due process of law and whether the state's
criminalization of abortion exacerbates the deprivation by in effect criminalizing the only viable means of self-help against the infringement. Here,
the question is whether the criminalization of abortion unduly burdens
liberty per se, not the comparative question raised earlier, to wit, whether
the criminalization of abortion imposes unequal burdens on pregnant
women to sustain the life of dependent others. Nevertheless, although
comparisons are not dispositive, they might well be helpful. As discussed
earlier, we do not generally require of citizens any good samaritanism
toward strangers. Nor do we require of parents who consensually bring
children into the world that they sacrifice even an ounce of their own
blood to aid even their own dying child. Perhaps we should—*but we don't.*
Why don't we? Presumably, because to require such physical sacrifice,
would constitute a deprivation of the very liberty we so highly value.
Because we highly value that liberty, we do not permit it to be taken by
any agency other than the state, and then only with due process.

Thus—imagine this scenario. One group of citizens decides to kidnap
and drug another group so as to extract from the second group the necessary organs, or bone marrow, or blood, all to benefit needy and innocent
citizens whose lives depend upon those organs, that marrow, or that blood
type. Laws are then passed criminalizing any action the kidnapped group
might take so as to ward off the kidnapping, all, perhaps, so as to protect
the value of the lives of those needful citizens. No laws are passed to criminalize the conduct of the kidnappers. Surely the kidnapped citizens have
been deprived of their liberty, and without due process of law. Surely, by
not arresting and punishing the kidnappers, the state has aggravated that
deprivation. Just as surely, it has further aggravated the deprivation by
passing laws that criminalize the victims' self-help.

Is this farfetched scenario really very different from laws criminalizing abortion, where the pregnancies are a result of rape outside marriage,
or forced intercourse within it? These women are first penetrated and

then impregnated against their will. They are then forced to carry the baby to term, supporting, nurturing, and physically caring for, as well as carrying, the fetus, at tremendous cost to their health, independence, and economic well-being. This nine-month term of forced good samaritanism is in some ways more, in some ways less restraining than a nine-month prison term: the pregnant woman has somewhat more mobility, maybe, than a kidnapped forced samaritan strapped to a gurney, but the pregnancy carries greater health risks and far greater long-term economic consequences. And of course, the pregnant woman has much less mobility than a nonpregnant and nonincarcerated citizen: pregnancy imposes serious constraints on mobility by virtue of the fatigue, injury, and sickness it engenders, as well as constraints on the ability to be economically self-sustaining. And, obviously, it is a deprivation of liberty that is imposed with no process of law: none of these women has been adjudged in a fair trial to be guilty of some malfeasance, the punishment for which is a nine-month-long interference with physical mobility and self-sovereignty. That the state then sees fit to criminalize the abortion that might alleviate this unsought condition simply further underscores the state's involvement. By criminalizing abortion in these circumstances, the state has not only deprived these citizens of their liberty without due process of law but also employed law toward the end of exacerbating rather than ameliorating that deprivation.

For these reasons, in my view, the refusal to allow raped women and women who have been forcibly impregnated inside marriage a lawful abortion is a violation of their right not to be deprived of liberty without due process of law under the Fourteenth Amendment.

III. Constitutional Roles and Remedies

Section 5 of the Fourteenth Amendment explicitly delegates to Congress the authority to pass necessary legislation should states violate Section 1 of that Amendment by denying individuals equal protection of the law or by failing to protect them against deprivations of their liberty, life, and property without due process of law. If a state's actions, or a state's laws, or a state's failure to take action, or a state's failure to pass laws violate citizens' rights to equal protection or liberty, then Congress is empowered to respond. It has both the explicit power to do so, under Section 5 of the Fourteenth Amendment, and the implicit responsibility to do so. Ideally, then, it is Congress, not this Court, that should respond to unconstitutional legal regimes such as those put in place by Texas and Georgia with respect to abortion. This Court should accord Congress considerable deference, when and if Congress acts so as to ameliorate or address unconstitutional conditions brought on by these state laws or any other. The power to take action so as to remedy constitutional violations brought on by state law must obviously include, as well, the authority to interpret the meaning of the constitutional mandate that has been violated. One cannot possibly enforce what one cannot interpret.

At the same time, and as Justice Marshall said in *Marbury v. Madison,* it is unavoidably as well as emphatically the Court's duty to say what the law is when the Court is called upon to enforce and apply it. 5 U.S. 137, at 177 ("It is emphatically the province and duty of the Judicial Department to say what the law is. Those who apply the rule to particular cases must, of necessity, expound and interpret that rule. If two laws conflict with each other, the Courts must decide on the operation of each."). Neither this Court nor any other court can possibly say what the Georgia law of abortion is, or what the Texas law of abortion is, without looking to the Constitution: if these laws that criminalize abortion violate the Constitution, then presumably these laws that so violate the Constitution are void. When faced with a seemingly unconstitutional, and hence void, state law, and a Congress that has failed to take any action regarding it, a judge cannot simply enforce it in the hope that Congress will some day address the constitutional infringement. Nor should a judge enforce a law in the face of his own conclusion that the law is unconstitutional in the vague hope that a national "conversation" will someday veer the country toward a more constitutionally palatable course of action. Nor is there any warrant within a constitutional democracy in which courts are responsible for expounding the law to move "slowly," or "piecemeal," or "pragmatically," toward a foregone constitutional conclusion so as not to preempt that conversation. If the law is unconstitutional, the Court must say so. That we have a Constitution, as Justice Marshall argued, directly implies that a judge or court should refuse to enforce flagrantly unconstitutional laws, while saying forthrightly what the grounds might be for doing so.

How, then, to square these conflicting responsibilities—the duty of courts to declare the law, and hence the constitutionality of law, on the one hand and the duty of Congress, under the Fourteenth Amendment, to pass legislation so as to enforce the substantive requirements of that Amendment on the other? Minimally, some measure of *comity* is clearly in

order. By declaring acts of Congress or acts of the various state legislatures void, this Court and courts in general enforce the Constitution. At
the same time, Congress is quite explicitly charged under Section 5 with
the primary task of addressing, *through legislation,* constitutional violations committed by the states. It must, then, perforce also have the authority to interpret those commands. It cannot possibly pass legislation so
as to enforce that which it is forbidden to interpret. Sometimes, these
responsibilities are not in conflict: obviously, there are some violations of
the Fourteenth Amendment that can be readily remedied by the Court's
power and responsibility to refuse to enforce unconstitutional state law,
without requiring any further legislative response by Congress. At the
same time—and we should explicitly acknowledge this—there may well
be breaches of our constitutional guarantees of liberty, life, or equal protection of the law that can be remedied only by legislation initiated by
Congress, rather than by the (relatively) quick judicial expedient of striking unconstitutional state statutes. The framers of the Amendment clearly
envisioned as much. It is imperative, then, that this Court be careful not to
overstate its authority to interpret the Constitution. Interpret it we must
—so as to perform the judicial function. But so must others, to perform
their constitutional functions. When doing the work of "saying what the
law is," we will perforce also be doing the work of saying what the Constitution says the law can and cannot be. But when doing so, we should permit, anticipate, and even welcome varying interpretations of our most
general constitutional guarantees and take care not to preclude their development with unnecessarily broad declarations of our own.

Specifically, here, I think it unnecessary and perhaps unwise to strike
these abortion laws, as they apply to pregnancies following consensual
intercourse, on two of the very broad grounds put forward by the Chief
Justice and alluded to in several of the concurring opinions as well: first,
that these laws violate a "right" not to be put to the choice between wanted
heterosexual intercourse unburdened by risks of pregnancy and celibacy,
whether such a right be called "privacy" or "liberty"; second, that these
laws unconstitutionally force women to embrace a life of motherhood that
is itself inconsistent with the duties and rights of citizenship. Both of these
asserted constitutional rights—a right to motherhood and citizenship,
and a right to companionate, rather than reproductive, marital sexuality
—if they exist, render constitutionally problematic entire social and cultural regimes and require remedial legislation far beyond the scope of anything this Court could conceivably order. Both rights, if they exist, will

require a full-scale reordering of basic social institutions and, most centrally, a full-scale reordering of the family. If, as the Chief Justice's argument implies, mothers are second-class citizens, then presumably that is acceptable to both some women and perhaps many more men, because of the special rewards and challenges of women's traditional place in family life. Likewise, if anti-abortion laws put women to the choice between sex with a risk of reproduction and celibacy, then presumably that is acceptable to many women and men because they regard sex as desirable and morally acceptable only within marriage and only when both parties are open to the possibility of creating new life. If either of these arrangements is itself unconstitutional, then there is a quite palpable conflict between our commitment to constitutional principle and our commitment to the social institution of the family. If we stay true to the one, we must reorder the other; if we are attached to the constitutional regime of citizenship, we will have to restructure family life. For this massive reordering of what is perhaps the central social institution of this society to occur because of orders promulgated by this Court, rather than because of the demonstrated will of a politically and constitutionally engaged public, could well prove disastrous.

Let me explain in more detail what I take the potential disaster to be, by taking the arguments one at a time. I fully agree that mothering children, as we presently socially construct that work, is incompatible with the basic rights and responsibilities of citizenship, as the Chief Justice quite explicitly argues, and as Justice Sunstein, Tushnet, and Rubenfeld all suggest, as well. And I fully agree that the incompatibility has constitutional implications. But what precisely is the consequence of *this Court* saying so, pursuant to a ruling on the constitutionality of laws criminalizing abortion, rather than Congress saying so, pursuant to a full-scale review of the constitutionality of our legal regulation of family life? For surely it cannot be, or should not be, that the constitutionally ideal *solution* to the conflict between citizenship and motherhood is to grant women a right to terminate pregnancies, thus avoiding the conflict altogether. That would be, frankly, a pathetically inadequate remedy. If there is a conflict between caring for one's children and being a citizen in this Republic of Choice, it is a conflict that will also burden mothers who enjoyed fully consensual, welcome pregnancies conceived in happy, consensual, joyful sex. By providing a constitutional right to avoid motherhood partly on the grounds that motherhood is inconsistent with citizenship, we would be legitimating, and with a vengeance, the inconsistency of motherhood and citizenship itself. We would perversely render the incompatibility of motherhood and citizenship, in effect, fully constitutional—by providing a constitutional right to avoid it.

Look at the possible implications, no doubt unintended, of accepting the Chief Justice's argument. If one *chooses* to mother—which all mothers will have presumptively done, should abortion be legalized—does that mean that one has voluntarily forgone one's rights to equal citizenship? Is the Constitution truly indifferent to an incompatibility between voluntarily mothering children and citizenship, so long as women have the option of opting out of the incompatibility by choosing abortion? The argument seems to suggest, first, that women lose citizenship rights by voluntarily becoming mothers, and, second, so long as the decision is indeed voluntary—which it is, if abortion is legal and available—then the loss of citizenship is not only politically and morally acceptable but fully constitutional, as well.

But this should give pause: it isn't morally acceptable, and it ought not be viewed as constitutionally acceptable, either. Surely, it can't be that our constitution envisions a two-caste society consisting of citizens on the one hand and mothers on the other, with that caste system in turn legitimated by the mother's choice not to abort. Rather, on any decent understanding of liberal constitutionalism, the *incompatibility itself* is unconstitutional, not just the forcing of women, against their will, into an adult life incompatible with citizenship. If we are all to enjoy equal protection of the law and constitutionally protected liberty and the privileges of citizenship, then those of us who voluntarily mother our children are surely as entitled to that equality, those liberties, and those privileges as those who voluntarily father children, or those who choose not to parent. It can't be that by choosing to mother a child, we have forgone rights, privileges, and responsibilities of citizenship. I suggest that if the incompatibility of motherhood and citizenship is of a constitutional magnitude, as the Chief Justice and I both believe it to be, it cannot be cured by providing a constitutional right to terminate pregnancies. Such a right may well, in fact, exacerbate it—as it would undoubtedly legitimate it.

Furthermore, if there is such an unconstitutional incompatibility between mothering and citizenship, there is very little this Court can do to address it. Mothering makes citizenship difficult or impossible, the Chief Justice suggests—but why? Presumably, it does so because our conception of citizenship presupposes either an adult without dependents or an adult with one dependent—a wife—who can and will then care for the others.

In either case, the citizen is free, time-wise, in Aristotelian fashion, to maintain his own independence and exercise his responsibilities, rights, and privileges of citizenship. Our conception of citizenship, apparently, does not presuppose, and cannot comfortably accommodate, an adult who is carrying around an infant who must be fed, rocked, held, changed, cleaned, and diapered virtually around the clock for at least six months, and then fed, rocked, held, changed, cleaned, diapered, and played with continuously for twelve-hour periods, seven days a week, for a couple of years, and then clothed, fed, housed, cleaned, and supervised closely for fifteen hours a day for the next couple of years, and then fed, housed, loved, nurtured, clothed, cleaned, and schooled for the duration of a quite lengthy childhood. The adult primarily charged with these responsibilities cannot be economically self-sufficient at all for the first two to six months of an infant's life. There is virtually no remunerative job in our office- and factory-focused workforce compatible with round-the-clock breastfeeding, cleaning, holding, rocking, and changing even a noncollicky newborn baby. Likewise, the new mother of an infant will be hard pressed to find the time or the freedom to vote, much less read newspapers or attend city council meetings. After her child moves from infancy to toddlerhood, she will continue to be severely economically constrained over the next five years, as well throughout the child's age of minority, and at a disadvantage politically and economically. A mother who has several children will be economically and politically handicapped in this regard for much, and perhaps most, of her adult life.

Now, why is this? Adults of both sexes obviously biologically *parent* and presumably could, if so inclined, share the work of parenting children, so as to decrease the incompatibility of mothering with citizenship. If there is a radical incompatibility between mothering and citizenship, and if that incompatibility is itself at odds with our constitutional ideals, then it is entirely because of the way in which we have constructed mothering or constructed citizenship, or both; it is not by virtue of *any* natural imperative. How, given that sort of glaringly obvious fact, should we respond to the incompatibility of motherhood and citizenship? Perhaps we should change the nature of mothering so that both parents do it, or so that the community does more of it, or so that women who do it have more social support. Alternatively, perhaps we should change the nature of citizenship so that, even if biological mothers continue to do the lion's share of the work of mothering, that work is not inconsistent with citizenship: we could insist on child-friendly workplaces and a child-friendly public sphere. Perhaps a judge might one day sit on the bench hearing a case, or a National Security Council chair might conduct a meeting, while at the same time breastfeeding and diapering a baby. Or, perhaps, we could insist on income support—in tax rebates, social security protection, health insurance, paid maternity or parenting leave—for women who mother, during those times of parenting when the incompatibility of motherhood and citizenship seems most severe and most rooted in economic imperatives. All of these responses would go some way toward alleviating the incompatibility of mothering and citizenship that the Chief Justice rightly bemoans. What is wrong, though, both for women who mother and for those who seek abortions, is that we attempt to paper over this profound problem of constitutionalism and social organization by giving it all a gloss of *voluntariness* through the somewhat brutal expedient of granting a right to opt out through legal abortion. Yet, that is what the Chief Justice apparently suggests we do.

To actually address the incompatibility of motherhood and citizenship, should we, as a community, ever get around to doing so, will require substantial congressional, not judicial, activity. The unconstitutional incompatibility of mothering and citizenship is not the result of an unconstitutional and hypothetical state law that *requires* mothers but not fathers to raise children, which this Court could simply strike down with the stroke of its pen. Rather, the incompatibility of mothering and citizenship is the cumulative result of scores of laws and legal regimes—employment law, social security law, family law, and criminal law, the interaction of those laws with social practice and cultural understandings, and much else besides. To address this problem will be a monumental congressional undertaking, demanding immense political skill and moral vision both. But, if it is true that citizenship is inconsistent with motherhood, and if it is also true that it is indeed unconstitutional to arrange society so that citizens by definition are not mothers and mothers by definition are not citizens, then it is an undertaking that Congress should commence pronto, no matter how arduous the task might prove to be. It is one that should not be impeded or obfuscated by the facile suggestion from this Court that the entire problem can be avoided by the simple expedient of giving women a right to an abortion—and, hence, a right not to be put to the Hobson's choice of motherhood or citizenship. Any decent society, and certainly any decent society with constitutional aspirations of liberty, equality, and the privileges of citizenship, ought to structure itself so as to facilitate both.

The same is true, I believe, of the Chief Justice's argument that the criminalization of abortion puts women (and presumably men, as well) to an unconstitutional choice between celibacy and heterosexual intercourse coupled with a fear of pregnancy. A constitutional right to sexual privacy, or sexual autonomy, if it exists, would upend social understandings of the relationship among family, sexuality, and reproduction. Our current legal regimes reflect a belief, perhaps now held by only a numerical minority, that sexual activity is proper and moral only within traditional marriage, and even then only when both parties are open to the possibility of conception being the result. This legal regime could obviously be displaced through legislative processes, and perhaps that displacement might eventually be reflected in our national, evolving Constitution: it may be, for example, that we have a constitutional right to a wide array of family structures, sexual choices, and marital arrangements and nonarrangements. It may be, as a constitutional matter, that "family" should be reconceived so as to focus on mutual care, intimacy, and the nurturance of children, rather than being defined by a hierarchic relation between man and wife and an authoritative and authoritarian relation between parents and their genetically connected children. But, if so, as is true of motherhood, this reconception of sexuality and its relation to the Constitution cannot happen by fiat from courts, and it certainly cannot happen solely because we declare it to be necessary en route to the discovery of a right to an abortion. To truly establish a right to sexual intimacy, entire bodies of law, again ranging through family law, employment law, and criminal law, will have to be rethought. By declaring a right to an abortion as a shortcut toward providing, in effect, a right to sexual pleasure unfettered by reproductive consequences, again we perversely validate, by constitutionalizing, our current sexual, marital, and familial regimes—so long as those regimes include the choice to have an abortion. This would do little but unduly truncate the development of constitutional thought, as it might more positively affirm a desirable and generous understanding of the diversity and range of our intimate sexual and familial lives.

There is no easy and certainly no determinate way to delineate the boundaries of judicial and legislative responsibility for implementation or enforcement of the Fourteenth Amendment's mandates. Nevertheless, it seems to me that we should at least be attentive to the problem and begin to articulate some perimeters. Where an apparent constitutional violation of equal protection or liberty involves a broad mesh, or tapestry, of law, social custom, entrenched belief, and habit, then Congress is better situated than this Court to address and remedy the constitutional violation.

Certainly, where such a violation can be addressed only through positive legislation, Congress and not this Court must be granted the latitude to both study and address the problem. At the other extreme, where the Constitution is clearly violated by force of a single law, and enforcement or nonenforcement of that law is necessary to the vindication of rights in courts, then it is clearly the Court's role, as Justice Marshall said, to enforce the Constitution and to deny enforcement of the law. Obviously, from time to time, a law might be unconstitutional on both narrow and broad grounds. In such a case, and I believe this is one such case, this Court should take care not to overstate its interpretive authority. More important, it should take care not to preclude or foreclose the most aspirational, generative, and simply generous understandings of the Constitution by providing clipped, abbreviated, and preemptive constitutional remedies.

I conclude with what I'm afraid might be a banal observation: the United States Constitution is many things. It is, for example, a founding document—a "speech event" that had enormous historical and political consequences. It is also, in part at least, the "Rule of Recognition" for our legal system: courts *must* look to it to determine whether a law is indeed a law in the course of the very ordinary judicial work of saying what the law is. By virtue of Section 5 of the Fourteenth Amendment, however, the Constitution is also a mandate to Congress to pass legislation so as to protect the equality and liberty of citizens against certain sorts of actions and inactions taken by states. Last, and by no means least, the Constitution, as understood by virtually all of our citizens, is the record of our country's moral and political history: it is the sieve through which we retain the best and the noblest moments of our history, transform them from narrative to imperative, and make them a part of our charter. Given this multiple identity, surely what the Constitution means, or says, or demands, or permits depends not only on who is doing the reading but on what we think it is that we are reading, and why. When historians or others read the Constitution as an event in history, it should be read with an eye toward understanding what the document did. When courts read it (or parts of it) as a part of our Rule of Recognition, it can, and perhaps should be, read literally, "legalistically," and narrowly: what does it constitute as a "law," and what not? What is not a law, by virtue of constitutional ordering? When read by Congress as a mandate pushing us toward equality and liberty, it should be read aspirationally: what are the liberty and equality that must be protected, and how might forward-looking legislation best achieve that goal? When read by any of us as the story of our ideals, it can and should be read capaciously. What does the Constitution demand of all of us—not just courts—as members of a free, individualist, and equal society?

Although this Court's understanding of the meaning of the Constitution must be authoritative, and final, in deciding what the Constitution precludes, it simply does not follow that either this Court, or courts in general, should be the sole interpreter of either the meaning of the Fourteenth Amendment's egalitarian and liberal mandate to Congress or the capacious and generous story of our country's moral development. It is not for this Court to authoritatively dictate the meaning of the liberty or equality Congress is charged with the duty of protecting. Even more clearly, it is not this Court's duty to authoritatively and exclusively expound the Constitution's moral story of our development, or in what direction our past, and its lessons, points us. The Constitution, read as a political and moral narrative, is the story of the country's development, not the story of this Court's jurisprudence. If we *don't* accord other political actors—legislators, senators, citizens—the right to engage these constitutionally interpretive practices, it is very hard to see how this legally binding, politically ambitious, and morally rich Constitution can possibly be compatible with democratic self-government. We simply must respect the right, the responsibility, and the duty of the other branches, and particularly Congress under Section 5 of the Fourteenth Amendment, to interpret the Constitution's mandates, and to do so in a way consistent with congressional roles, no less than Congress must respect the right and need of the Court to parse the Constitution finely, consistent with the Court's quite different obligation to expound the content of law.

Sunstein, J., concurring in the judgment.

I concur in the judgment, but I cannot join the Court's unnecessarily broad opinion. This nation is in the midst of a large-scale debate about the proper role of the state in the protection of unborn life. Reasonable people reasonably disagree. This Court should not resolve that debate all at once. It should be especially reluctant to do so in light of the fact that our precedents, and the Constitution itself, are far from conclusive on the underlying issues.

In this case, our task is not to decide the abstract question whether the state's interest in the protection of unborn life is sufficient to justify a limitation on a pregnant woman's decision whether to bring the child to term. Instead, we are asked to assess the constitutionality of specific statutes from Texas and Georgia. I believe that both statutes have a fatal flaw: they are not narrowly tailored to protect the legitimate interests at stake. I would leave the harder questions, about what balances states may permissibly strike, for another day.

I agree with the Court's conclusion that an intrusion on a woman's freedom of choice in this particular domain cannot survive constitutional scrutiny merely because it is rational. To be sure, we have abandoned the idea that the Due Process Clause permits us to second-guess rational legislative judgments in the ordinary domains of social and economic life. See *Ferguson v. Skrupa*, 372 U.S. 726 (1963). The idea of "substantive due process" should be invoked very rarely. But *Griswold v. Connecticut*, 381 U.S. 479 (1965), stands for the proposition that, in the context of the choice whether to bear or beget a child, minimal rationality is not enough. Certainly this is so when the interference with reproductive choice is, by its very nature, aimed at women alone. See *Reed v. Reed*, 404 U.S. 71 (1971). Our jurisprudence makes clear that, at a minimum, a statute that constrains the reproductive choices of women, and not of men, must be justified as narrowly tailored to the protection of legitimate state interests.

The Texas statute cannot satisfy this test, and for one simple reason: it is fatally overbroad. See *Thornhill v. Alabama*, 310 U.S. 88 (1940).[1] Texas forbids abortion even in cases in which the mother would face serious health problems from bringing the child to term, even in cases in which the pregnancy resulted from rape, and even in cases in which the pregnancy was a product of incest. The legitimate interest in the protection of fetal life cannot be sufficient to justify so massive an intrusion on women's freedom of choice. Surely it cannot be sufficient where, as here, the state has not shown that the intrusion will, in fact, provide meaningful protection to fetal life. We may take judicial notice of the fact that restrictions on abortion have questionable effectiveness in protecting unborn children,[2] especially when women would suffer severe consequences, physical or psychological, from carrying the fetus to term. When pregnancy has resulted from rape or incest, abortion, whether or not lawful, will often result whatever the law says. See L. Lader, Abortion (1966). And the problem goes much deeper than ineffectiveness. As many as 10,000 women per year are reported to die each year from unlawful abortions. See L. Lader, supra at 3; R. Schwarz, Septic Abortion 7 (1968). It cannot reasonably be doubted that many adverse health effects, and a significant number of deaths, will result from Texas's blunderbuss prohibition.

It follows that, by forbidding abortion in cases involving rape and incest and those with serious health consequences, Texas cannot meet its burden of showing that its legislation is justified as a narrowly tailored means of protecting unborn life. We have no occasion to resolve the question whether a state could justify a more narrowly drawn statute that overcomes the problem of overbreadth.

At least at first glance, the Georgia statute presents a closer question, simply because it allows pregnant women to choose abortion in a wider array of circumstances. I would nonetheless invalidate the statute. The reason is that Georgia has surrounded the woman's nominal freedom with a constitutionally unacceptable panoply of obstacles and burdens, going far well beyond what is necessary to protect the state's legitimate interests. In fact, these statutory obstacles and burdens, taken as a whole, are so severe that they threaten to undo whatever rights are created by the statutory protections in cases involving rape and physical endangerment.

Under Georgia law, three doctors—not one or two—must certify, on the basis of their own *separate* medical examinations, that the abortion meets the statutory criteria. See Ga. Criminal Code 26-1202(a)(3). In cases of rape, pregnant women must, under risk of criminal penalties, identify their assailant—even though, in many cases, women reasonably fear that such identification will subject them to further risks of criminal violence. Id. at (a)(6). The abortion must be approved, not only by individual doctors but also by a committee of a hospital's medical staff (not including the performing physician). Id. at (a)(5). To add insult (and further injury) to injury, third parties, including relatively distant relatives, are permitted to go to court to enjoin the abortion if it would "violate the constitutional or other legal rights of the fetus." Id. at (c). The idea of "legal rights" evidently includes rights under the statutory and common law of Georgia. This provision thus creates a continuing risk that grave uncertainty, and unpredictable new burdens, will face any woman who seeks an abortion under the exceptions apparently recognized by the state. It is plain that Georgia has gone far beyond what is necessary to protect the interest in safeguarding fetal life. I would not rule that the Constitution forbids Georgia from protecting that legitimate interest; but the state may not do so in a way that intrudes, in a dramatic and even gratuitous way, on the countervailing interests that are at stake.

I would not take this occasion to specify the permissible procedural obstacles that might be placed in the way of pregnant women who seek abortions. That is a task for legislatures, not for this Court. I also recognize the good faith, and the deep commitments, of many Americans, including those in Texas and Georgia, who seek to protect unborn life. In this case, I would rule only that any such protection must be narrowly tailored, allowing reasonable exceptions and imposing procedural barriers that do not exceed what is necessary to protect the interests at stake.

I concur in the judgment.

NOTES

1. In the unusual circumstances of these cases, I would permit a challenge, on grounds of overbreadth, to statutes that forbid so much conduct that seems to me constitutionally protected.

2. Studies suggest that in the 1960s, there were between 1.0 and 1.5 million abortions in the United States each year. See L. Lader, *Abortion* 2 (1966) (referring to the estimate of 1.5 million); Whittemore, "The Availability of Non-Hospital Abortions," in *Abortion in a Changing World* 217 (P. Hall ed. 1970) ("the oft-quoted figure of one million criminal abortions in the United States is a fairly reasonable estimate"); R. Schwarz, *Septic Abortion* 7 (1968) (in the late 1960s, more than 20 percent of pregnancies terminated in illegal abortions, resulting in approximately

1.2 million unlawful abortions per year). Police reports reveal that in some years, illegal abortion has been the third largest illegal enterprise in the United States, after gambling and narcotics. See E. Schur, *Crimes Without Victims, Deviant Behavior and Public Policy* 25 (1965).

AMAR, J., concurring in the judgment in part and dissenting in part in *Roe v. Wade,* No. 70-18, and dissenting in *Doe v. Bolton,* No. 70-40.

There is an important difference between the two abortion laws at issue before the Court today, both of which impose heavy burdens on women as women without saddling men with comparable burdens. The Texas law, enacted in the 1850s, was passed by an all-male legislature that was in turn chosen by an all-male electorate. This old law cannot stand. The recently adopted Georgia law, by contrast, was enacted at a time when women could and did vote for and serve in the legislature. This new law raises issues that should be addressed in the first instance by Georgia courts, which have not yet had a chance to rule on various important questions of statutory construction and state constitutional law.

I. Roe v. Wade

Constitutional law must have some basis in the Constitution itself. U.S. Const. art. VI ("This Constitution . . . shall be the supreme Law of the Land."); *Marbury v. Madison,* 5 U.S. (1 Cranch) 137 (1803); *McCulloch v. Maryland,* 17 U.S. (4 Wheat.) 316 (1819). Every member of this Court has sworn a personal oath to uphold the letter and the spirit of the Constitution—as distinct from, say, the precepts of Hippocrates or the views of the AMA. See U.S. Const. art. VI ("all executive and judicial Officers . . . shall be bound by Oath or Affirmation, to support this Constitution."). And even if we were not oath-bound to do so, I believe that we should carefully consult the Constitution and, indeed, lavish attention on its text, history, and structure, because this document distills a great deal of the collective and hard-won wisdom of the American people over the centuries. This wisdom, no less than the wisdom of the AMA or Hippocrates, can powerfully inform our judgment even where the text does not unambiguously dictate an outcome.

A. Due Process and the Ninth Amendment

Today's opinion by Chief Justice Balkin mentions, among other things, the Ninth Amendment and the Due Process Clause of the Fourteenth Amendment. In relevant part, these two Amendments read as follows: "The enumeration in the Constitution, of certain rights, shall not be construed to deny or disparage others retained by the people." U.S. Const. amend. IX. "No state shall . . . deprive any person of life, liberty, or property, without due process of law." Id. amend. XIV, sect. 1. See also id. amend. V ("No person shall be . . . deprived of life, liberty, or property, without due process of law.")

As for the Ninth Amendment, although the opinion of The Chief Justice waves in the direction of this text, this opinion fails to make clear exactly how rights of "the *people*" in the Ninth Amendment become rights of individual *persons* to privacy; or how judges are to figure out what is and is not a Ninth Amendment right; or how this Amendment, with its roots in anti-Federalist anxieties about the new federal government (and its courts), invites federal judges to strike down state laws. Cf. *Barron v. Baltimore*, 32 U.S. (7 Pet.) 243 (1833). Perhaps there are satisfying answers to such questions, but today's opinion does not provide them. It's also worth noting that the District Court decision relying on the Ninth Amendment could point to no Supreme Court case ever decided that used this Amendment to strike down a statute. If today's Court is truly serious about breathing judicial life into the Ninth Amendment, it owes us more elaboration. In pondering whether a law violates the rights of "the people," might it be relevant to see what that "the people" have in fact claimed for ourselves in critical legal documents such as state constitutions? I would have thought so. Yet, today's Court does not undertake any serious survey of these sources.

As for the Fourteenth Amendment's Due Process Clause, the Court reads this clause as embodying an "abstract guarantee[] of liberty." But the Amendment's words (and the companion words of the Fifth Amendment) say no more about guaranteeing liberty than about guaranteeing property. Under the words of this clause, a government may indeed deprive a person of liberty or property, but it must provide "due process of law." *Process* of law—due *process,* not due substance.

Liberty and property are spacious concepts. Almost all laws implicate, and in some measure restrict, some arguable liberty interest or property interest. If the mere existence of a liberty interest or property interest is enough to allow this Court to invalidate any law that (according to us) intrudes too far upon those interests or that (as we see it) lacks persuasive policy justification, we shall be very busy indeed. (During this Court's *Lochner* era, we invalidated roughly 200 regulatory statutes that violated this Court's sense of property rights.) More to the point, I do not believe that the text, history, and spirit of the Due Process Clause authorize us to embark on such an adventure. Nor is there anything in the word "liberty" or in the history behind it that decisively differentiates erotic liberty or family-related liberty from many other aspects of liberty—of movement, of employment, of contract, and so on. Many forms of liberty—of speech and of worship, for example—also find refuge in specific language elsewhere in the Constitution, above and beyond the Due Process Clause. But, as Justice Rosen explains, most of the provisions of the Bill of Rights—the First, Fourth, and Fifth Amendments, for example—are rather far afield of the facts at hand today.

I am aware that this Court has on other occasions read the word "process" to mean "substance." See, e.g., *Dred Scott v. Sanford,* 60 U.S. (19 How.) 393 (1857); *Lochner v. New York,* 198 U.S. 45 (1905). But the fact remains that the Constitution simply does not give this Court the right to ignore the word "process" and substitute "substance." Nor can it be said that there are strong reliance interests in "substantive due process" that now preclude our questioning of this judicial approach.

B. Privileges or Immunities

I do not reject the outcome of every case in which the Court has invoked "substantive due process." Many of these cases, on their facts, may well be defensible by reference to other constitutional words and structures. For example, in *Griswold v. Connecticut,* 381 U.S. 479 (1965), we recast *Pierce v. Society of Sisters,* 268 U.S. 510 (1925), and *Meyer v. Nebraska,* 262 U.S. 390 (1923), as cases rooted in First Amendment rights of speech and expression. In my view, personal First Amendment rights are properly held applicable against the states via the following constitutional language: "No State shall make or enforce any law which shall abridge the privileges or immunities of citizens of the United States." U.S. Const. amend. XIV, sect. 1.

These privileges and immunities include, at their core, individual rights and freedoms affirmed elsewhere in the Constitution, such as the privilege of habeas corpus, the right not to be subject to unreasonable search or seizure, and the liberties of speech, press, petition, and assembly. Indeed, the special linkage between First Amendment freedoms and the Privileges or Immunities Clause is obvious on the very face of the clause, which borrows no fewer than five of its words—"No, shall, make, law, abridge"— from the First Amendment itself. More generally, as Justice Black has forcefully noted, Reconstruction history supports the view that the Fourteenth Amendment largely "incorporates" against the states most of the individual rights provisions of the Bill of Rights. See *Adamson v. California,* 332 U.S. 46, 68 (1947) (Black, J., dissenting); *Duncan v. Louisiana,* 391 U.S. 145, 162 (1968) (Black, J., concurring).

Like Justice Black, I do not believe that precedent properly precludes our returning to the core meaning of the Privileges or Immunities Clause. Much of what the Court said about the clause in the 1873 *Slaughterhouse Cases,* 83 U.S. (16 Wall.) 36, ranged far beyond what was necessary to decide these cases on their facts; in any event, many of our subsequent decisions are best justified by open recourse to this clause. Over the past generation, we have effectively incorporated most of the Bill of Rights against the states, and these holdings are best grounded not in the language of the Due Process Clause but in the words and spirit of the Privileges or Immunities Clause.

My own views about the details of this incorporation process differ somewhat from Justice Black's. Had the framers of the Fourteenth Amendment meant simply to incorporate Amendments One to Eight, no more and no less—or all rights affirmed in the Constitution (including, for example, the habeas right in Article I), but nothing more—there would have been clearer ways of saying so. As I read the clause's text, and its underlying history, it aimed to prevent states from abridging Americans' fundamental rights above and beyond those specifically mentioned in Amendments One through Eight, or elsewhere in the Constitution.

Are we, then, precisely back to where we started, with "substantive due process" under a different label? Not quite. The Privileges or Immunities Clause of the Fourteenth Amendment offers a democratically superior and judicially manageable alternative to our past experience with substantive due process.

In the substantive due process arena, Justices have typically consulted their own viscera, the views of their own social strata, and this Court's precedents. The reasons for this judiciary-centered approach are not hard to fathom. Because the very phrase "substantive due process" teeters on self-contradiction, the words of this phrase provide neither a sound starting point nor a directional push to proper legal analysis. The phrase does not clarify thought. It is a judicial Rorschach blot. Granted, once the first due process cases are on the books, these decisions may launch the general doctrinal project. But, since the entire concept is a judicial fabrication, the judicial phrase "substantive due process" unsurprisingly ends up encouraging the judiciary to consult itself as the ultimate source of meaning. This judge-centered approach fails to do justice to the underlying vision of the Fourteenth Amendment itself, which reflected uneasiness about judicial adventurism. (The first sentence of the Amendment, after all, aimed to overrule parts of the infamous *Dred Scott* decision.)

Instead of beginning with a phrase of our own making—substantive due process—I suggest that we begin with the words actually used by the Amendment and ponder the vision that underlies these words. There was indeed a core set of fundamental freedoms that the people aimed to affirm in the Fourteenth Amendment's Privileges or Immunities Clause: freedom of expression and of religion, protection against cruel and unusual punishments, the safeguards of habeas corpus, and so on. These clear instances of inclusion, embraced by the people themselves when they ratified the Amendment, give us core cases—paradigm cases, so to speak—from which we can properly begin the doctrinal process of generalization, interpolation, and analogic reasoning.

Moreover, the Privileges or Immunities Clause suggests a more populist and less court-centered method for finding other fundamental rights not specified in the Bill of Rights. The Fourteenth Amendment does not exhaustively list all the privileges and immunities of American citizenship, but it presupposes that such fundamental rights are catalogued elsewhere in documents that the *American people* have broadly ratified, formally or informally. In the eyes of those who drafted and ratified the Fourteenth Amendment, the federal Bill of Rights was one of these catalogues, a compilation of fundamental rights that the Amendment would henceforth guarantee ("incorporate") against states. But the Bill of Rights was not the only epistemic source of guidance. In other words, the Fourteenth Amendment incorporates more than the Bill of Rights. Magna Carta, the English Petition of Right, the Declaration of Independence, state bills of rights—all these, too, were proper sources of guidance for interpreters in search of fundamental rights and freedoms. Rather than a system in which

Justices simply look to what they or their predecessors have declared fundamental in self-absorbed opinions, a more attractive and document-supported approach to the Privileges or Immunities Clause would invite this Court to canvass nonjudicial legal sources—the documents just listed, state laws and constitutions, federal legislation, and so on—as critical sources of epistemic guidance. Such a law-canvassing approach would focus the members of this Court not on ourselves or our own individual or institutional wisdom but on the wisdom of the American people more generally. Where it can be said that a law offends a principle that *the American people* have generally understood as fundamental, such law would invite judicial invalidation.

This law-canvassing approach helps explain the rightness of our decision in *Griswold v. Connecticut.* As Justice Harlan emphasized, the Connecticut contraception law at issue was utterly outlandish, as measured by the laws of all the other states. "[C]onclusive, in my view, is the utter novelty of this enactment. Although the Federal Government and many States have at one time or other had on their books statutes forbidding or regulating the distribution of contraceptives, none so far as I can find, has made the *use* of contraceptives a crime."

But this ground for reaffirming the basic holding of *Griswold* today furnishes a dubious basis for invalidating abortion laws that, as Justice Rosen's dissenting opinion makes clear, are far from unusual or outside the mainstream of American legislation.

One final note on the law-canvassing approach. Suppose that this Court were to strike down a state law as wholly outside the mainstream of American fundamental freedom, as defined by actual legal practice. Suppose further that after this ruling, many other states were to enact similar laws—say, with delayed effective dates so as to allow for anticipatory judicial review—in order to spark a judicial reconsideration of the issue. On my view, these later enactments could properly call into question our initial grounds for invalidation and give rise to a genuine dialogue between the judiciary and the larger polity on the issue of evolving unenumerated rights. Indeed, America is now in the middle of just such a democratic dialogue on the death penalty, prompted in part by our recent decision in *Furman v. Georgia,* 408 U.S. 238 (1972). Just as the word "unusual" in the Eighth Amendment invites this Court to consult the broad penal practices of America in order to get a sense of the contemporary American ethos of punishment and the broad public understanding of cruelty, so the words "privileges or immunities of citizens" invite this Court to listen to what citizens actually believe their fundamental rights to be, as expressed in key legal texts and practices.

C. Privacy and Precedent

The Chief Justice's basic analysis of liberty and privacy is not fundamentally textual, or historical, but rather doctrinal, relying mainly on *Pierce, Meyer, Skinner v. Oklahoma,* 316 U.S. 535 (1942), *Griswold,* and *Eisenstadt v. Baird,* 405 U.S. 438 (1972).

None of these cases on its facts involved abortion. None involved the destruction of an unborn embryo or fetus. Generally speaking, one of the virtues of doctrinalism is that it proceeds in small steps from like case to like case. But today's ruling, going far beyond a series of cases that are inherently different, lacks this traditional doctrinal virtue.

The Court marches ahead under the banner of "privacy." "Privacy" would seem an apt word for the claim, say, of two or more consenting adults (whether married or not, and whether or not of the same sex) to engage in forms of intimate physical contact behind closed doors in a manner that imposed no direct injury or "harm" on others. (I use "harm" here in a way elaborated by John Stuart Mill in *On Liberty.*) But the Chief Justice's opinion, as I read it, does not go so far as to confer constitutional protection on all such self-regarding/no-harm-to-others behavior. More to the point, in the abortion context, "privacy" seems an inapt concept unless we simply define away the harm to the fetus. "Privacy" may be a good word to describe a claimed right to contraception, but in the abortion context the word seems to beg the question of the status of the fetus. Surely, for example, there is no "privacy" right to commit infanticide or child abuse.

There are indeed plausible textual reasons for not treating the unborn as "persons" within the meaning of the Constitution. (The Fourteenth Amendment itself begins with a reference to "born" persons, as I elaborate later.) But even nonpersons may have interests that deserve legal protection. A pet dog is not a person, yet the law may protect it from cruelty or wanton destruction; society does not view this purely as a question of the owner's "privacy." If persons have no "privacy" (or "liberty") right to set aside laws that prohibit cruelty to animals, why do persons have a "privacy" or "liberty" right to set aside laws that prohibit cruelty to human fetuses? If fetuses are simply imagined away in a privacy analysis, does this mean that a state would be barred from punishing as murder or intentional manslaughter the actions of a thug who shoots a pregnant women in the abdomen and thus knowingly kills the fetus? (Such would seem to be the implication of Justice Tushnet's dismissive views of unborn human life. With a judicial coup de main, his separate opinion simply sweeps the previable fetus off the table, relying heavily on nonjudicial writings of former Justice Clark. Perhaps Justice Tushnet would, outside the abortion/privacy context, allow the state to protect the unborn against the hypothesized thug. But, if so, then talk of a pure privacy right to abortion would seem to have a touch of circularity about it.)

The Chief Justice argues that Texas does not really care about protecting unborn human life because its law also reflects cross-cutting and countervailing concerns (as does Georgia's law). Justice Rosen's dissenting opinion exposes some of the problems with the Court's analysis here; laws often reflect and balance a cluster of legitimate concerns. See generally Note, Legislative Purpose, Rationality, and Equal Protection, 82 *Yale L.J.* 123 (1972). Is the Chief Justice serious when he suggests that were Texas to punish women themselves who seek to self-abort, such an extension of its abortion laws would render its legal code *more* constitutionally defensible? (Justice Sunstein also casts doubt upon whether Texas's abortion law "will, in fact, provide meaningful protection to fetal life." But he points to no evidence that those states that prohibit abortions in fact have the same rate of actual abortions as those that allow it. Would he find Texas's law more constitutionally defensible if Texas cracked down harder on illegal abortions?)

The Chief Justice also quotes language from our decision last Term in *Eisenstadt v. Baird*: "If the right of privacy means anything, it is the right of the *individual*, married or single, to be free from unwarranted governmental intrusion into matters so fundamentally affecting a person as the decision whether to bear or beget a child." I do not think we crossed the abortion bridge in *Eisenstadt*, which was a contraception case, not an abortion case. To the extent that the Chief Justice might seek to place super-strong weight on the word "bear" as distinct from the word "beget," a permissible alternative reading of these words is that in *Eisenstadt* we affirmed the right of individual *men* not to procreate ("beget"), just as we affirmed the rights of women not to *procreate* ("bear"). In support of this male-female reading of *Eisenstadt*, I should note that the case that we cited immediately after this sentence was a case about a man and his erotic activities, *Stanley v. Georgia*. And, to repeat, the bear/beget language appeared in the context of a contraception case where no fetus in being existed. Thus, I do not think we should treat a stray word or phrase in *Eisenstadt* as having somehow squarely faced and answered the momentous legal and moral questions that surround abortion. Indeed, the words "fetus" and "embryo" do not even appear anywhere in the case. Thus, it would be irresponsible—a kind of judicial bait-and-switch—to treat one word in that case ("bear") as dispositive of the issues we confront today for the first time.

It is also worth noting that the quoted *Eisenstadt* language did not command the support of five Justices in that case. Even if it had, the question today would remain, from whence did *Eisenstadt* derive this right? To repeat, our ultimate fidelity must be to the Constitution itself; if our cases were themselves not properly grounded in the document, we need not slavishly follow and extend these cases, or their broadest dicta.

D. Prudence and Humility

Given the vast legal and moral complexities and profundities implicated by the abortion question, and given that today is this Court's first real occasion to consider the topic, members of this Court should proceed with extraordinary humility and caution. This Court has made many mistakes in its past—especially in the context of substantive due process. See, e.g., *Dred Scott v. Sanford*; *Lochner v. New York*. We Justices are not infallible. And today we confront some of the deepest questions of human existence, issues on which many thoughtful men and women of good will have strongly disagreed and may continue to do so for years to come. On these issues, it is not clear to me that judges and Justices are any wiser than others. Unless the Constitution speaks with crystal clearness on the issue at hand—and I confess that I do not see perfect clarity, even as I offer my own best preliminary judgment—there are good reasons for us not to decide more than is necessary today.

E. Women's Equal Citizenship

For me, a key constitutional point to keep in mind today is that abortion laws impose severe burdens on women, burdens that are not imposed on identically situated men (a null set) or even on analogously situated men. Moreover, these burdens may well make it difficult for women as a group to participate on fully equal terms in political life—as lawmakers and jurors, for example.

The Fourteenth Amendment begins by affirming that "All persons born or naturalized in the United States . . . are citizens." This sentence squarely aimed to repudiate some egregious language in the *Dred Scott* case, where Chief Justice Taney had proclaimed that blacks, even if free, could never be citizens. The Fourteenth Amendment emphatically rejected this racist suggestion in *United States Reports.* The Amendment thus affirms that all blacks born in America are indeed citizens. And not just citizens, but *equal* citizens—that is the deep premise of this sentence, understood in its historic context. Writing for the Court in 1896, the first Justice Harlan (who understood the Fourteenth Amendment far better than did his brethren in cases such as *Plessy v. Ferguson,* 163 U.S. 537 (1896), and *The Civil Rights Cases,* 109 U.S. 3 (1883)) glossed the first sentence of the amendment as follows: "All citizens are equal before the law." *Gibson v. Mississippi,* 162 U.S. 565, 591 (1896). In the next sentence of the Amendment, the word "equal" appears prominently and for the first time in the Constitution: "No state shall . . . deny to any person within its jurisdiction the equal protection of the laws." A companion statute, the Civil Right Act of 1866, also speaks of the right of "citizens" to the "full *and equal* benefit" of various civil rights.

In the minds of those who drafted and supported the Fourteenth Amendment, this equality of citizenship, of civil rights, and of legal protection was not limited to racial equality. The word "race" nowhere appears in the Fourteenth Amendment, as it does in the Fifteenth. Surely, if the framers of this Amendment had meant to limit the idea to race, they knew how to say so. But they intentionally chose broader words. What kind of equality, broader than mere racial equality, is affirmed in this Amendment? The word "born" in the first sentence helps us to see the core textual idea: government should disavow laws that heap disadvantage on a person because of that person's *status at birth.* Government should not penalize or discriminate against a person because he was born black, or a slave, or poor, or Jewish, or out of wedlock. Or because she was born female.

The history the surrounds the adoption of the Fourteenth Amendment shows that issues of sex equality were intertwined with issues of race equality in the 1860s. The very language of the Fourteenth Amendment in fact resembled wording that Elizabeth Cady Stanton herself endorsed in 1865, which she in turn borrowed from the Seneca Falls Declaration of 1848. (Stanton called for an amendment in which "the women as well as the men shall be secured in all the rights, privileges, and immunities of citizens." The Seneca Falls Declaration had demanded that women receive "all the rights and privileges which belong to them as citizens of the United States.")

Although the burgeoning women's rights movement disliked the sexism of Section 2 of the Fourteenth Amendment, which inserted the word "male" into the Constitution for the first time and excluded women from states' presumptive electorates, women generally embraced the letter and spirit of Section 1, which aimed to affirm "civil rights"—as distinct from "political rights" such as voting, office holding, and jury service. Indeed, the very distinction between civil and political rights—a distinction at the foundation of the Fourteenth Amendment—drew upon the model of women's rights: unmarried white women enjoyed most civil rights but not political rights. In effect, the Fourteenth Amendment's opening words promised blacks the historic rights of these women, whose legal entitlements thus helped define the central meaning of Section 1's organizing category of full and equal civil rights.

Granted, it is doubtful that in the 1860s all discriminations against women were viewed in exactly the same way as discriminations against blacks. Traditional marriage law subordinated the woman to the man, but a law that allowed a black and a white to join together as business partners only so long as the white was the senior partner would plainly violate the Amendment. Withholding the vote (and the associated rights to serve on juries and to sit in the legislature) from women because of their birth status was not seen as an impermissible discrimination, even though similar discriminations against black men were soon prohibited by the Constitution, in its Fifteenth Amendment.

But, as I read the Constitution *as a whole,* the eventual adoption of the Nineteenth Amendment, granting women the suffrage in virtually identical language to the Fifteenth Amendment's grant to blacks, argues for a robust reading of women's equal protection and women's equal citizenship. (The Nineteenth Amendment reads as follows, in relevant part: "The right of citizens of the United States to vote shall not be denied or abridged by the United States or by any state on account of sex." Whereas this amendment ends with the word "sex," the Fifteenth Amendment ends with the words "race, color, or previous condition of servitude." Otherwise, the two provisions are identical.) In my view, these kindred Amendments aimed to make blacks/women the full equals of whites/men in the political domain, including not simply the right to vote for legislators but the right to vote in a legislature—the right to be a legislator, the right to be voted for—and likewise the right to serve and vote on juries and to hold other political office.

Once the Constitution vested women with full and equal political rights, shouldn't entitlement to the full and equal enjoyment of lesser civil rights follow a fortiori? Discriminations that might once have seemed legitimate on the basis of an old-fashioned view of woman's role and capacities become illegitimate when the *Constitution itself,* in a later amendment, affirms a very different and more robust vision of women as full and equal members of the political People who govern America. In essence, we must read the words of the Fourteenth Amendment in light of a later chapter of America's constitutional saga, namely the Nineteenth Amendment. (For an early example of a case reading the Fourteenth Amendment rights of women more sweepingly in light of the Nineteenth, see *Adkins v. Children's Hospital,* 261 U.S. 525 (1923).)

F. Pregnancy and Abortion

With this understanding of the letter and spirit of the Fourteenth and Nineteenth Amendments' affirmation and reaffirmation of women's equal citizenship, I now turn to the vexing question of abortion. Although abortion laws often operate directly upon physicians of both sexes (as is true in Texas), the primary burden of the law lands upon the pregnant woman herself, who is in effect obliged to carry her unwanted pregnancy to term. The obligation to bear an unwanted pregnancy is a heavy one, both literally and figuratively. As a practical matter, it can require a woman to end her education or career, at least temporarily. It can impose serious financial burdens and medical risks. It can put her at risk of physical attack from the biological father or for a man who suspects that he is not the biological father. It can dramatically interfere with her general freedom of movement, her daily routine, her diet, her relations with others around her, her mental state, and her body generally. Especially in cases of rape and incest, the pregnancy itself can impose severe mental trauma on her. After she has given birth, psychological and social pressures may make it difficult for her to give the baby up for adoption. In that event, the serious burden of an unwanted pregnancy is only the beginning of the obligations that she will bear and the possible sacrifices she may be obliged to make.

Texas's justification for imposing such heavy burdens on the pregnant woman—even in cases of rape and incest—is to protect the life of the unborn and innocent human life inside her womb. Her liberty is abridged so as to protect its life. In effect, the Texas law has chosen life over liberty.

The problem, however, is that Texas has chosen to impose these life-sustaining burdens only on women. It is at least possible to imagine alternative ways of promoting unborn human life. For example, in the case of unmarried women, the law could require the biological father to remunerate the woman for half of the total financial and physical burdens that she must bear during the course of her pregnancy. This more gender-neutral approach would require him to compensate her for her childbearing expenses, work, and labor, and thus to bear his fair share of the burden. (The law could of course allow any woman who so desired to opt out of this compensation entitlement.) In response, it might be said that "nature" imposes the burden on her, not him. But "nature" also makes abortion possible. If the law intervenes to limit her "natural" freedoms, why not his?

Indeed, in the act of procreation itself, men would seem to bear equal if not more responsibility, on average. It is possible to imagine sexual intercourse in the absence of full male consent (as in the case of statutory rape involving an adult female and an underage male). Nevertheless, sex in the absence of full consent by the woman—because of male coercion that rises to the level of legal rape, or some lower level of force or fraud—is more common than sex in the absence of full consent by the man. Thus, one could argue that conscription of a father's income stream is actually *easier* to justify than conscription of a mother's womb. In almost every case, his commission of the sex act was voluntary, whereas, in many cases, hers may not have been. And yet, to repeat, the law saddles her with special burdens while exempting him. Texas obliges her to give up nine months of her life to sustain the unborn life but does not oblige him to give up even nine dollars.

Of course, it can be argued that pregnancy is simply a unique case: "This is not really discrimination between women and men, but simply discrimination between pregnant persons and nonpregnant persons." I wonder. Surely, government should not be free to subordinate women so long as it does so via laws that use women's unique biology to disadvantage them as a class. Imagine, for example, a law that said that pregnant people cannot vote, or cannot serve on juries, or be elected to office. Would not such a law plainly violate the Nineteenth Amendment? But, if so, isn't this a square admission that laws that heap disabilities on pregnant persons are indeed laws that discriminate "on account of sex"?

Of course, in some situations, our governments have conscripted men.

However, when male soldiers have been drafted—deprived of their liberty to protect others' lives—government has at times furnished them with educational and other benefits after their term of service has ended. But when pregnant women are asked to disrupt their careers and education in order to protect unborn life, government has not showered comparable benefits upon them. There is no Mothers' Bill of Rights akin to the G.I. Bill of Rights. Indeed, in Texas and many other places, public schools and public employers have generally been allowed to expel or fire unmarried pregnant women but have not expelled or fired the men involved with equal vigor. If Texas meant to minimize its imposition on the life and liberty of women, I suspect the state could also do much more than it has done to facilitate and encourage adoption (perhaps even through publicly supported institutions that would help any woman who so desired to keep the pregnancy itself, as well as the later adoption, confidential). I further suspect that Texas could do far more to support public institutions that provide medical assistance and other services to indigent women who are bearing unwanted pregnancies.

Indeed, if Texas truly aims to minimize the burdens of unwanted pregnancy it imposes on females, why has the state chosen to make it especially difficult for certain rapes to be proved? Under Texas law, in certain rape cases the victim's testimony cannot suffice to convict a rapist in the absence of physical corroboration or "fresh complaint." No comparable rule exists for male victims of nonsexual assault. In virtually all other Texas criminal cases, a single witness's uncorroborated testimony may lawfully suffice to convict. But not for certain rapes. These extant Texas evidence laws have their origin in an explicitly gendered set of rules about "female[s] alleged to have been seduced." Such laws—just like the Texas abortion law at issue today—were passed at a time when no woman was allowed to vote in Texas. These old evidence laws in effect singled out some persons on the basis of their birth status and declared that they, uniquely in our criminal justice system, were not fully reliable witnesses. To me, this seems an obvious status insult to the equal citizenship of women. More than that, such laws seem to deny rape victims the genuine equal protection of laws, a concept that at its core affirms the rights of victims to be equally protected by government from criminals. (The Fourteenth Amendment thus barred a state from looking the other way when white Klansmen murdered and pillaged black folk.) Indeed, Texas's evidence laws in rape cases eerily resemble the infamous Black Codes that forbade the conviction of whites on the testimony of blacks. All this casts in a troubling light the burdens that Texas has chosen to impose on pregnant women (even rape victims), while showing more solicitude for the liberty interests of men (even rapists).

In this connection, certain aspects of the law we properly condemned in *Griswold* are also worth highlighting. Like the Texas anti-abortion law before us today and the Texas rape-corroboration law already mentioned, the Connecticut anticontraception law in *Griswold* was adopted before women had the vote and imposed serious risks on women—risks of unwanted pregnancy—that men did not bear. Indeed, the law specifically exempted contraceptive devices designed to prevent venereal disease. A condom was okay (as it might protect the man from unwanted infection), but a diaphragm was not (as it would only protect the woman from unwanted pregnancy). Thus, men could shield themselves from future disease, but women could not equally shield themselves from future dis-ease. (Pregnancy and childbirth are, as I have stressed, not exactly easy.) The Connecticut law entrenched traditional gender roles, implicitly treating women as baby machines and using their unique biology as a basis for legal disadvantage. I am worried that the Texas law may do the same thing.

No members of the *Griswold* Court even spotted the gender issue. No women sat on the Court in *Griswold*. Only four years before *Griswold*, this Court unanimously upheld a Florida law that explicitly treated women differently from men and that predictably led to gross underrepresentation of women on juries—and not a single Justice so much as even mentioned the Nineteenth Amendment. See *Hoyt v. Florida*, 368 U.S. 57 (1961). All this is unfortunate, to say the least. And, for me, it suggests that this Court should try to approach the issues in this case in a manner that invites women in general to make their voices heard; a conversation about women's rights needs to involve women themselves. (That is one of the reasons today's opinion should begin a dialogue with the American people, not end it.)

The Texas law itself was not the product of a dialogue in which women participated equally. It was adopted at a time when no woman voted. As I see it, this law should be judicially set aside for three interlocking reasons. *First, this law when enacted did not reflect women's equal input. Second, this law imposed and continues to impose serious and gender-specific burdens on women. And, third, this law continues to impose burdens that, by disrupting women's lives and careers, may make it less likely that they will be able to be full political equals in legislatures, judiciaries, and other positions of government power.*

My proposed framework of analysis builds upon the lessons of this Court's race cases. For example, my approach can help us to see, from yet another angle, the compelling rightness of *Brown v. Board of Education,* 347 U.S. 483 (1954), and its companion cases. In those cases, it should be recalled, this Court confronted Jim Crow laws that (a) when enacted generally did not reflect black's equal input (because blacks were widely disfranchised, often in unremedied violation of the Constitution); (b) imposed serious and race-based burdens on blacks denied the chance to associate on equal terms with more privileged whites; and (c) imposed exclusions that made it harder for blacks to participate as full political equals.

A critic of my approach might say that because women today can vote in Texas, the burden should be on them to repeal this law if they feel it in effect discriminates against them. See, for example, today's dissent by Justice Rosen. But I read the Nineteenth Amendment more broadly. This amendment sought to make amends. It sought to end a past practice of exclusion that was viewed as unfair, wrongful, erroneous. To the extent that the Texas law may well be a legacy of that wrongful era, we should not perpetuate it. We should wipe the slate clean for a new conversation that involves men and women on equal footing.

A critic from the opposite direction might say that we Justices should decide the full meaning of women's equality for ourselves, rather than remand the question to the Texas political process. This critic might be aghast at the idea of "putting constitutional rights up to a vote." This critic might even propose to go far beyond Chief Justice Balkin—say, by constitutionalizing a detailed regulatory grid based on pregnancy trimesters. But, to repeat, one way of respecting women's equality is for us Justices to pay particular attention to conversations in which women participate as equals—in a way that, alas, they do not yet do on this Court.

Such conversations need not be confined to the separate states. Congress itself may choose to weigh in on behalf of women's rights in the context of pregnancy and abortion, as it has recently weighed in on behalf of women's rights in other areas. It bears emphasis that the Fourteenth Amendment vests Congress with sweeping, *McCulloch*-like powers to enforce the equal rights, freedoms, privileges, and immunities of women and to safeguard those interests in the domains of pregnancy and abortion. See U.S Const. amend. XIV Sect. 5 ("The Congress shall have power to enforce, by appropriate legislation, the provisions of this article.") See also id. amend. XIX para. 2 (similar). In the event that Congress were to pass a woman-protective law that limited various state abortion statutes, this Court should treat Congress's enactment with great deference, in keeping with Section 5's words and its underlying history; Reconstruction Republicans plainly envisioned a role for Congress alongside courts in safeguarding American civil rights. (*The Civil Rights Cases* of 1883 do not properly stand in the way of such deference. These old and dubious cases have been superceded—indeed, implicitly overruled in part—by our more recent decisions in *Katzenbach v. Morgan,* 384 U.S. 641 (1966), and *Jones v. Alfred Mayer, Co.,* 392 U.S. 409 (1968).)

In Texas, and in other similarly situated states, the result of the new conversations I am envisioning may well be new laws that restrict some kinds of abortions in a variety of ways. These laws will probably at some point come before this Court for further review. Cf. *Furman v. Georgia.* And, when they do, this Court may well confront a range of hard questions. Exactly what does equality demand on issues related to real biological difference, such as the capacity to become pregnant? Should it matter how many women are actually members of the legislature that adopts a new statute and how they vote? If a state acts by initiative or referendum, in which presumably fully half of the voters were female, should this fact count especially in its favor? More generally, what kind of standard of review is appropriate, given that women are not a "discrete and insular minority"? See *Reed v. Reed,* 404 U.S. 71 (1971); cf. *United States v. Carolene Products,* 304 U.S. 144, 152 & n. 4 (1938). (Note, of course, that this Court has yet to confront related issues about the proper judicial stance toward laws that seek to benefit rather than burden blacks and other historically disadvantaged racial minorities.)

I do not seek to anticipate and answer these and other questions today. For one thing, my views do not command a majority of the Court today, so nothing that I might add here would provide definitive guidance. More important, I have criticized the Court for going too far too fast today, in a manner that goes well beyond the facts of the Texas case before us. I must take care to avoid a similar mistake in this separate opinion. The issues that surround women's equality, especially in the context of the unique and profound questions implicated by pregnancy, are multifarious. I expect to learn a great deal from the American people as this dialogue unfolds. And, in turn, I hope that this dialogue may benefit from public attention to those aspects of the Constitution that genuinely do bear on the abortion question, especially the women's equality norms of the Fourteenth and Nineteenth Amendments.

II. Doe v. Bolton

Unlike the statute at issue in *Roe v. Wade,* supra, the Georgia law was passed only recently. Indeed, this law is so new that Georgia courts have yet to define some of its central terms or to consider possible state constitutional objections to it. I would therefore vacate the District Court's decision and instruct that court to abstain from decision until the state courts have had an opportunity to weigh in. See *Railroad Commission of Texas v. Pullman Co.,* 312 U.S. 496 (1941).

ROSEN, J., dissenting.

"I like my privacy as well as the next one," said Justice Black. See *Griswold v. Connecticut*, 381 U.S. 479, 530–31 (1965) (Black, J., dissenting). I like my own a good deal more. The right to be let alone by government is indeed "the most comprehensive of rights and the right most valued by civilized men." *Olmstead v. U.S.*, 277 U.S. 438, 471 (1928) (Brandeis, J., dissenting). And today it is valued by women, as well. This country is in the middle of the most important transformation of the relations between the sexes in our history, and I expect that the consequences of this social and legal revolution will be viewed, in time, as second in importance only to the end of racial segregation and the dismantling of the legacy of Jim Crow. Congress has proposed an Equal Rights Amendment to the Constitution; men and women are learning to interact as equals in the workplace; and state legislatures have begun to repeal the draconian restrictions on abortion that, although passed in the nineteenth century to protect fetal life, have the effect of restricting employment choices for women and channeling them into roles that they might not have chosen for themselves. I recognize that increasing numbers of women view these laws as violations of their personal autonomy, as well as of their civic equality. For myself, I sympathize entirely with their sentiments. And because I have no doubt that Tocqueville was correct when he predicted that American society would move inexorably in the direction of greater and greater equality, I expect that most state legislatures, in time, would have come to recognize these laws as a barrier to the full equality of women and would eventually have joined the handful of states that have already decided to repeal them.

I say that the states would have repealed these laws, because they are no longer free to do so. Instead, this Court, by rushing to short-circuit the political debate about abortion, has relieved the states of the opportunity to make a democratic choice. And, although some will applaud the Court for having served the cause of liberty and equality, I fear that they will come to regret their impatient demand for judicial salvation. By inventing a new right to abortion before a consensus in favor of liberalization has had an opportunity to crystallize, I fear that the Court will energize an anti-abortion majority to press its cause with renewed fervor, converting what would have been eventual losers in the political arena into aggrieved and determined opponents of judicial power. The costs to this Court, and to the federal judiciary in general, may become obvious enough in time.

But, although the pragmatic arguments against judicial intervention are powerful, they are not the reason I dissent today. Instead, I cannot join the majority for a simple reason: after consulting all of the conventional methods of constitutional interpretation—constitutional text, original understanding, evolving traditions, and precedent—I conclude that none of them supports the sweeping right that the Court recognizes in these cases—namely a right to abort a fetus during the first trimester of pregnancy. On the contrary, each of these methodologies supports the opposite conclusion—that no broad right to abortion can be easily discerned.

I.

I begin, of course, with the text. Although the word "privacy" doesn't appear in the Constitution, several amendments protect different dimensions of privacy clearly and unequivocally. But each of those dimensions has intelligible boundaries, and none can be easily stretched to cover the cases before us. The First Amendment protects "the right of the people peaceably to assemble," as well as certain related expectations of anonymity from state surveillance. But the right of political assembly can't be plausibly extended to insulate the decisions of couples and their physicians from state regulation. The Third and Fourth Amendments protect the people from unreasonable searches and seizures of their "persons, houses, papers, and effects." We held recently that the Fourth Amendment protects "people, not places," see *Katz v. U.S.*, 389 U.S. 347, 351 (1967), recognizing that certain searches and seizures of persons, papers, or effects might be unreasonable whether or not they take place in the home. But this case does not involve a bodily search or seizure, let alone a trespass on the sanctity of the bedroom. The restrictions on therapeutic abortion at issue here concern voluntary, not involuntary, procedures and therefore don't implicate either the Fourth Amendment or the related common law rules that prohibit the state from imposing unwanted medical treatment. Compare *Jacobson v. Massachusetts*, 197 U.S. 11, 26 (1905), with *Skinner v.*

Oklahoma ex rel. Williamson, 316 U.S. 535 (1942). The Fifth Amendment protects persons from being "compelled in any criminal case to be a witness against himself." Like the First Amendment, it protects a zone of mental privacy—rooted in the framers concern about the unique indignity of interrogation under oath. This doesn't get us very far down the road toward sexual autonomy.

Privacy, in other words, has many distinct dimensions (which is why the Court's abstractions are especially malleable and unhelpful). For better or for worse, two of the dimensions of privacy that our Constitution does not obviously protect concern personal dignity and personal autonomy. Privacy conceived as a form of dignity focuses on the social forms of respect that citizens owe each other. It is protected in tort by the law of slander and libel and by the cluster of privacy actions that grew out of Justice Brandeis's famous article, see Samuel Warren and Louis Brandeis, "The Right to Privacy," 4 *Harv. L. Rev.* 193, 214 (1890), such as intrusion on seclusion and the publication of private facts. But the Constitution does not provide an obvious remedy for offenses against dignity and honor, as Brandeis and Warren recognized when they called for the creation of new common law privacy rights in the first place. In any event, the restrictions at issue in this case involve intrusions by government, not private citizens, and therefore do not centrally implicate the dignitary aspects of privacy.

They do, however, strike at the core of personal autonomy. Privacy conceived as a form of autonomy concerns the individual's ability to maintain a sphere of immunity from social norms and state regulation. It is precisely this sphere that is invaded when the state presumes to tell a woman that her own decisions about the course of her private life and public career must give way to her fetus's interest in potential life. But our Constitution does not provide any obvious protections for privacy conceived as a form of autonomy. The police powers of the state have traditionally given local communities broad discretion to regulate health, safety, and morals in the public interest, and these traditional regulations have never been seen as inconsistent with the liberty protected by the Due Process Clause of the Fourteenth Amendment.

Of course, the fact that a particular form of privacy or liberty is not explicitly enumerated in the constitutional text does not tell us definitively one way or the other whether it is protected by the Constitution. The Fourteenth Amendment says that no state shall "abridge the privileges or immunities of citizens of the United States," and the Ninth Amendment reminds us that the constitutional enumeration "of certain rights shall not be construed to deny or disparage others retained by the people." But neither the Ninth Amendment nor the Privileges or Immunities Clauses is an empty vessel into which judges can pour any vision of privacy that strikes their fancy. When the Fourteenth Amendment was ratified, the privileges or immunities of citizens were not viewed as an ambiguous set of abstract rights that judges could define at their whim; on the contrary, they were viewed as a fairly determinate set of fundamental rights rooted in the common law and relatively consistent from state to state. In the nineteenth century, they were widely understood to include the common law rights enumerated in the Civil Rights Act of 1866 and in Justice Bushrod Washington's opinion in *Corfield v. Coryell,* including the right to make and enforce contracts, to sue and be sued, and to engage in the ordinary occupations of life. See *Corfield v. Coryell,* 6 F. Cas. 546, 551–52 (1823). None of these private law rights (which some framers viewed as an antidiscrimination principle and others as a substantive guarantee of fundamental rights) were originally understood to include a right to terminate pregnancy free of state regulation.

The Court suggests that, by requiring pregnant women to be mothers, the Texas and Georgia laws deny their opportunity to engage in the occupations of their choice, thereby implicating the privileges or immunities of citizenship. But this is a metaphor, rather than the kind of legal argument that would have been intelligible to the framers of the Fourteenth Amendment: motherhood is not one of the ordinary occupations of life recognized in the nineteenth century as a privilege or immunity of citizenship, and there are no formal barriers that keep pregnant women from pursuing whatever occupations they choose. The pressures that they feel are social, rather than legal, and in the nineteenth century, everyone agreed that the Fourteenth Amendment protected civil, not social, rights.

Just as the text and original understanding of the Fourteenth Amendment fail to support a right to terminate pregnancy, so do the constantly evolving traditions of our people. At the time of the framing through the mid-nineteenth century, abortion was regulated by common law and was not considered a criminal offense if performed before quickening. In the years after the Civil War, however, states began with increasing frequency to restrict abortion by statute without reference to quickening. When the Fourteenth Amendment was ratified in 1868, thirty of the thirty-seven states in the Union had passed laws restricting abortion. All but three of these states—Arkansas, Minnesota, and Mississippi—banned abortion throughout pregnancy. Seven of the twenty-seven states that banned abortion throughout pregnancy punished abortions after quickening more severely than those before quickening, but the other twenty states punished abortions equally regardless of when they were performed. The effect of these laws was to ban abortion from conception, unless necessary to save a mother's life—precisely like the Texas law before us today. Since the statute before us today had been adopted by a majority of states when the Fourteenth Amendment was ratified, it clearly does not violate the Fourteenth Amendment as originally understood. And, unlike the Alien and Sedition Acts, which were adopted soon after the First Amendment but whose unconstitutionality was clear to many constitutional framers and legislators at the time, I know of no authority in the late nineteenth century who suggested that abortion restrictions violated the Due Process or Equal Protection Clauses.

Tradition, of course, is not a static thing: it evolves dramatically every decade, reflecting the social changes that are constantly transforming American society in the direction predicted by Tocqueville. We are, at the moment, undergoing one of the most dramatic gains for women's equality in our history, and the inexorable logic of equality is transforming our politics, our workplaces, and the way that men and women interact in the public and private sphere. A minority of states have begun to repeal their draconian restrictions on abortion: thirteen states (including Georgia) have adopted the American Law Institute's Model Penal Code approach, which allows a licensed physician to terminate a pregnancy "if he believes that there is substantial risk that continuance of the pregnancy would gravely impair the physical or mental health of the mother or that the child would be born with grave physical or mental defect, or that the pregnancy resulted from rape, incest, or other felonious intercourse." See Model Penal Code Sec. 230.3. And four states—New York, Washington, Alaska, and Hawaii—now permit doctors to perform first-trimester abortions with almost no restrictions but set limits later in pregnancy. If a supermajority of states chose, in time, to follow this lead, leaving a state like Texas virtually alone in retaining the nineteenth-century model of permitting abortions only to save the life of the mother, then we as judges might plausibly conclude that our national traditions about abortion had decisively changed. Texas would be like Connecticut in the *Griswold* case —one of the only states that clung to an atavistic view of procreation that had been rejected by the rest of the nation. In such a situation, we might conceivably strike down the Texas law, as Justice Harlan suggested we should have struck down the Connecticut law, for its sheer novelty alone. See *Poe v. Ullman,* 367 U.S. 497, 554 (1961) (Harlan, J., concurring).

But the shift in tradition that the Court rushes to recognize has hardly begun to materialize. The overwhelming majority of states continue to share Texas's view of abortion, rather than rejecting it. Today, thirty states still allow abortion only to save the life of the mother—more than in 1868, not less. See Ariz. Rev. Stat. Ann. §§ 13-211, 13-212 (1956); Con. Gen. Stat. Ann. § 53-29 et seq. (West Supp. 1972); Idaho Code §§ 18-601, 18-602 (Supp. 1972); Ill. Rev. Stat. ch. 38, paragraph 23-1 (1971); Ind. Code Ann. §§ 35-1-58-1, 351-58-2 (Burns 1971); Iowa Code §§ 701.1 (1950); Ky. Rev. Stat. Ann. § 436.020 (Michie/Bobbs Merrill 1962); La. Rev. Stat. Ann. § 14:87 (West 1964); Me. Rev. Stat. Ann. tit. 17, § 51 (West 1964); Mich. Comp. Laws Ann. § 750.14 (West 1968); Minn. Stat. Ann. §§ 617.18, 617.19 (West 1971); Mo. Ann. Stat. § 559.100 (Vernon 1969); Mont. Code Ann. §§ 94-401, 94402 (1969); Neb. Rev. Stat. §§ 28-404, 28-405 (1964); Nev. Rev. Stat. §§ 200.220, 201.120 (1967); N.H. Rev. Stat. Ann. §§ 585:12, 585.13 (1955); N.J. Stat. Ann. § 2A:87-1 (West 1969); N.D. Cent. Code §§ 12-25-01, 12-25-02, 12-25-04 (1970); Ohio Rev. Code Ann. § 2901.16 (Baldwin 1953); Okla. Stat. Ann. tit. 21, §§ 714, 861, 862 (West 1971); Pa. Stat. Ann. tit. 18, §§ 4718, 4719 (1963); R.I. Gen. Laws §§ 11-3-1 (1956); S.D. Codified Laws Ann. §§ 22-17-1, 22-17-2 (1967); Tenn. Code Ann. §§ 39-301, 39-302 (Supp. 1956); Tex. Penal Code Ann. §§ 1191 et seq. (West 1961); Utah Code Ann. §§ 762-1, 76-2-2 (1953); Vt. Stat. Ann. §§ 101 (1958); W. Va. Code §§ 61-2-8 (1966); Wis. Stat. §§ 940.04 (1969); Wyo. Stat. §§ 6-77, 6-78 (1957). Far from being a national outlier, Texas continues to represent an overwhelming national consensus. As for the Georgia statute, it is even less vulnerable to being attacked as an atavistic remnant from a distant era. Georgia actually liberalized its abortion law in 1968, and, far from choosing the New York model of allowing abortions in the first trimester, the citizens selected instead the more restrictive Model Penal Code model, which allows abortions only to preserve the life and health of the mother. The choice made by the citizens of Georgia reminds us that the future of abortion rights in this country is being fiercely contested in the political arena, and the outcome is by no means certain. By rushing brazenly to circumvent this political debate in the name of a consensus that does not yet exist, this Court is aggrandizing itself at the expense of the still divided American people.

It seems clear to me, in other words, that constitutional text, original understanding, and evolving traditions do not easily support a right to terminate pregnancies in the first trimester. That leaves precedent. The

Chief Justice asserts confidently that "Our decisions from *Meyer* to *Eisen-stadt* demonstrate a continuous concern with the right of the people to make decisions about whether to have children, and to make choices about how those children will be raised." But he reaches this conclusion only by indulging in a kind of abstract expressivism, reading our precedents at such a high level of generality that the differences among them are airbrushed away. A more careful description of our precedents from *Meyer* to *Eisenstadt* makes it hard to discern a right to choose abortion. Let's begin with *Meyer* and *Pierce*. I would have thought that these chestnuts of the *Lochner* era would have been viewed with some wariness, but, in any event, they don't support a right to abortion. In the relevant passage from *Meyer*, Justice McReynolds wrote: "Without doubt, [the liberty guaranteed by the Fourteenth Amendment] denotes not merely freedom from bodily restraint but also the right of the individual to contract, to engage in any of the common occupations of life, to acquire useful knowledge, to marry, establish a home, and bring up children, to worship God according to the dictates of his own conscience, and generally to enjoy those privileges long recognized at common law as essential to the orderly pursuit of happiness by free men." *Meyer v. Nebraska*, 262 U.S. 390, 399 (1923), citing *Slaughter-House Cases*, 16 Wall. 36; *Butchers' Union Co. v. Crescent City Co.*, 111 U.S. 746; *Yick Wo v. Hopkins*, 118 U.S. 356; *Minnesota v. Barber*, 136 U.S. 313; *Allgeyer v. Louisiana*, 165 U.S. 578; *Lochner v. New York*, 198 U.S. 45; *Twining v. New Jersey*, 211 U.S. 78; *Chicago, Burlington & Quincy R.R. Co. v. McGuire*, 219 U.S. 549; *Truax v. Raich*, 239 U.S. 33; *Adams v. Tanner*, 244 U.S. 590; *New York Life Ins. Co. v. Dodge*, 246 U.S. 357; *Truax v. Corrigan*, 257 U.S. 312; *Adkins v. Children's Hospital*, 216 U.S. 525; *Wyeth v. Cambridge Board of Health*, 200 Mass. 474. This is consistent with the original understanding of fundamental liberties under the privileges or Immunities Clause, which were limited, as I've noted, to basic common law rights, relatively uniform from state to state, and available as a matter of right rather than legislative discretion. But the inclusion of the right to marry in this list does not imply a broad shield for all sexual decisions about whether or not to bear or beget a child within marriage. Fundamental liberties, as McReynolds noted in the next sentence, were subjected to "reasonable" regulation under the police power (as determined by the courts)—that is, regulations that promoted the public interest (as opposed to the interest of a particular class) by improving health, safety, or morals. It was well established by 1923 that the police power included not only the right to restrict categories of people who could marry (such as siblings) but also the right to proscribe abortions throughout pregnancy, as a majority of states had done. Nor did McReynolds suggest that the right to marry included the right of parents to choose whether to have children and to decide how they should be raised. He stressed "[t]hat the State may do much, go very far, indeed, in order to improve the quality of its citizens, physically, mentally and morally," but it could not single out non-English speakers for discriminatory treatment. The Nebraska law prohibiting the teaching of foreign languages in public and private schools, in other words, was a not a violation of the parent's autonomy to make important decisions about whether and how to raise children, as the Chief Justice suggests; instead, it violated the far more familiar and well-established right to make contracts relating to the common occupations of life: "Plaintiff in error taught this language in school as part of his occupation," McReynolds noted. "His right thus to teach and the right of parents to engage him so to instruct their children, we think, are within the liberty of the Amendment." Id. at 400. Two years later, in *Pierce v. Society of Sisters,* McReynolds invoked the same liberty of contract to strike down an Oregon law that required parents to send their children to public school. See *Pierce v. Society of Sisters,* 268 U.S. 510, 535–36 (1925). Whatever the vitality of these *Lochner*-era decisions about the New Deal, they do not come close to supporting what the Chief Justice calls "a general right of individual autonomy in matters related to bodily security, family, reproduction and child rearing."

Nor does the *Skinner* case, which the Chief Justice says "explicitly expanded the rights guaranteed by *Meyer* and *Pierce* to encompass the right to procreate and have children." Justice Douglas's opinion is not a model of clarity, and it is hardly obvious that his dictum that "marriage and procreation are fundamental to the very existence and survival of the race" intended to expand the common law rights recognized in *Meyer* and *Pierce.* If it did, it is hard to see on what grounds Justice Douglas meant to justify his decision, since he provided none in the opinion. The only argument that would be consistent with the substantive due process methodology that the Chief Justice embraces here was that sterilization laws somehow clashed with long-standing common law rights to refuse unwanted medical treatment that involves physical incursions into the body. See, e.g., *Rochin v. California,* 342 U.S. 165, 172 (1952) ("Illegally breaking into the privacy of the petitioner, the struggle to open his mouth and remove what was there, the forcible extraction of his stomach's contents . . . is bound to offend even hardened sensibilities"); *Union Pacific R.*

Co. v. Botsford, 141 U.S. 250, 251 (1891). Our Fourth Amendment cases have a similar concern. See *Schmerber v. California,* 384 U.S. 757, 772 (1966) ("The integrity of an individual's person is a cherished value of our society"). But a law that forbids abortion (as opposed to mandating abortion) hardly violates the right to refuse unwanted medical treatment. And even the right to refuse unwanted medical treatment is not absolute: it must yield when there is a clear health benefit to society as a whole. "Real liberty for all could not exist under the operation of a principle which recognizes the right of each individual person to use his own, whether in respect of his person or his property, regardless of the injury that may be done to others," the first Justice Harlan observed in upholding compulsory vaccinations in *Jacobson.* "In *Crowley v. Christensen,* 137 U.S. 86, 89, we said: 'The possession and enjoyment of all rights are subject to such reasonable conditions as may be deemed by the governing authority of the country essential to the safety, health, peace, good order and morals of the community.'" See *Jacobson,* 197 U.S. at 26. This is why Justices Stone and Jackson, concurring in *Skinner,* took care to stress that the sterilization law might be consistent with the Fourteenth Amendment if it had provided an individualized hearing to establish whether or not criminal propensities were in fact genetically transmissible in particular cases. See *Skinner,* 316 U.S. 535 (1942) (Stone and Jackson, JJ., concurring). All this is a long way from the Chief Justice's fundamental right of unregulated procreative autonomy, and it is perfectly consistent with the long-accepted understanding that women's reproductive choice may be restricted to protect fetal life.

Which brings us to *Griswold.* Justice Douglas's opinion, once again, was impressionistic in its derivation of a fundamental right to use contraception, eliding very different conceptions of privacy protected by different amendments of the Bill of Rights. His opinion was vulnerable to criticism not because it recognized an unenumerated right to privacy but because it conflated several different enumerated privacy rights at such a high level of generality that the free-floating privacy penumbra that emerged had little obvious connection to the textual principles from which it supposedly emanated. Yet, even Justice Douglas did not assert a general right of procreative autonomy; instead, the "notions of privacy" that he said were fundamental were those "surrounding the marriage relationship." See *Griswold,* 381 U.S. at 486. As a result, his opinion was heavily rooted in Fourth Amendment notions of the privacy of the home and the impossibility of enforcing Connecticut's law prohibiting the use of contraceptives by married couples without unreasonable intrusions into the "sacred precincts of the marital bedroom." Id. at 485. The case before us today, by contrast, is hardly a case about intrusive forms of information gathering in the home; its proscriptions are centered on medical professionals in a hospital, a traditional area of state regulation.

Justice Harlan, in any event, provided a more convincing rationale for striking down the Connecticut law in his concurring opinion in *Poe v. Ullman,* where he stressed "the utter novelty" of the law as the "conclusive" argument against it. "Although the Federal Government and many States have at one time or other had on their books statutes forbidding or regulating the distribution of contraceptives, none, so far as I can find, has made the use of contraceptives a crime," he stressed, nor had any other nation done so, even those that shared Connecticut's moral policy. *Poe v. Ullman,* 367 U.S. at 554–55 (Harlan, J., dissenting). The situation is very different, as I've suggested, in the case of abortion, where restrictions like those of Texas are still the rule rather than the exception.

Finally, there is *Eisenstadt.* Although counsel at oral argument in the *Griswold* case assured us that the right of privacy he was pressing for would not encompass a right to abortion, the Court in *Eisenstadt* included a dictum that suggested otherwise. "If the right of privacy means anything, it is the right of the *individual,* married or single, to be free from unwarranted governmental intrusion into matters so fundamentally affecting a person as the decision whether to bear or beget a child." See *Eisenstadt v. Baird,* 405 U.S. 438, 453 (1972). As a legal matter, this statement is unconvincing: the privacy right in *Griswold* was centrally concerned with the privacy of the marital bedroom, rather than a broad right of sexual autonomy for single and married people alike. Moreover, the *Eisenstadt* Court supported its dictum with a citations to cases involving mental privacy and the right to refuse unwanted medical treatment. See id., citing *Stanley v. Georgia,* 394 U.S. 557 (1969), *Skinner v. Oklahoma,* 316 U.S. 535 (1942), and *Jacobson v. Massachusetts,* 197 U.S. 11, 29 (1905). None of these cases easily supports a broad right of procreative autonomy.

The most plausible interpretation of *Eisenstadt* is that it did not recognize (or create) a new fundamental right at all but that it merely struck down as irrational the law that prohibited the distribution of contraceptives to unmarried people if the same distribution was not forbidden to married people. It was the arbitrariness of the distinction that violated the Equal Protection Clause; after *Griswold,* the statute simply lacked a rational basis. This is a far more modest conclusion than the Chief

Justice's effort to read *Griswold* and *Eisenstadt* for all they might, in theory, be worth.

It's easy enough, if you are a judge who is determined reach a particular destination, to read every constitutional precedent at such a high level of generality that the differences among them evaporate into air. Before long, you will have produced a principle very different from the one the Court thought it was recognizing. If you practice this particular sleight of hand repeatedly, you can get yourself from point A to whatever point B you like without too much trouble. But, in addition to being glib, this particular exercise will be transparently unconvincing to those who don't share your preconceptions. And it is likely to anger and energize your opponents, who will feel, properly, that they have been played for dupes.

II.

I've argued that text, original understanding, tradition, and precedent don't support the claim that there is a fundamental right under the Due Process Clause of the Fourteenth Amendment to choose to terminate early-term pregnancies. But perhaps due process is not the best argument for opponents of the Georgia and Texas laws. The Chief Justice suggests that "Criminal prohibitions on abortion not only restrict the liberty of individuals; they also violate fundamental notions of equality between men and women." The Fourteenth Amendment, he argues, was passed to extend equal civil rights to all citizens, including women, and it was based on the principle that the state should not be permitted to pass laws that maintain an inferior caste of citizens. Although the civil equality of women was undermined by nineteenth-century coverture rules, many of the remnants of these disabilities have been recently abolished by civil rights statutes. He cites Congress's decision to propose the Equal Rights Amendment to the states as evidence that "Congress has concluded that discrimination based on sex is inherently invidious." He then blithely short-circuits the states' opportunity to ratify or reject the amendment by taking it upon himself to enact the Equal Rights Amendment by judicial fiat, announcing that "state laws or practices that discriminate against women or which help maintain their subordinate status are suspect under the Equal Protection Clause." Undaunted by having cut short the most important constitutional debate of our generation, he finishes the job by announcing that "by refusing women a significant choice in the direction of their lives, as well as by denying them control of their bodies, restrictions on abortion reinforce women's subordinate status in society and therefore deny them equal citizenship."

I agree as a descriptive matter, as I mentioned earlier, that restrictions on abortion exert strong pressures on women to delay or abandon their entry into the job market, potentially redirecting the course of their lives in important ways. I also agree that increasing numbers of women perceive restrictions on abortion to be important restrictions on their own equality as citizens, which is why I am confident that if the political process were allowed to work itself pure without this Court's eager assistance, laws like the ones we review today would, in the course of time, be repealed. But I cannot agree with the Court's constitutional analysis, which is no less freewheeling under the Equal Protection Clause than it was under the Due Process Clause.

The Court's decision to enact the Equal Rights Amendment by judicial fiat is brazen. What is the point of submitting important proposals for constitutional change to the people if the Court is determined to deny the people an opportunity to make their constitutional views clear? Of course, the Equal Protection Clause, even without the addition of the Equal Rights Amendment, guarantees equal civil rights, or privileges and immunities of citizenship, to all citizens without reference to sex. But we have never held that laws that discriminate on the basis of sex are subject to the same strict scrutiny as laws that discriminate on the basis of race. In *Reed v. Reed*, we struck down a law that mandated a preference for men over women in the appointment of estate administrators under rational basis review. We were willing to invalidate a law that discriminated "solely on the basis of sex" because it failed to recognize similarities between men and women. *Reed v. Reed*, 404 U.S. 71, 76–77 (1971) The Texas and Georgia laws at issue here, by contrast, do not discriminate solely on the basis of sex. They discriminate between pregnant women on the one hand and women and men who are not pregnant on the other. Because we have not in the past viewed these two classes as similarly situated for the purposes of equal protection analysis, nothing in our precedents suggests that the dissimilar treatment between them raises a constitutional claim.

We might, of course, reconsider our evolving approach to sex discrimination. Two years ago, in a case that ultimately became moot, we were urged in a brief to accept the principle that "[s]ex discrimination exists when all or a defined class of women (or men) are subjected to disadvantaged treatment based on stereotypical assumptions that operate to foreclose opportunity based on individual merit." Brief of Petitioners at 15, *Struck v. Secretary of Defense*, 409 U.S. 1071 (No. 72-178). The case involved a constitutional challenge to Air Force regulations requiring the discharge of pregnant officers from the Air Force; petitioners argued that the Air Force regime differentiated invidiously by allowing men who became fathers but not women who became mothers to remain in the service and by allowing women who had undergone abortions but not women who delivered infants to continue their military careers. (The Air Force, not an institution known as a vanguard of social experimentation, made abortions available to women in Air Force hospitals, suggesting that even without this Court's eager assistance, even the most conservative institutions may evolve on their own.) This approach would allow a plaintiff to show that the policy under dispute rested on stereotypes about the proper roles of men and women without the need to point to similarly situated men or women who faced different treatment.

Even if, at some point in the future, we were to adopt a novel equal protection inquiry that asked whether a defined class of women was being subject to disadvantaged treatment because of their sex on the basis of stereotypical assumptions about the way women should be, I am still not convinced that this would easily lead to the invalidation of restrictions on early-term abortions. To find a violation of the Equal Protection Clause, I presume, we would still insist on evidence of intentional discrimination— evidence, in other words, that women were being disadvantaged because of their sex, not for some other reason. The historical evidence, however, suggests that most of the states that banned first-trimester abortions in the mid-nineteenth century did so to protect human life, not because of stereotypical views about the proper roles of women. In the mid-nineteenth century, the newly formed American Medical Association relied on recent discoveries about human development to reject the common law quickening distinction and to extend legal protections for all unborn children. (The mammalian egg was identified in 1827; the cell was first recognized as the foundation of organisms in 1839 and the egg and sperm as cells during the following twenty years.) The text of the mid-nineteenth-century laws supports this understanding: twenty of the thirty-six states that adopted abortion laws by the end of 1883 provided for greater punishment if the abortion was proved to have caused the death of the unborn child. The most plausible explanation for this difference is that state legislatures were more concerned about protecting the life of unborn children than the health of the pregnant woman.

It is true that some of the doctors who lobbied for restrictions on abortions during the mid-nineteenth century clearly harbored what would be considered today stereotypical views of women; they talked about the importance of motherhood as a way of guaranteeing the survival of the race, and they also had a professional interest in monopolizing medical procedures that had previously been provided by midwives. But the fact that some of a law's proponents may have held views about gender equality that seem, in retrospect, stereotypical can hardly justify a court's invalidating the law because of its allegedly impermissible purpose. The only evidence we have of the purpose of the legislators who passed the abortion laws (as opposed to the doctors who lobbied for them) is their text, and that text clearly suggests that the primary purpose of the laws was to protect fetal life. Moreover, those legislators and citizens who support restrictions on abortion today, as opposed to those in the mid-nineteenth century, explicitly justify their arguments in terms of the protections of fetal life and disavow any interest in channeling women toward or away from particular careers. We must, I think, take them at face value; any search for hidden purposes to enforce stereotypes would be empirically fraught and hard to sustain. For this reason, regardless of the descriptive power of the claim that restrictions on abortion violate women's equality, I do not find it legally convincing.

We might also, I suppose, invalidate abortion laws that were passed in the nineteenth century and have not been revised since then in order to smoke out failures in the political process. Because women could not vote before the passage of the Nineteenth Amendment, the argument might go, laws that burden women but that were passed before 1919 bear a presumption of constitutional suspiciousness, and this presumption can be overcome only by giving women today a chance to vote on laws that uniquely implicate their own interests. Although this argument seems more intelligible to me than the claim that abortion restrictions are a form of sex discrimination, I still cannot accept it. We judicially know that support for abortion restrictions today, as in the nineteenth century, is widespread among both women and men, both of whom claim to be centrally concerned with protecting fetal life. Because there is no inherent reason that men are more likely than women to support abortion restrictions in order to preserve fetal life, I am not persuaded that the extension of women's suffrage at the beginning of the twentieth century changed the constitutional landscape in a decisive way. It appears that the recent growth in women's social (as opposed to political) expectations of equality during the 1960s (together with the widespread acceptance of the birth control pill) may have led to a significant decrease in support for abortion restrictions among women in particular. But this is a political, not a constitutional argument, and if the political landscape has indeed changed, the political branches should have been given the opportunity to recognize the shift without having their prerogatives usurped by this Court.

III.

I've argued that constitutional text, original understanding, tradition, and precedent fail to support the claim that restrictions on abortion implicate fundamental rights guaranteed by the Due Process Clause or the Equal Protection Clause. We must, therefore, uphold the Texas and Georgia laws unless they are irrational, and the claim that they are irrational is hard to accept. The Texas law holds doctors, but not pregnant women, liable for performing abortions, and the Chief Justice suggests that the failure to hold women liable for abortions undermines the state's claim that it is devoted to fetal life. Under rational basis review, however, there is no question that the exemption can pass muster. The truth is that many Americans who believe that life begins at conception also believe that it would be cruel to punish women who are desperate enough to perform abortions on themselves, and cruel also to punish women criminally for seeking illegal abortions from doctors. The laws are designed to deter doctors from performing abortions and therefore to make abortions more difficult to obtain; at the same time, many citizens believe that women who manage to obtain abortions anyway should not be imprisoned for their decision. This position may not satisfy a canon lawyer—it may not be consistent, in other words, with an absolute devotion to fetal life in all circumstances—but it is a perfectly rational way of balancing a devotion to fetal life with other moral concerns, and it is a balance that many of our citizens and most of our states continue to embrace. To dismiss this complicated moral judgment with syllogistic impatience, as the Chief Justice does, shows how poorly equipped the Due Process Clause is to evaluate the actual moral intuitions of actual citizens and actual legislatures. In any event, the Texas law clearly passes muster under rational basis review, which doesn't presume to grade our citizens' moral judgments as if they were submitted as part of an undergraduate exam in moral philosophy.

Along the same lines, the Georgia law allows an exception for pregnancies due to rape, an exception that counsel suggests is also intended to prevent pregnancies due to incest. With similar overconfidence, the Chief Justice concludes that this exception undermines Georgia's interest in protecting fetal life at all costs. But Georgia, like Texas, has not asserted an interest in protecting fetal life at all costs; its citizens, like many Americans, have made a judgment that the burden of pregnancies that result from coerced or illegal sex should not be imposed on women who deserve no responsibility for having become pregnant. This is the way real human beings balance complicated and competing moral claims, and, for that reason, it is constitutionally rational.

IV.

I began by suggesting that the Court may come to regret its decision today on pragmatic as well as constitutional grounds. When we take sides in a highly polarized and closely divided national debate, we had better be especially confident that we have all our ducks in a row and that we can justify our decision in the most convincing constitutional terms. Instead of being unable to point to powerful arguments rooted in text, original understanding, tradition, and precedent, as we are today, we should second-guess the political branches only when all these methodologies point in favor of judicial intervention. Constitutional arguments alone, of course, will never mollify those whose position has been ruled out of bounds, but the arguments should be strong enough to be intelligible to people of good faith, even those who disagree. This decision, by contrast, presents the losers with a very different situation. The reasoning is so adventurous, the treatment of legal materials so glib, and the sweep of the invalidation so unnecessarily ambitious that those who continue to believe in good faith that fetal life deserves legal protection are unlikely meekly to accept their defeat. Now their political energies will be turned on the courts rather than the legislatures, and they will resolve to do everything in their power to ensure the appointment of justices who will take a position on abortion more to their liking. It is not impossible to imagine every confirmation battle for decades to come being consumed with abortion and nothing else. First nominees to the Supreme Court and eventually (as interest groups mobilize around this single issue) nominees to lower courts as well may be asked by supporters and opponents of our decision today to embrace or repudiate it. Prospective nominees to this Court and candidates for promotion on lower courts may even feel pressure to modify their positions to satisfy one side or the other in the permanent abortion wars, knowing that their selection will depend on their views on this issue alone. The flimsiness of our legal reasoning will put nominees on both sides in an especially awkward position, since they will be asked to swear fealty not to a principle but to a political result. Eventually, as the wave of equality continues to expand and women and men across the nation becomes more supportive of the right to choose, the judicial battle over abortion will lose its practical salience, but it will continue to inspire passions far out of proportion to the actual stakes. Women's equality will flourish, but the judiciary will be enfeebled by a self-inflicted wound.

Or maybe I am wrong. Judges are not good at predicting the future. But they are even worse at coaxing it into being ahead of schedule. For all these reasons, I respectfully dissent.

COLLETT, J., dissenting.

I fear that by their opinions today the majority of my fellow justices have set our beloved country and this Court upon a path to a time when reasoned dialogue regarding our nation's common life will be rendered almost impossible. This is true, notwithstanding that each writes with a firm view toward ensuring the common good of all Americans whether female or male, whether members of present or future generations. In disregarding the political consensus that has been forged through the constitutionally recognized processes of the citizens of Texas and Georgia, members of this Court have inadvertently cast themselves as platonic guardians of the republic. But a republic by its very nature is to be governed by the elected representatives of the people, not the unelected members of this Court. I respectfully dissent.

The legislatures of Texas and Georgia have enacted laws that limit the practice of abortion. In Texas, all abortions are prohibited except those performed in order to preserve the life of the mother. Tex. Penal Code arts. 1191, 1194. Georgia's laws admit more exceptions, allowing abortions in cases of rape, threat to the mother's health, or grave, permanent, irremediable birth defects. Ga. Crim. Code §§ 26-1201, 26-1202(a). Additionally, there are procedural requirements that test the validity of any claims to these exceptions. Id. at 26-1202(b). The Chief Justice, writing for the plurality, strikes down the Texas statutes and the procedural requirements of the Georgia statutes on the basis that these laws violate equal protection and substantive due process, as well as the Privileges and Immunities Clause. In a nod toward the people's right of political self-determination, the Chief Justice grants that "a woman's right of abortion is not unlimited" and that the legislatures may impose some regulations upon the procedure. Balkin, C.J., supra at 52. Yet, as the remainder of the Chief Justice's opinion clearly illustrates, this regulatory authority is largely illusory, since not even the implementation of a recognized medical organization's guidelines such as the Joint Council for the Accreditation of Hospitals passes constitutional muster. Id. at 55.

What force could possibly motivate eight men and women of such integrity and legal acumen as the Chief Justice and those concurring with him to disregard their oaths of office, the political structure of the country, the text of the Constitution, the history and traditions of our people, legal precedent, and the possibility that this Court is, in the words of Justice Paulsen, "unleashing an American Holocaust" that may result in forty-five million human deaths in the next thirty years? Paulsen, J., post at 212. Their opinions reveal the answer—an unshakeable conviction that women can prosper only under a regime that allows liberal access to abortion. Justices Rosen and Paulsen show how the constitutional text, original understanding, tradition, and precedent fail to support the claim that restrictions on abortion implicate fundamental rights guaranteed by the Constitution. I write to address what I perceive to be the more pernicious claim—that liberal access to abortion is necessary for the liberty and equality of women.

I.

I begin where my sister justice, Justice Siegel, began much of her analysis: by recalling the history of women's struggle for political equality in the United States, but, unlike Justice Siegel, I linger long enough on the early history of woman suffrage in this country to note that our feminist foremothers were uniformly opposed to abortion. They saw it as a tool of oppression, manifesting men's domination and mistreatment. Elizabeth Cady Stanton wrote, "When we consider that women are treated as property, it is degrading to women that we should treat our children as property to be disposed of as we see fit."[1] Susan B. Anthony was of the same opinion. "Guilty? Yes. No matter what the motive, love of ease, or a desire to save from suffering the unborn innocent, the woman is awfully guilty who commits the deed. It will burden her conscience in life, it will burden her soul in death; But oh, thrice guilty is he who drove her to the desperation which impelled her to the crime!"[2] In their newspaper devoted to women's equality, *The Revolution,* Matilda Joslyn Gage wrote, "[This] subject lies deeper down in woman's wrongs than any other. . . . I hesitate not to assert that most of [the responsibility for] this crime lies at the door of the male sex."[3] So strongly did these women reject abortion that they put the solvency of their publication, *The Revolution,* at risk rather than accept advertisements from abortionists.

By their rejection of abortion, these women demanded something more meaningful (and more radical) than what a majority of this Court has ordered today—they demanded equality as full women, not as chemically or surgically altered surrogates of men. It is this vision of full equality that we glimpse in Justice West's opinion when she writes of changing the nature of citizenship so that the work of mothering is not inconsistent with full citizenship. West, J., supra at 143–44. Left to the ordinary political and economic processes, I am optimistic that the immense gifts and talents that women offer would entice the American people to find ways to better accommodate the demands of parenting and public life.

We already see harbingers of change. According to a 1972 report by the United States Census Bureau, "Women who had completed 4 years or more of college were as likely as men with the same education to be professional, technical, administrative, or managerial workers."[4] Only nine years ago, Margaret Chase Smith became the first woman in our nation's history to be nominated for the presidency of the United States at a national political party's convention. Six years ago, Muriel Seibert became the first woman to own a seat on the New York Stock Exchange, and just last year Juanita Kreps became the first woman director of that eminent institution. Women are making great progress in our society, and it is not by means of denying their capacity to conceive and bear children. By adopting this Court's counsel of despair, employers and society at large lose all incentive to adapt to women's unique nature.

II.

Notwithstanding the visible progress of women, Justice Allen suggests that "[c]ontraception and abortion are tools women can use to take charge of their lives, subject, of course, to men's loosing their—at times violent and oppressive—grip on women's minds and bodies." Allen, J., supra at 96. Justice West writes of pregnancy as alienating women from their bodies. West, J., supra at 124. I dispute these conclusions. It is artificial birth control and abortion that treat women's bodies as unnatural, something to be altered to conform to the male model. Most forms of birth control are used by the woman alone and seek to alter some natural process within her body. Abortion is even more alienating, requiring, as it does, the physical invasion of the woman's body by a surgical instrument or chemical solution.

When contraception fails, men may rightfully claim that they believed that no child would be conceived and that, with the availability of abortion, they certainly should not be responsible for support during the child's minority. How will this Court answer men's equal protection and substantive due process claims when they assert their right to be free of the obligations of parenting, having taken all "reasonable" steps to avoid pregnancy short of celibacy? Justice Rubenfeld opines, "No one would defend a law that left men with a comparable choice—either abstain from sexual intercourse or accept the state's power to force labor upon you—on the ground that the state had left men 'free to choose.'" Rubenfeld, J., supra at 112. If no one would defend such a law, we must conclude that men will be free to walk away. Thus, privacy becomes isolation and isolation becomes abandonment, and the woman is left alone to cope with the consequences.

III.

This is the logical result of the individualistic sexual ethic that this Court wrote into the Constitution last Term with its decision in *Eisenstadt v. Baird*: "If the right of privacy means anything, it is the right of the *individual,* married or single, to be free from unwarranted governmental intrusion into matters so fundamentally affecting a person as the decision whether to bear or beget a child."[5] Justice West echoes this philosophy when she describes America as "a free, individualist, and equal society." West, J., supra at 147.

Contrary to *Eisenstadt,* our jurisprudence has not traditionally been based upon an individualist understanding of the human person. Rather, the line of cases relied upon by the plurality from *Meyer v. Nebraska*[6] through *Pierce v. Society of Sisters,*[7] *Skinner v. Oklahoma ex rel. Williamson,*[8] and *Griswold v. Connecticut*[9] reflects a more communal understanding. Each reference to procreation in these cases is within the context of marriage and family, with its attendant joys, sorrows, rights, and responsibilities. Marriage, whatever its flaws, is the civil institution by which men and women assume legal responsibility for children conceived during marital intercourse. This most intimate of unions has been protected by law in every age, and it is this union, not the sexual act per se, that is at the heart of the constitutional protection this Court has traditionally afforded the procreative act. Cf. *Poe v. Ullman*, 367 U.S. 497, 522 (1961) (Harlan, J., dissenting). We gravely erred in *Eisenstadt v. Baird*.

IV.

In any case, contraception differs from abortion because of the presence of the fetus. I agree with Justice Paulsen about the humanity of the unborn. Paulsen, J., post at 207. Justice Rubenfeld counters this assertion, and indeed all of the evidence supporting the humanity of the fetus presented to this Court, by responding that "[i]t confounds the potential with the actual." Rubenfeld, J., supra at 114. His reply disregards both legal and medical authorities.

Since 1946, in a series of more than thirty cases, states have recognized a child's right to sue for prenatal injuries.[10] Family law courts have recognized the right of the unborn child to sue for the financial support of his parents.[11] Unborn children have long been included as heirs and testamentary beneficiaries of decedents.[12]

The medical authorities are even more impressive. At five and a half weeks the fetal heartbeat is similar to that of an adult, and at forty-three days of gestation brain waves can be noted.[13] "By the end of the first trimester (12th week) the fetus is a sentient moving being. We need not pause to speculate as to the nature of his psychic attributes but we may assert that the organization of his psychosomatic self is now well under way."[14]

How, then, can we explain the impressive array of medical organizations that support appellants in their effort to strike down the Texas statutes?[15] Two possible explanations come to mind. First, the physicians attack only the Texas statutes and make no comment on the Georgia statutes, evidencing their real objection—the absence of ultimate control on this question by the medical profession.

Second, some in the medical profession, like some of my fellow jurists, have fallen victim to their emotional responses to the claims of the women before them.[16] The panic and depression that some pregnant women exhibit has moved these men and women to try to alleviate the suffering of their most visible patients through abortion. Yet, as studies of women denied abortions indicate, for most women, fear and depression are passing phases and the birth of the child brings contentment.[17] The proper response to the temporary fears of a few is comfort and encouragement, not destruction of the unborn child.

V.

Justice West suggests that, even if the fetus is human, absent full consent by the woman to the act in which the child was conceived, she would be justified in taking the life of the unborn child. "[F]orced 'good samaritanism' required of these victims of criminal violence is an utter anomaly in our law." West, J., supra at 129. See also id. at 137–38, and Amar, J., supra at 164. This mischaracterizes both the situation and the law that controls.

Consider the following scenario: a kidnapper drugs a woman and sets her adrift in a small craft in the middle of the ocean with a limited supply of fresh water and food. In the craft is a young child who bears a physical resemblance to the kidnapper but who is also a victim of the kidnapper. The child is capable of feeding and caring for herself. Without the child, the food and water would last longer, and the woman would be more comfortable in the craft since there would be more space and the constant reminder of the kidnapper would be gone. Is the woman justified in killing the child?

Anglo-American law says no. In *United States v. Holmes*, 26 F. Cas. 260 (E.D. Penn. 1842), the Court rejected the ability of shipwreck survivors to sacrifice their shipmates in order to save the remainder, except upon strict necessity and then only when the victims were selected by lot. Similarly, in *Queen v. Dudley and Stephens*, 14 Q.B. 273, 286–87 (1884), the English court rejected a claim by two sailors that necessity justified their slaying and cannibalizing a cabin boy after a shipwreck since the act was necessary to preserve their lives. "Who is to be the judge of this sort of necessity? By what measure is the comparative value of lives to be measured? Is it to be strength, or intellect, or what? It is plain that the principle leaves to him who is to profit by it to determine the necessity which will justify him in deliberately taking another's life to save his own. In this case the weakest, the youngest, the most unresisting was chosen. . . . [I]t is quite plain that such a principle once admitted might be made the legal cloak for unbridled passion and atrocious crime." Id. at 287–88.

In both of these cases, the trial courts imposed punishments, and in each case, clemency was shown. These cases reflect both the need for a clear rule that punishes oppression of the weak and vulnerable and a recognition of the limits of the human capacity to endure suffering. Similarly, the Texas and Georgia laws draw moral lines that attempt to satisfy the need for justice and compassion when dealing with women who experience their pregnancies as traumatic.

The fact that the legislatures of these states arrive at differing conclusions does not alter the constitutionality of their conclusions insofar as both present rational answers to the question "When is a woman privileged to use force to free herself from the demands of the unborn child within her?" Texans have decided that this balance allows force to be used only when both the woman's and the child's lives are at stake. Georgians have decided that lethal force may be used when the woman's health is at stake, when the woman did not consent to the creation of the child, or when the child will have permanent, grave, and irremediable defects. While my personal beliefs are more closely aligned with the views expressed in the Texas statutes, I cannot say in the context of the present case that the balance struck by the Georgia legislature is irrational in light of the unique dependence of the unborn child on the mother during the pregnancy. These complex issues require careful attention to the interests of the child, her parents, and the community.[18]

Texas defends its prohibition of abortion on the grounds that unborn children have constitutional rights, an argument, that if accepted, would have put the constitutionality of laws that legalize abortion into question. Had the Court reached the proper conclusion in the present case, there would be time enough to consider this claim. Statutes that allow women to take the life of the fetus for any reason whatsoever clearly fail to evidence the necessary respect due the unborn child, his or her father, and the broader community. While I am inclined to agree with Justice Paulsen that the Fourteenth Amendment includes the unborn in its protections, I am unprepared to so hold until the issue is properly before us.

I am troubled that Georgia allows the killing of the disabled and children conceived in rape. See *United States v. Carolene Products,* 304 U.S. 144, 152–53 n. 4 (1938) (judicial review may be necessary to protect discrete and insular minorities). I am also concerned about the seeming elasticity inherent in the word "health," which might be employed by doctors to perform abortions in a wide variety of cases.

Yet, even assuming that the unborn are constitutional persons, the situational differences of children *in utero* and *ex utero* may warrant some constitutional distinction. A single example illustrates this point. The law would not tolerate draining all the blood of an infant in order to preserve the mother's life through a blood transfusion, yet every jurisdiction allows (but does not compel) abortions to save the mother's life.

Judicial prudence and respect for the political process require me to leave for another day the difficult question of how to demarcate the permissible constitutional exceptions to the state's general obligation to protect innocent life. It may well be that in cases when abortion is not immediately necessary to protect the mother's life, some judicial process is required to ensure that the woman is free of duress and that the child's interests are adequately weighed, but that decision awaits another day.

Today, we embark on what I fear will prove to be a tumultuous and troubling experiment initiated by this Court in the name of equality for women. A majority of my fellow justices have chosen to preempt the political dialogue in this country that surrounds the practice of abortion, substituting their moral judgment for constitutional analysis. In doing so, they have embraced a notion of women's equality that will ultimately prove barren. Like the early feminists, I refuse to accept that women must deny their fertility and slay their children in order to obtain equal access to the marketplace and the public square. I respectfully dissent.

NOTES

1. Letter to Julia Ward Howe, October 16, 1873, recorded in Howe's diary at Harvard University Library.

2. Susan B. Anthony, *The Revolution*, 4(1): 4, July 8, 1869.

3. Matilda Joslyn Gage, *The Revolution*, 1(14): 215–16, April 9, 1868.

4. U.S. Bureau of the Census, Current Population Reports, Series P-20, No. 242, "Educations Attainment: March 1972," at 2. U.S. Government Printing Office, Washington, D.C., 1972.

5. 405 U.S. 438, 453 (1972) (emphasis in original).

6. 262 U.S. 390 (1923).

7. 268 U.S. 510 (1925).

8. 316 U.S. 535, 541 (1942).

9. 381 U.S. 478, 486 (1965).

10. Prosser on Torts at 365–66 (3rd ed. 1964).

11. See *Kyne v. Kyne*, 28 Cal. App. 2d 122, 100 P.2d 806 (1940), and *People v. Hestergard*, 457 P.2d 698 (Colo. 1969).

12. E.g., *James v. James*, 174 S.W. 46 (Tex. Civ. App. 1914), and *Doe v. Clarke*, 2 H. Bl. 299, 126 Engl. Rep. 617 (1795).

13. Appellee's Brief, pp. 37–38.

14. Arnold Gesell, The Embryology of Behavior 65 (1945), quoted in Brief Amicus Curiae of Certain Physicians, Professors and Fellows of the American College of Obstetrics and Gynecology in Support of Appellees (1971) at 19.

15. See Amicus Brief of the American College of Obstetricians and Gynecologists et al. (1971).

16. I can offer no other explanation for the obviously inflated number of 5,000 deaths due to illegal abortions in this country per year used by some of my fellow justices and amici, not withstanding that a report by the National Center for Health Statistics reported that in 1965, when abortion was still illegal nationwide except in cases of life endangerment, 193 women died from illegal abortions. National Center for Health Statistics, Vital Statistics of the United States, 1965: Vol. II—Mortality, Part A. Washington, D.C.: U.S. Government Printing Office, 1967.

17. "84% were later glad that the pregnancy was not terminated, 9% were uncertain, and only 7% were discontent." P. Kolstad, "Therapeutic Abortion: A Clinical Study Based upon 968 Cases from a Norwegian Hospital, 1940–53," in the *Proceedings of the Scandinavian Gynecological and Obstetrical Society,* 36 (1957), quoted in Amicus Curiae Brief of Women for the Unborn et al. in Support for the Appellees, at 13 (1971).

18. Cf. *Doe v. Bolton,* 319 F.Supp. 1048, 1055 (N.D. Ga. 1970).

PAULSEN, J., dissenting.

A majority of the justices of this "packed" Court[1] today concludes that the Constitution of the United States provides a substantive individual liberty to obtain or commit an abortion of a human life—that is, to terminate the life of a human embryo or fetus.

Let us be clear about that fact, to begin with. *Abortion ends the life of a living human embryo or fetus.* There really can be no serious doubt about that. Plainly, abortion kills a living being. It is equally plain that the living being killed by an abortion is a *human* living being: abortion kills a living *human* embryo or fetus. The act of abortion thus ends a human life. To be sure, it is a human life that, at the earlier stages of pregnancy at least, is not matured to the point where the human embryo or fetus can live on its own, outside of his or her mother's womb. But that does not alter the fact that what is being killed is a human life. It merely means that the human life is being killed at a very early stage in its life cycle.

To repeat: a majority of this Court concludes that the Constitution creates a substantive individual liberty to terminate the life of a human embryo or fetus. That right is, of course, nowhere set forth in the text of the Constitution. Indeed, there is no remotely plausible argument that the text of the Constitution creates such a right. It is somewhat amusing (but also somewhat pathetic and dispiriting) to observe the other members of this Court flailing around, so desperately and so very creatively—and so inconsistently with one another!—and with such evident desire to reach a predetermined preferred result, trying to torture an argument out of the Constitution's text in support of a "right" of some kind (the members of the Court disagree as to what kind of right it is and why it exists) to kill human fetuses gestating in their mothers' wombs.

Their efforts do not succeed. The Constitution quite obviously does not contain a right to abortion. No rule or principle supplied by a fair reading of the text of the Constitution; no rule or principle fairly derived from the Constitution's structure or internal logic or deducible from other clear propositions contained therein; no rule or principle traceable as a matter of history or intention to an authoritative decision made by the people with respect to this issue, remotely supports the result reached by the other members of this Court.

With regret, I must say that the majority's divergent opinions represent the very worst of American constitutional legal thinking. They consist of poor sophistries, masking raw assertions of power, in violation of the judges' very oaths and of the Constitution they purport to serve, and in the ultimate service of terrible injustice and terrible harm. In terms of "constitutional law," the decision of the majority is utterly and entirely illegitimate and deserves to be treated as such by the people whose Constitution it is, and by the other branches of the national government whose shared responsibility it is to be faithful to that Constitution. In terms of justice, the Court's decision is even worse. Without justification in law, the members of this Court would create a plenary right of some human beings to kill other human beings for any reason or for no reason at all. Resistance to the Court's decision is not only legally justified. It is a moral imperative.

I.

I begin where no other member of this Court, save one, appears to feel it necessary to begin: with the Constitution of the United States.[2]

And I begin with "the judicial Power" set forth in Article III of the Constitution, since that provision is the source of this Court's authority. The judicial power includes the power to finally decide, as a judicial matter, cases where the disposition depends upon resolution of a point of law set forth in the Constitution, see U.S. Const. Art. III, sec. 2; the obligation, implied by the structure of the Constitution, to give a rule of law set forth in the Constitution priority over other federal law and the parallel obligation, made express in the text, to give such rules priority over anything in the constitutions or laws of the states contrary to it, U.S. Const. Art. VI, cl. 2; and, finally and perhaps most important, the sworn duty to do so in accordance with "*this* Constitution" and none other. U.S. Const. Art. VI, cl. 3.

It follows from this brief description of the power, obligation, and duty of this Court, and from the sound logic of *Marbury v. Madison*, 5 U.S. (1 Cranch) 137 (1803) applying these provisions, that any act, order, decree, or judgment by a judge not warranted by and consistent with the language of the Constitution, is *ultra vires*—beyond the judge's legitimate power—and *void*. Id. at 177 (deducing proposition that "an act of the legislature, repugnant to the constitution, is void"). Compare *The Federalist No. 78* (Alexander Hamilton) ("all acts contrary to the manifest tenor of the constitution [are] void"). Simply put, there is no legitimate constitutional power for a federal court to enter a judgment or decree, in the name of the Constitution, that is not in fact justified by the document itself. Courts cannot—or at least cannot properly—"interpret" the Constitution so as to create powers or rights that are not there.

Where is the supposed constitutional right to abortion to be found in the Constitution? It is not among the enumeration of rights contained in Article I, section 9, of the Constitution. It is not among the enumeration of rights contained in the first eight amendments to the Constitution.

Nor is it contained (as some allege) in the Ninth Amendment to the Constitution, which is plainly not itself a *grant* of (unspecified) further rights but a rule of construction about the legal effect of the Constitution's enumeration of other rights. The Ninth Amendment is a rule of non-pre-emption; the enumeration of certain federal constitutional rights does not itself operate to displace or vitiate other legal rights, resting on *other* legal authority. Most obviously, such retained rights consist of individual rights that exist by virtue of state law, including state common law and state constitutions. The enactment of a federal Bill of Rights, the Ninth Amendment says, does not repeal such other rights. But the amendment scarcely creates new, unspecified, substantive *federal* constitutional rights.

This is especially obvious given the historical backdrop of the Federalists' initially having argued that a bill of rights was not only unnecessary but affirmatively dangerous in that it could be taken to imply, contrary to the Constitution's original design, a general assignment of *all* rights and powers into the hands of the new national government. See *The Federalist No. 84* (Alexander Hamilton). The Ninth Amendment clarifies what might not have needed clarification—that the enumeration of rights should not be understood as having any such effect—had Federalist opponents of a bill of rights not initially made the argument that such an inference might be possible. (The Ninth Amendment is a cognate provision with the Tenth Amendment, which adopts an analogous rule of non-pre-emption by clarifying that unenumerated governmental *powers* are reserved to the states or to the people. The Tenth Amendment clarifies for state powers what the Ninth Amendment clarifies for state citizens' rights.)

The Supremacy Clause of the U.S. Constitution, U.S. Const. Art. VI, cl. 2, makes clear that such retained or reserved state-law rights and powers do not have the same federal constitutional status as federal rights and powers. State law rights and state law powers remain *state* law rights and powers. The Ninth Amendment does not create substantive federal constitutional rights, nor does it vest state law rights, common law rights, or claimed natural law rights with federal constitutional law status.[3]

Is the alleged right to abortion contained in the Fourteenth Amendment?[4] The most plausible such suggestion (and it is not all that plausible) is that the constitutional right of one person, alone or in cooperation with others, to kill a living human fetus or embryo is among "the privileges or immunities of citizens of the United States" that a state may not abridge. U.S. Const. Amend. XIV, sec. 1. Just what are the "privileges or immunities" of citizens of the United States? The reference is either to a corpus of rights of determinate content or to a corpus of rights of indeterminate content—an open-ended delegation to someone (or a group of someones) to define and prescribe the "privileges or immunities of citizens of the United States." The latter construction is problematic precisely because of the vagueness of the potential delegation and the lack of clarity as to whom the defining power is delegated. If "privileges or immunities" is completely open-ended—if the text prescribes (or incorporates) *no* constraining standards as to what might count as a privilege or immunity of citizens—then literally *anything* that the relevant decision maker decides is such a privilege, or immunity, goes. On this view, however, one could as readily find a constitutional privilege to torture puppies in one's basement (or, its opposite, an immunity from being subjected to the affront of such conduct by one's neighbor) as one could find a constitutional privilege to commit abortion (or an immunity from the affront of such private violence committed by others). If "privileges or immunities" consist of *whatever* one decides, there are no standards constraining whateverism.

I suppose it would be possible for the People to have adopted such a constitutional provision, and if this is the proper understanding of the clause it would be the obligation of the judiciary to give it its full effect. But this seems an especially unlikely understanding of the text. It seems to render the specific, textually-identified individual privileges and immunities set forth in Article I, section 9, and in the Bill of Rights, superfluous (or maybe even subject to being overridden by the interpreter's unconstrained explication of the later-enacted Fourteenth Amendment's privileges or immunities) and to render the rest of section 1 of the Fourteenth

Amendment without much clear effect. The Omnipotent Privileges or Immunities Clause would swallow up everything else. It seems unlikely that this was the public meaning of the phrase "privileges or immunities of citizens" at the time it was adopted as part of the Fourteenth Amendment. (In fact, as I discuss presently, there is a much more obvious source for understanding the public meaning of this phrase at the time the amendment was adopted.) It does not seem consistent with notions of constitutionalism and government at the time. And there is no historical evidence that suggests that this is what was intended or understood, or what any ordinary (or specialized) user of the English language would have understood those words to have meant, at the time the amendment was adopted.

It also seems especially unlikely that these words would have been understood, in context and at the time enacted, as delegating *to the judiciary* the power to define and prescribe the "privileges and immunities of citizens," given the U.S. Supreme Court's notorious, rightly-reviled decision in *Dred Scott*, which held that an entire class of persons did not have and never could be given the rights and status of citizens of the United States—which, of course, is precisely the holding that the first sentence of the Fourteenth Amendment is designed to reverse, see U.S. Const. Amend. XIV, sec. 1 ("All persons born or naturalized in the United States, and subject to the jurisdiction thereof, are citizens of the United States and of the State wherein they reside.")—and which further held that one of the privileges of citizens was to own blacks as slaves and one of the immunities of citizens was to be free of federal legislation impairing such property rights when the citizen went into a Territory of the United States. *Dred Scott v. Sanford*, 60 U.S. (19 How.) 393 (1857). *Dred Scott* cast a long shadow of illegitimacy over the judiciary, and the Fourteenth Amendment was enacted in that shadow, and (as noted) in part to repudiate that case. It strains credulity more than a little to assert that the amendment's provisions ought to be read as an open-ended delegation of privileges-and-immunities-defining power to the federal judiciary.

Again, this is not to say that the people could not have delegated such a power to the judiciary. It simply means that this is a most improbable intended or understood meaning of the text, and thus a dubious and disfavored one in light of historical context, unless such a meaning is unavoidable in light of the words chosen. It plainly is not: given section 5's delegation to Congress of the power "to enforce, by appropriate legislation, the provisions of this article," if the content of the "privileges or immunities of citizens of the United States" is to be supplied by anyone, the most obvious repository of this privileges-defining power is Congress. (It would not be surprising, given the history of the times, if the Reconstruction Congress that proposed the Fourteenth Amendment designed a series of constitutional provisions the most natural linguistic meaning of which dramatically enhanced its own legislative power vis-à-vis state government action that affects individual rights.)

But there is good reason to believe that the term "privileges or immunities of citizens" was *not* radically indeterminate and would not have been read that way by Constitution-adopters or intended as such by Constitution-drafters at the time. Article IV, section 2, of the Constitution uses essentially identical language to describe the entitlement of "[t]he Citizens of each state" to "all Privileges and Immunities of Citizens in the several States." Quite obviously, this is the provision after which the Privileges or Immunities Clause of the Fourteenth Amendment was modeled.[5] And the received baseline understanding of *this* original constitutional provision (some judicial interpretations went further, but none to the point of open-ended delegation) was that a state must grant to citizens of other states the privileges and immunities that the state granted its own citizens. Thus, just as the Full Faith and Credit Clause of Article IV, section 1, meant that Virginia must honor the "public Acts, Records, and judicial proceedings" of Maryland, the Privileges and Immunities Clause of Article IV, section 2, meant that Virginia must accord to Marylanders the core privileges and immunities it gave its own citizens. Presumably, those privileges and immunities would be identified by reference to Virginia statutory, common, and constitutional law. To put it colloquially, the Privileges and Immunities Clause makes Virginia treat Marylanders as having the full rights of Virginians; Virginia is enjoined not to discriminate against Marylanders in making and enforcing the law of Virginia.[6]

The Privileges *or* Immunities Clause of the Fourteenth Amendment makes Virginia treat *Virginians* (and all other citizens of the United States) as having the full rights of citizens *of the United States*. In effect, it is a self-executing "full faith and credit" provision with respect to the privileges or immunities that a citizen of the United States possesses against the *United States* government by virtue of being a citizen of the nation. The now-accepted doctrine that the individual privileges or immunities contained in the Bill of Rights (and in Article I, section 9) are "incorporated" by the Fourteenth Amendment as limitations on the substantive power of state governments against their own citizens or the citizens of any other state seems to rest most naturally in the Privileges or Immunities Clause of that amendment, see *Duncan v. Louisiana,* 391 U.S. 145, 166 (1968) (Black, J., concurring), and that conclusion gives relatively determinate content to the Privileges or Immunities Clause. Such a conclusion is textually justified and certainly coheres better with the rest of the Fourteenth Amendment than the notion that the clause is radically open-ended.

Going slightly beyond incorporation of the Bill of Rights and Article I, section 9, one might argue that the "privileges or immunities of citizens of the United States" includes *all* legal rights and interests that a citizen possesses by virtue of federal law—statutory and treaty rights, as well as constitutional ones. The Privileges or Immunities Clause thus operates as a kind of constitutional rule of automatic, self-executing federal preemption of state law that abridges federal law rights created by Congress, reinforcing and augmenting the Supremacy Clause's directive that federal law always trump inconsistent state law. Finally, one might press slightly further yet and argue that other individual privileges or immunities are implicit in notions of United States citizenship—that is, that they are sound inferences from the structural relationship between government and citizen in an extended republic. Things like voting, office holding, rights of political participation, and even "travel" and the like, cf. U.S. Const. Art. IV, sec. 2, *might* fairly be argued to be privileges or immunities incident to national citizenship that, consequently, state governments may not abridge. But see *Minor v. Hapersett,* 88 U.S. (21 Wall.) 162 (1874) (finding that voting is not a privilege or immunity of national citizenship).

But one need not worry about which of these formulations marks the precise outermost reach of the clause; for a right to have or commit an abortion does not come close, under *any* of these formulations, even extended to its broadest. Abortion is not a right conferred by any other federal constitutional, statutory, or treaty law provision. It is not a privilege incident to citizenship in the United States. It is even less plausibly so, one would think, than the asserted privilege of operating a different kind of slaughterhouse, rejected by this Court a century ago. *Slaughter-House Cases,* 16 Wall. (83 U.S.) 36 (1873).[7]

Appellants do not really look to the Privileges or Immunities Clause of the Fourteenth Amendment as the font of the alleged constitutional right to abortion. Instead, they look to the Due Process Clause of that amendment, and to this Court's decisions invoking that provision. Brief for Appellants at 92. On its face, this would appear the *least* plausible basis in the text of the Fourteenth Amendment for such a claim. The Due Process

Clause provides that no state shall "deprive any person of life, liberty or property, without due process of law." U.S. Const. Amend. XIV, sec. 1. *Without due process of law.* The text does not say that states may never deprive persons of their property, or that they may never deprive persons of their liberty, or that they may never deprive persons even of their lives. It says that they may not do so *without due process of law.* That is, a state may not deprive people of such rights in an irregular, extralegal, procedurally defective manner. But the Due Process Clause on its face does not restrict the *substance* of validly enacted state laws that affect the life, liberty, and property of persons subject to a state's authority. To so read the clause would be to read the words "without due process of law" entirely out of the text.

I suppose, of course, that one *could* say that an enactment that too greatly interfered with the *substance* of the right to life, liberty, or property "could hardly be dignified with the name of due process of law" such that the requirement of due process itself entails substantive limitations on legislative power. This Court, indeed, has said exactly this in the past— indeed, using exactly these words—in a landmark, watershed case decided more than a century ago. That case, of course, was *Dred Scott v. Sanford,* 60 U.S. (19 How.) 393, 450 (1857). A decision to fashion a right to abortion out of the words "due process of law" would share much in common with *Dred Scott,* which is, methodologically, the single best supportive precedent for such an invention. (It is also a close, supportive precedent substantively—that is, in the *substance* of the substantive due process it creates: a right of some human beings to dispose of other human beings as they see fit.) Were it not for the fact that *Dred Scott* is so thoroughly discredited, its substantive due process methodology so plainly indefensible, its result so illustrative of the dangers of judges assuming quasi-legislative authority, *Dred Scott* would be the precedent most nearly in point for the proposition appellants assert. (*Lochner v. New York,* 198 U.S. 45 (1905), also thoroughly discredited, would probably be the next most directly supporting authority.)

Instead, of course, appellants cite *Griswold v. Connecticut,* 381 U.S. 479 (1965), and *Eisenstadt v. Baird,* 405 U.S. 438 (1972). The chief virtue of *Griswold* in this regard is the obscurity of its reasoning. It is not clear what the controlling rationale of the case *is.* The chief virtue of *Eisenstadt,* on the other hand, is its dishonesty. It "extends" *Griswold,* on nominally Equal Protection Clause grounds, to create a broad "right to privacy" that ends up being tied to no text of the Constitution.

There is much more that could be said by way of distinguishing and/or criticizing these cases. But, in the end, these precedents do not matter much. It is plain that neither *Griswold*'s nor *Eisenstadt*'s holding is *controlling* here. In any event, the experience of such cases as *Dred Scott, Lochner,* and (to cite another important example) *Plessy v. Ferguson,* 163 U.S. 537 (1896), should make clear what should be obvious on first principles: an erroneous judicial interpretation of the Constitution cannot properly displace the correct understanding of the Constitution's text itself, and wrongly decided precedents (or cases announcing bogus legal principles) cannot properly be given *any* generative weight in future cases in opposition to what the correct constitutional rule would be on the basis of first principles. Any jurisprudence that would assert that this Court's precedents, simply by the force of being precedents, *require* extrapolation to textually unsound results or *compel* reaffirmation of wrong principles would require that *Brown v. Board of Education,* 347 U.S. 483 (1954), have reaffirmed, rather than disapproved, the pernicious principles of *Plessy.*

This, of course, has never been the rule in American constitutional law. And it could never be the rule, consistently with first principles: as this Court (correctly) held in *Marbury v. Madison,* 5 U.S. (1 Cranch) 137 (1803), courts must give effect to *the Constitution,* rather than the acts of mere subordinate agencies that are not consistent with the Constitution. (As noted earlier, a *judicial* act contrary to the Constitution, no less than a legislative one, is void.) It follows that, just as the Court may not give effect to an Act of Congress contrary to the Constitution, the Court may not give effect to one of its own precedent decisions contrary to the Constitution. All the more so is it true that the Court should never *extend* a precedent to produce results not consistent with the Constitution. Thus, I conclude that the doctrine of "substantive due process," rightly discredited as a matter of text, structure, and history, cannot properly supply any support to appellant's position, regardless of whether precedent decisions of this Court could be thought to endorse such a doctrine.[8]

Finally, what of the Equal Protection Clause of the Fourteenth Amendment? Is there some plausible basis in the command that "[n]o state shall . . . deny to any person within its jurisdiction the equal protection of the laws" for the conclusion that state laws prohibiting or restricting abortion are unconstitutional in that they deny "equal protection of the laws" on the basis of a person's sex? Cf. *Reed v. Reed* , 404 U.S. 71 (1971). The proposition is too extravagant to be maintained. Abortion restrictions impose legal burdens not on the basis of gender but on the basis of the asserted presence and value of a human life *in utero.* To be sure, only women become pregnant. But an abortion restriction's target category—pregnancies (or some subset thereof)—embraces all relevant instances of the identified harm that the restriction seeks to prevent. It is tightly drawn to its purpose of protecting the human life-*in-utero* (to some degree or another); it does not regulate *women* as a class; it regulates the *conduct* of *men and women* relevant to commission of or assistance in abortion; it affects no women who are not pregnant.

As a matter of legal doctrine, the equal protection argument makes little sense. But its premise is even more outlandish. It is offensive in the extreme to even suggest (as some of my colleagues unfortunately appear to do) that a woman's ability to function as an equal member of society requires that she have the right to kill her children *in utero*—that a woman lacks the "equal protection of the laws" unless she possesses such a license to kill. It is degrading and offensive to women to adopt the (dare one say) *paternalistic* attitude that a woman cannot be the equal of a man politically, economically, or socially unless she is able to kill her unborn child. If one is concerned, perhaps with cause, that *men* often can rid themselves of social responsibilities with respect to children more easily than can women, one must recognize that this is a mere social construction. States surely may impose on men (and many do) legal obligations in this regard. Even if one thought that abstract notions of equality required more equal legal burdens on men and women, the remedy would not be to create a constitutional right to abortion. The remedy would be to impose more equal burdens or responsibilities on men.[9]

Instead, by vesting such a right in the woman alone, as a matter of her unfettered choice, some of my colleagues would create a sad, socially destructive irony: a man, wishing to free himself of child support obligations or other paternal responsibilities, could merely invoke the woman's right to have had an abortion as a defense to such obligations. After all, if the choice is purely that of the woman, why should the man be responsible in any way for the woman's choice? Even prior to that, it is not at all hard to imagine that, under a regime where abortion is a matter of essentially unrestricted choice, a husband or boyfriend who desires not to be a father could subtly encourage the pregnant woman to abort their child or ruthlessly insist on such a course of action. The man could threaten to walk away from the relationship if an abortion is not committed. Or the man could simply walk away. If one takes the premises of so many of my colleagues seriously, women will feel pressured by economic and social

conditions, and the oppression of others, to bear burdens that they otherwise would not wish to bear. For how many might that not mean that they
will feel compelled, by their new-found "freedom," or by men, to kill their
unborn children? The judges of this court, and perhaps one day a substantial part of society, tell them that abortion is their sacred "right." And others—men—for whom the creation of this right appears to terminate their
own responsibilities, will tell women that abortion is their sacred *duty.*
One shudders at the prospect that women (whom some of my colleagues
disparagingly assume to be less than fully equal to men without a right to
abortion) might be pressured by husbands or boyfriends or elite society
into having abortions when they would not otherwise be inclined to kill
the unborn child but for the legal regime my colleagues would create—in
the name of "equality" and "protecting" women.

Worse yet, if the right to abort an unborn human child (in the name of
"equal protection" of the laws and remedying asserted gender discrimination) is made a matter of legally unrestricted "choice," that choice could be
exercised *on the basis of the gender of the unborn child,* if (as is virtually certain) medical technology one day soon makes it possible to know such a
fact during pregnancy. The claimed right to abortion assumes that the
unborn child ought not be entitled to be treated as a human being, vested
with protection against the private violence of others, including the inflic-
tion of fatal violence. (I address presently why this assumption is wrong.)
Given this assumption that the human fetus has no human status that
anyone else must respect, it follows that, within whatever range of pregnancy the right to "choose" abortion exists (e.g., the first six months), it
may be exercised *for any reason.* My colleagues thus appear to allow (and
constitutionalize) that right to be exercised because the unborn child is *a
girl.* The logic of a constitutional right to abortion, based on notions of
equal protection and remedying gender discrimination, thus tends to double back on itself. Those who invoke women's equality to create a constitutional right to abortion in the end permit mothers (influenced, perhaps,
by others) to selectively kill their unborn children because of the child's sex.

Now, those who contend for a constitutional right to abortion (from
whatever implausible textual source in the Constitution derived) dare not
concede that abortion constitutionally could be prohibited if based on
the sex of the child. For such a concession implicitly would recognize the
humanity of the fetus. *It's* a *girl.* Or a *boy.* And once the humanity of the
fetus is recognized, the game is up. Even under any of the embarrassingly
atextual theories advanced by my colleagues, a claimed individual right

(such as a right to abortion) must yield to a sufficiently compelling or important interest on the other side. Recognition of the humanity of the fetus would appear sufficient to trump the claimed right to abortion in all but the most limited circumstances of true medical necessity. In short, if the human embryo or human fetus is a *living human being*, it becomes virtually impossible to justify a constitutional right of certain individuals to kill that human being whenever they so choose, in order to advance their own "liberty," "equality," "privileges," "sexual freedom," "reproductive freedom," or (in a most Orwellian usage of the terms) "privacy" or "autonomy." The essential question therefore, *even if* one were to concede the legitimacy of the assorted illegitimate theories advanced on behalf of a claimed constitutional right to abortion, is whether the fetus is a *living human being*.

None of the opinions of my colleagues fully comes to grip with this question. Yet, surely this is the crux of the entire matter. The whole question—the question on which every other aspect of *any* legal analysis necessarily depends—is whether the unborn human fetus or embryo is a member of the human family, to whom the state *may*, or perhaps *must*, provide basic protection of the laws, including protection of his or her right to life, as against private violence.

The answer to this question is straightforward. A conceived human embryo is, biologically, human life. It is a separate, unique living human being. Embryology, fetology, all of medical science attest to this basic fact. There is simply no room for disagreement with the scientific and medical evidence concerning the biological beginning of human life. The full genetic makeup of a unique living being of the species *homo sapiens* is present at conception, and that makeup constitutes a human life. The human embryo is a new, distinct human life. It is clearly *life*, and it is clearly *human* life.[10]

To be sure, that living human being may die *in utero*, before birth, as a result of any of a number of causes. But that does not mean that the human embryo or fetus is (in the words of some of my colleagues) "potential life." Such a proposition is simply confused—displaying either ignorance of basic biological facts or a stubborn (perhaps dishonest?) refusal to accept them. The living human embryo is already *alive*, and it is a *human* life. Abortion does not destroy potential life. Abortion kills a living human being.[11]

Now, the question whether that living human being possesses affirmative constitutional or other legal rights—for example, whether prenatal human beings are legal "person[s]" entitled to "the equal protection of the laws"—is a separate and distinct matter. One might plausibly argue that the word "person" in the Fourteenth Amendment does not include living human beings, alive and gestating in their mothers' wombs but not yet born. (I say more about this presently.) But I do not understand that to be the form in which the argument is made, by Texas for example. While it is doubtless true that, if the unborn child is a "person" within the meaning of the words of the Fourteenth Amendment, this would defeat the asserted constitutional liberty of a woman and her doctor to choose to kill it (outside of some extreme justification of tragic necessity), such a legal conclusion is not necessary: it is sufficient that the human embryo or fetus is human life (whether or not a legal "person" in the sense in which the Fourteenth Amendment uses the word). For surely there is a "compelling" or "subordinating" state interest in protecting human life, at all stages, from being killed by other human beings.

That is all that is necessary to decide this case, even were one to concede the (textually and historically indefensible) premise that some provision of the Constitution grants a presumptive right, privilege, or "interest" to women to obtain or commit an abortion of a human embryo or fetus. The State of Texas surely may, as it has, protect living human beings from being killed before birth. That interest trumps any claim of "liberty" to commit such a killing, under any sensible analysis.[12]

It is worth pausing for a moment to let this simple point sink in. If *anything* constitutes a "compelling state interest," it is the protection of human life from being killed. One can torture the provisions of the Constitution for pages, desperately attempting to generate an argument that supplies a presumptive liberty or equality interest in avoiding pregnancy, but that interest must yield in almost every circumstance if what is in the mother's womb is an actual human life.

Now, what if Texas *didn't* protect such human lives from the private violence of others? Or (in what advocates of a right to choose "whether to bear or beget a child" appear to believe is a knock-down hypothetical), what if a state law *required* abortion? The answer is not, in either case, that parents (or mothers) have a substantive due process right, as against the state, to choose whether their unborn child gets to live or is condemned to death. Rather, in such a case, the answer then really *would* depend on whether the unborn child is a legal "person" entitled to the equal protection of the laws under the Fourteenth Amendment. For to withdraw from a class of persons the protection of the state and to abandon such persons to the private violence of others (or, as a majority of my colleagues today would do, to grant such private violence the affirmative legal sanction and protection of the state) is surely the *very core* of the Constitution's prohibition of state denial of the "equal *protection* of the laws." Such an act by the state would be to abandon to Hobbesian private violence, or for the state itself to commit violence against, a class of persons.

The question then would be whether unborn human beings are "persons" within the meaning of the Equal Protection Clause. The word "person" does not appear to have this meaning when used in other texts of the Constitution (those referring to age requirements or census requirements, for example), but the contexts in which the word is used in those other provisions are quite different and do not themselves compel the conclusion that "person" could not bear a different meaning when talking not about traditional rules for computing age or counting heads but about entitlement to the equal protection of the state against the violence of others. Nor is the question strictly one of the subjective "original intent" of the amendment's framers or the subjective "original understanding" of its ratifiers. There is a logical and important difference between the content of a legal rule and the expected consequences of the rule in the minds of (some of) its drafters and advocates. The search is not for the contents of dead draftsmen's heads but the meaning the words they used would have had, in context, to an ordinary speaker and reader of the English language at or about the time those words were adopted. Thus, for example, the fact that the drafters of the Fourteenth Amendment might not have intended or expected that the meaning of the words they employed logically entailed a principle the consequence of which would invalidate state-sponsored racial segregation is not dispositive. See, e.g., *Brown v. Board of Education*, 347 U.S. 483 (1954).

There is no decisive evidence of the meaning of the word "person," at the time the Fourteenth Amendment was adopted, as applied to the protection of the laws for human fetuses and embryos against the private violence of others. The meaning of the word "person" was not the focus of interpretive controversy, and abortion was not a major legal issue, with thirty-six states or territorial legislatures prohibiting it in many or most situations. In short, the meaning of the word "person" in the Fourteenth Amendment is ambiguous. It could include living but not-yet-born human beings, but not necessarily. Other uses of the word within the Constitution are not determinative, context is not determinative, and evidence of intention is not determinative.

The most natural meaning of the word "person" in the Fourteenth Amendment, as distinguished from "citizen" or other terms of limitation used in the amendment (e.g., "male citizens twenty-one years of age"), is that "person" refers to *all* living human beings. It is a general, inclusive word. It constitutes a category broader than "citizens" (the term employed in the amendment's Privileges or Immunities Clause). It is not limited to *adults*—the term contains no minimum age requirement. See *In re Gault*, 387 U.S. 1 (1967) (constitutional protections of due process of law apply to minors). Given that a human embryo or a human fetus is a living human being—a member of the species *homo sapiens*—it would seem that the better, more natural usage of the term is that he or she is also a "person." This may not have been specifically intended by the amendment's framers, but it appears to be a logical consequence of the use of the general word "person" as embracing all human beings subject to the authority of a state.[13]

At least one three-judge court has recently reached essentially this conclusion. In *Steinberg v. Brown*, 321 F. Supp. 741 (N.D. Ohio 1970), the court found that the claimed right to abortion must yield to the right to life of the unborn child and to the state's obligation to safeguard that life. The court found that, as a matter of basic biology, a new human life comes into being upon conception. "Once human life has commenced," the court continued, "the constitutional protections found in the Fifth and Fourteenth Amendments impose upon the state the *duty* of safeguarding it." 321 F. Supp. at 746–47 (emphasis added).

It thus may well be the better view that the Fourteenth Amendment is a self-executing constitutional requirement that the states protect all living human beings within their respective jurisdictions, both born and unborn, from the private violence of others.[14] Even if not a self-executing requirement, the range of meaning of the word "person" certainly appears to permit *Congress,* pursuant to section 5 of the amendment, to pass a statute forbidding states from refusing to protect the unborn. Congress, possessing power "to enforce, by appropriate legislation, the provisions of this article" (U.S. Const. Amend. XIV, sec. 5) could act pursuant to the view that unborn human beings are "persons" who may not be denied equal protection of the laws by the states, whether or not the judiciary, acting alone, properly could enforce the provisions of the Equal Protection Clause on behalf of unborn children. See *Katzenbach v. Morgan*, 384 U.S. 641 (1966).

As noted, it is not necessary for the Court to decide any of this here and now. No one challenges Texas's statute as denying equal protection of the laws to unborn human beings. Quite the reverse, appellants challenge the constitutionality of Texas's protections of such life. But as noted above, if there is even a good basis for *believing* that the human fetus is a human life, then surely the state *may* protect that life. Indeed, the state's interest in protecting that innocent human life is truly compelling, and must triumph as against mere "privacy" or "autonomy" claims of freedom to choose to kill that life, for reasons sympathetic or unsympathetic. And if it is *clear* that the human fetus is human life, there is a serious and strong case that a state *could not* refuse to protect such life.

II.

No opinion rejecting appellants' claims in this case would be complete without some comment on the human implications—the implications for *justice*—of my colleagues' creation of a constitutional right to abortion. There is a danger in this, to be sure, for the question of *law*—the meaning of the Constitution's commands, prohibitions, and empowerments of democracy—is distinct from the question of *justice,* which is whether those provisions are used, by the people possessing powers and rights under them, for good or for evil. The Court's power is only with respect to law. If, under the Constitution, constitutional powers are used to produce unjust ends, that problem of justice is (for better or worse) not for the courts. It is for the People, and for their chosen representatives. I fear that my colleagues have lost sight of this, and twisted the law, beyond recognition, to produce results they desire. They apparently feel that these results are just, and so they violate their oaths in order to achieve them.[15]

It is a significant indictment of the idea that judges should pursue their own visions of justice, rather than apply the law, that it can produce results like these. Today's decision is not just. In fact, its result is as nearly the complete opposite of justice as it is possible to be. If my account of the law, set forth above is correct; and if it is true that the unborn human embryo or human fetus is a *living human being,* then what the majority of my colleagues has done is create out of whole cloth a super-protected constitutional right of some human beings to kill other human beings, for essentially whatever reasons they may have for doing so, including caprice, spite, convenience, or the child's gender, race, or other physical characteristic.

This, I must observe, is the most horrible thing this Court has ever done in its history. The Court may very well have unleashed an American Holocaust in which private violence is authorized, permitted—encouraged, even—by a fundamentally lawless decision of this Court. And the Court has authorized that violence on a truly cataclysmic scale. If a proximate result of this Court's decision is the de facto end of abortion prohibitions, it is possible to imagine one million to one-and-a-half million human lives being exterminated a year as a consequence. Imagine if this goes on for thirty years: This would mean that a decision of this Court is responsible, directly or indirectly, for a substantial share of *forty-five million human deaths* between now and the year 2003.

This is worse than *Dred Scott* and slavery, as a fire is worse than a frying pan. Slavery is a horrible human wrong. But as bad as that was, murder is worse. *Dred Scott*'s chief evils were two: the declaring of a certain class of the human race as incapable of citizenship or of possessing human rights that other Americans must respect; and the evisceration of the possibility of legislative limits on the *extension* of the evil institution of slavery. What my colleagues do today is similar in form, and worse in substance. They declare a certain class of the human race as non-human, or at least as possessing no moral status that other humans must respect, so that they may be *killed* at will; and they eviscerate the possibility of legislative limits or prohibitions of such killing, and do so based on the Big Lie that the Constitution says that this is required. In terms of the magnitude of the evil inflicted, its wrongness morally and its wrongness legally, the atrocity inflicted by the Court today must be ranked among the greatest wrongs in American, indeed in world, history.

It is personally hard for me to accept the fact that men and women whom I otherwise respect, and call my *friends,* embrace constitutionalized private mass murder. The temptation is to back off a bit, to pull the punch so as not to breach social etiquette and fracture personal relationships, perhaps even to adopt a "live and let live" attitude (a phrase sadly ironic in this context) for the sake of some ostensibly larger value of social peace—or acceptability in polite elite company.

Now I have a better sense of how the German people could have allowed Nazism and the Holocaust to occur. Before today's decision, I had always reacted to the tragic, awful history of World War II with incredulity, with amazement: How could a civilized people have allowed such a thing? How could the German people have tolerated the evisceration of their legitimate governing institutions, and the incubation of evil, for so long? How could they have just looked the other way? Or just gone along? *What was the matter with them?!*

The answer, I fear, is that it is hard to believe, almost impossible to believe, that one's respected elite peers, people whose intellect and passion one may well admire—one's *friends*—are advancing what is almost unqualifiedly *evil*, even when it is staring you squarely in the face. The cognitive dissonance is almost too much to bear. And so we tend to forbear from saying what we know is true and must be said. Evil marches on, unchecked, because to question it breaks the conventions of polite society. Thus it is that a civilized society may well display a "screaming silence" in the face of atrocity.[16]

Today's decision is wrong. It is wrong legally—perhaps the most indefensible "constitutional" decision ever reached by this Court to date. It is wrong morally—the most awful human atrocity inflicted by the Court in our Nation's history. It is not the law, and it is not right. It does great violence to the Constitution, and it authorizes great violence against innocent human life. The members of this Court, today, must be called to account for their actions in no uncertain terms, and those of the rest of society today, and of succeeding generations, must not acquiesce in, or act in complicity with, or offer an apology and defense for, the truly hideous injustice inflicted by this Court. To embrace the result reached today is to commit an act of great evil. To accept the result—to remain silent, to acquiesce, to offer only tepid critiques—is to act in cowardly complicity with great evil.

And so I must, with deep regret, render my honest judgment not only about this case but also concerning the men and women who have today authored the opinions in support of a constitutional right to abortion.

Jack Balkin is a man of violence.

Anita Allen is a woman of violence.

Jed Rubenfeld is a man of violence.

Reva Siegel is a woman of violence.

Cass Sunstein is a man of violence (one case at a time).

Mark Tushnet is a man of violence.

Robin West is a woman of violence.

Akhil Amar is a coward and a collaborator.

As James Madison wrote in *The Federalist No. 49*, "[t]he several departments being perfectly co-ordinate by the terms of their common commission, neither of them, it is evident, can pretend to an exclusive or superior right of settling the boundaries between their respective powers." *The Federalist No. 49.* "[T]he people themselves," Madison continued, are "the grantors of the commission" who "can alone declare its true meaning and enforce its observance." This Court is empowered by the Constitution faithfully to interpret the Constitution. But it is not alone in that power, and when it exceeds it and violates it, it is the responsibility of other actors in our constitutional system to check the abuse.

The decision reached by the Court today, being manifestly and atrociously contrary to the Constitution, should be resisted by the legislative branch and should be refused enforcement by the executive branch, because it is not the law. Indeed, it would violate *their* oaths of office for these officials to act in complicity with, or subserviency to, my colleagues' violations of their oaths to support the Constitution. Ultimately, the People declare the true meaning and enforce the observance of the Constitution that is theirs. It is my hope that the People, through whatever means, will one day soon rescue their Constitution, and the lives of millions, from the decision of this Court today.

NOTES

1. The justices were appointed by Chief Justice Balkin, in blatant violation of Article II, § 2, cl. 2, of the Constitution. It is no accident that a majority of the Justices agree, in whole or in part (and invariably in essence), with Chief Justice Balkin's view. It is also worthy of note that the Court is packed with legal academics—a small group of elites not renowned either for its diversity of opinion on abortion or its commitment to interpreting the Constitution in accordance with the meaning its language would have had to ordinary, reasonably well-informed readers and speakers of the English language at the time the document's provisions were adopted. The result is predictable, and lamentable. I appear to be the only "jurist" selected to sit on this case not to be picked for the attribute of having a likely predetermined commitment to Chief Justice Balkin's desired outcome in this case. Rather, I appear to have been appointed to provide token opposition to that outcome, without meaningful risk that such views would be published as the majority view of the members of this tribunal (a role in which I have been joined, over a year after the public argument in the case, by Justice Collett, in an attempt to mitigate, belatedly and to the smallest extent possible, the force of this observation). Whether these defects in the manner of appointment undermine the legitimacy of the views expressed by this kangaroo "Court," I will leave for the reader to judge.

2. One of my colleagues, with commendable candor, seeks faithfully to interpret the Constitution and follows the law where it leads him, even though it is contrary to his own pro-abortion political views. But the remainder of my colleagues' opinions either make no serious attempt faithfully to apply the language of the Constitution or engage in transparently dishonest, result-oriented reasoning.

One of my colleagues remarks, with unintended irony, that "[c]onstitutional law must have some basis in the Constitution itself" (as if "constitutional" "law" could have "some basis" in anything else)! Sadly, this colleague is the one that comes the next closest to serious consideration of the language of the Constitution itself. Or, at least he does for two-thirds of his opinion, before taking a bizarre turn and conjuring the Nineteenth Amendment's language protecting a constitutional right for women "to vote" into a constitutional right to abortion in whose wake all state abortion regulations adopted before 1920 are unconstitutional but identical regulations enacted in 1921 might (?!) be constitutional. Whatever the (questionable) virtues of such an approach—it at least would leave the substantive constitutional validity of abortion prohibitions an open question—having "some basis in the Constitution itself" is surely not among them.

3. Even if the Ninth Amendment were thought to create a federal constitutional common law of "natural rights," the claim that the right of a woman (or of someone else, acting with the woman's consent or acquiescence) to kill a living human fetus, gestating, living, growing in his or her mother's womb is a *natural law right* would have to be regarded as at best facetious and, at worst, evidence of grossly defective moral reasoning. See section II of this Opinion, infra.

4. I pass quickly over the Thirteenth Amendment, since it cannot seriously be maintained that restrictions on abortion constitute the imposition of slavery or involuntary servitude within the meaning those words had, in context, at the time they were adopted. Notwithstanding certain philosophers' arguments about the propriety of imposing duties on one person to sustain the life of another against his or her consent (see, e.g., Judith Jarvis Thompson, "A Defense of Abortion," 1 *Philosophy & Public Affairs* 47 (1971)), the law imposes on parents duties to their children all the time. Society may also impose duties on its members to engage in military service, risking and sometimes losing their lives or limbs, in defense of the lives and safety of others. If all such legal impositions constitute "slavery" or "involuntary servitude," the terms have no meaning. Any such suggestion would be an affront to the language of the Constitution, to those who suffered in *true* slavery, to those who fought and died for freedom and Union in the Civil War, and indeed to all those who have served their nation's military in just wars. Regrettably, some of my colleagues on the Court come close to making exactly such a suggestion (though, of course, without trying to rest this conclusion in the text of a specific provision of the Constitution).

5. It is natural and appropriate to interpret words and phrases within a legal

document with reference to how those words and phrases are used elsewhere in the document—especially if the provision in question is an amendment to the original document and borrowed language used elsewhere in the original. One might call such a method of textual interpretation "intratextualism." It contrasts sharply with the methodology that at least one of my colleagues employs in interpreting the Privileges or Immunities Clause, which would look not to Article IV, § 2's Privileges and Immunities Clause but to other documents outside the Constitution. I suppose one should call such an approach "extratextualism."

6. The modern judicial understanding of Article IV, § 2, appears to depart in some respects from the original meaning of the provision (and not to improved effect), but that is mostly irrelevant for present purposes, and I will set that question to one side.

7. There is much that one could criticize in this Court's opinions in the *Slaughterhouse Cases,* but rejection of the proposition that the privilege to operate a slaughterhouse in a particular place within the state is one of the "privileges or immunities of Citizens of the United States," exempt from state legislation, is not one of them.

8. I agree with those members of this Court who have argued so persuasively that *Griswold* and *Eisenstadt,* even on their own terms, come nowhere near justifying a constitutional right to abortion. I think the broader point is important. Even if those cases *did* support such a claim, they should not be followed if the claim is wrong as a matter of first principles.

9. As noted earlier, one of my colleagues rests the argument for a constitutional right to abortion, for the benefit of women, less in abstract notions of "equality" loosely moored to the Equal Protection Clause than (even less plausibly, as a matter of text) in the Nineteenth Amendment's grant to women of the constitutional right to vote, on the theory that pregnancy makes it harder (I am not making this up) to vote, hold office, or serve on juries. However cast, the suggestion that women are not fully the political or social equals of men unless they have a constitutional right to kill their unborn children is as idiotic as it is offensive. If one is concerned about the special burdens of pregnancy and motherhood, the remedy is better social and political *accommodation* of pregnancy and motherhood. To treat like things differently is to discriminate. But to insist that differences are evils to be removed, rather than to be accommodated, is to discriminate in a different way. If I am a black man and am excluded from a state law school because of my race—my difference is disqualifying—that is discrimination. If I am a blind man and am required by a state law school to read printed texts like everyone else—my difference is again disqualifying—*that, too,* is discrimination. In the former case, the proper remedy is to eliminate unjustifiably disparate treatment. In the latter case, the proper remedy is to eliminate unjustifiably pseudo-"equal" treatment—to stop the unjustifiable refusal to accommodate. Pregnancy, childbirth, and parenthood impose unique burdens and special obligations. The

proper response of society is reasonable accommodation of those who bear these burdens and assume these obligations so that they may be fully equal citizens and participants in the life of the nation, *not* to create a legal right to eliminate pregnancy by exterminating an unborn child. (On this point, and perhaps no other, Justice West and I appear to be in ironic substantial agreement.) Sadly, the same reasoning that some of my other colleagues use to justify creation of a constitutional right to abortion—the need to relieve women of the burden of pregnancy and the *lifelong* burden of motherhood(!)—could as well be used to justify creation of a constitutional right to infanticide.

10. Texas, in its brief, has included photographs of the human embryo and fetus at various stages of development. See the appendix to this opinion.

11. One of my colleagues quips that this is like saying "a planted acorn is an oak tree," apparently believing this to be a refutation of the medical facts of abortion. This is a truly silly sophism. That A' might not be a true case of A does not mean that B' is not an instance of B. "A" and "B" may be entirely different animals, such that what applies for species (or genus, or phylum, or kingdom) A does not apply to B. Lo and behold: "A" (acorns and oaks) is not merely an entirely different animal from "B" (humans); A is a *plant.* The acorn analogy proves little except that its author is a poor biologist (and an even worse moral philosopher), if he is unable to distinguish scientifically or morally between plant reproduction and human reproduction or to identify the different moral status of the two species of life. (As an aside, I note that a planted acorn *is* an oak tree seed and thus *is* an oak tree, just one at an early stage. And, I reiterate, a human embryo is a *human being* embryo. It is the same human being it will later be, just at an earlier stage of development.)

12. There may well be other sufficiently compelling state interests as well: maintaining the ethical integrity of the medical profession; guarding against eugenics (or, put differently, protecting and respecting the lives of persons with disabilities); safeguarding against devaluing the lives of the poor or of racial minorities; protecting women from oppression and/or abandonment; and guarding against a slippery slope to infanticide.

13. Indeed, there is at least some historical support for this usage. Though the evidence is not without ambiguity, it indicates a broad conception and understanding of the meaning of "person" within the Fourteenth Amendment. John Bingham, one of the principal authors of section 1 of the Fourteenth Amendment, said, in discussing the Constitution's language protecting "person[s]": "Before that great law the only question to be asked of the creature claiming its protection is this: Is he a man? Every man is entitled to the protection of American law, because its divine spirit of equality declares that all men are created equal." *Congressional Globe,* 40th Cong., 1st Sess. 542 (statement of Rep. Bingham).

14. The Chief Justice seems to think it a persuasive *reductio ad absurdum* that this view might entail the further consequence that abortions not be permitted on

grounds of medical necessity to save the life of the mother, unless the unborn child's rights are represented by counsel or a guardian *ad litem*. But there is nothing at all absurd about this inadvertently insightful suggestion. It is simply *unfamiliar* in the abortion context. In an appropriate case in which a state permitted aborting the child to save the mother but failed to provide procedural safeguards to ensure equal protection of the child's life, it would certainly be open to this Court to consider whether the requirement of equal protection of the laws was not satisfied (assuming it having first been decided that the unborn child was a "person" within the meaning of the Fourteenth Amendment). Similarly, the Chief Justice seems to think it a refutation of any claim that the Fourteenth Amendment protects the legal personhood of unborn human fetuses that this might mean that some state laws are *too permissive* in the circumstances in which abortion is allowed. Indeed it might, but this is not a *refutation* of the Equal Protection personhood contention, if otherwise valid, but an *implication* of it. The Chief Justice does not seem to have similar concerns about the far more sweeping implications of his own "constitutional" analysis, which invalidates every state abortion restriction, with far less plausible textual basis.

15. Were the situations reversed, and the Constitution in fact required an unjust result, I would think it not open to me, in the office of judge or justice, to advance my personal notions of justice in opposition to the law I was sworn to uphold. The correct response for the judge in such an instance is to recuse himself, or resign, if following sworn duty would mean imposition of grave injustice. When faced with grave injustice, a proper response may well be to rush, as it were, "to the barricades." But the barricades and the bench are not the same thing. And though justice may require a refusal to act in complicity with injustice, that refusal marks the limits of the appropriate response that may be made by a man or woman *qua* judge. Cf. Robert M. Cover, Book Review, 68 *Colum. L. Rev.* 1003 (1968) (reviewing R. Hildreth, Atrocious Judges: Lives of Judges Infamous as Tools of Tyrants and Instruments of Oppression (1856)). As Professor Cover's review makes clear, it is atrocious for the judge himself or herself to be the deliberate and willing instrument of oppression created by others, or by an unjust regime. But I submit that it is yet worse for the judge himself or herself to be the lawless creator *and* dispenser of injustice and oppression that *the law*, faithfully interpreted and applied, in fact did not inflict.

16. Professor Cover has written eloquently and passionately of "the screaming silence of the German people." Id. at 1005.

The images in the following appendix were donated by Priests for Life. The original photographs were taken by Andrzej Zachwieja and Jan Walczewski, under the direction of Professor Andrzej Skawina of Collegium Medicum Jagiellonian University, Krakow, Poland, and Antoni Marsinek, M.D., of the Czerwiakowski Gynecological and Obstetrics Hospital, Krakow, Poland.

Photo Appendix to the Opinion of
Michael Stokes Paulsen

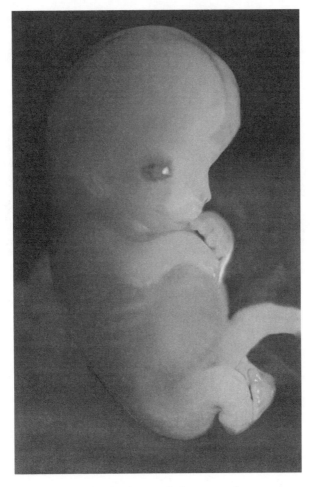

Developing human baby at 7 weeks.

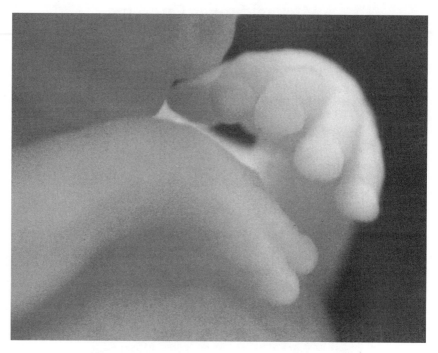

Developing baby's hands at 7 weeks.

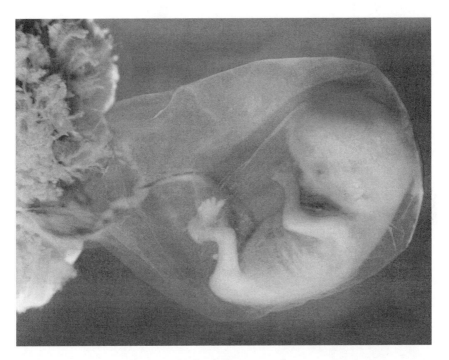

Developing baby at 8 weeks.

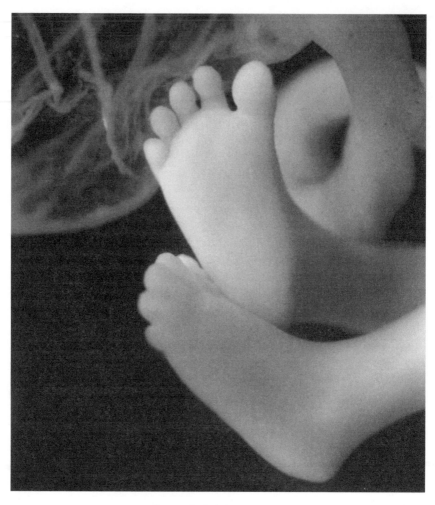

Developing baby's legs at 11 weeks.

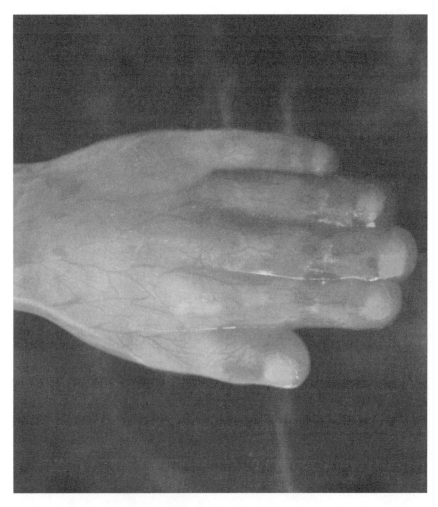

Developing baby's hands at 12 weeks.

Developing baby at 3.5 months.

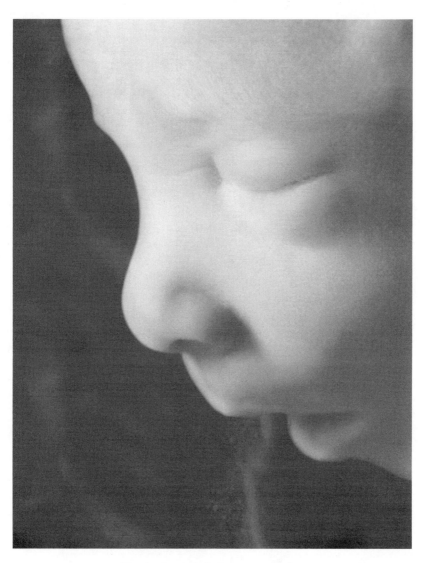

Developing baby's face at 4 months.

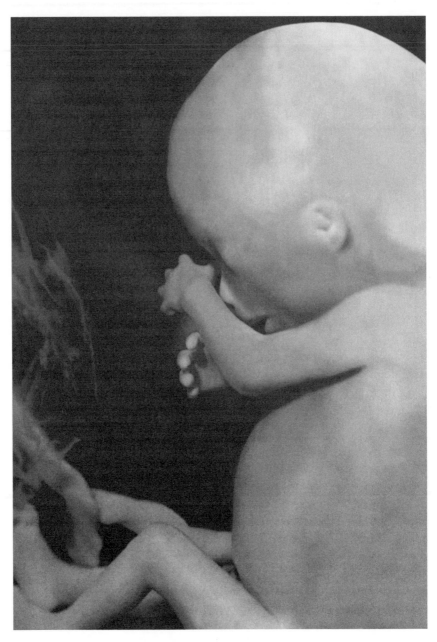

Developing baby at 4 months.

Developing baby's face at 5 months.

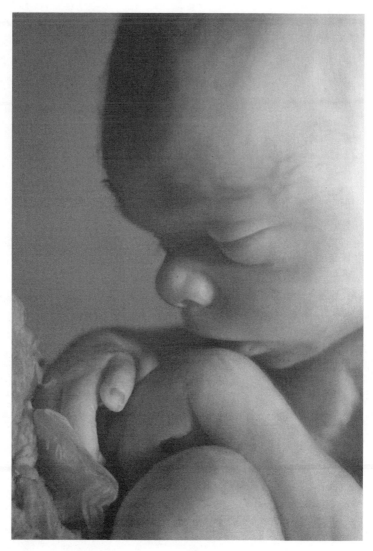

Developing baby at 5 months.

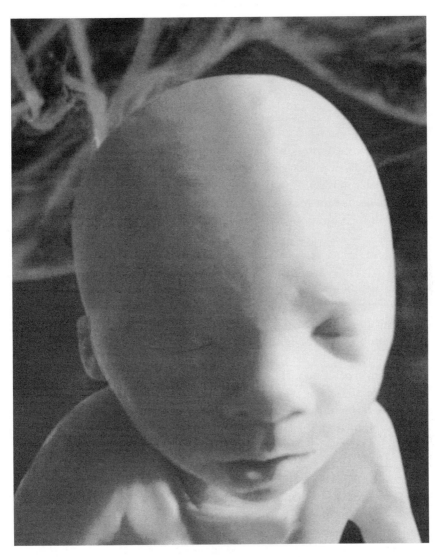

Developing baby's face at 6 months.

Comments from the Contributors

I asked the contributors to this book to give a short account of why they wrote their *Roe* opinion as they did and to describe the goals they were trying to accomplish. I also wanted them to give a chance to give credit where it was due for sources written after 1973, which they could not quote directly in their opinions. Here are their responses.

Anita L. Allen

The first time I heard a woman say that she would get an abortion if she were ever pregnant again, I was about thirteen and thoroughly indignant. "How could she," I thought. "What are women for if not having babies?" Never mind that the woman in question was a high school dropout with no job and six children. Half a dozen years later, *Roe v. Wade* was decided. I do not recall how or why I changed my mind about abortion. However, like most women of my generation, I came to view *Roe* as a mostly positive development in the law.

In the past ten years, I have served on the boards of Planned Parenthood of Metropolitan Washington, the Planned Parenthood Federation of America, and, more recently, the Family Planning Council of Philadelphia. Work for these prominent charities has been an outlet for my moral and political commitment to the ideal of family planning, including sex education, contraception, and early medical abortion. The opinion I drafted has an intentionally passionate tone, designed to mirror the tone of concern for women's health and well-being that I have observed among the health care providers and pro-choice activists with whom I have had the privilege to work.

I have closely followed the fate of *Roe v. Wade.* I was on the steps of the Supreme Court as a legal commentator for CNN television on the day in 1989 that the decision came down, in *Webster v. Reproductive Health Ser-*

vices, to permit states to place restrictions on abortion. I was on the steps of the Court again in 1992 when the Court released its decision in *Planned Parenthood v. Casey*, this time as a paid commentator for CBS News. I was disappointed, but not surprised, that the Court upheld controversial waiting periods and opened the door to further restrictions deemed not to "unduly burden" the abortion right.

What should *Roe* and *Doe* have said? As my fantasy opinion indicates, I believe the opinions ought to have said more about both women's inequality and their lack of privacy and private choice. They should have rehabilitated the messy privacy jurisprudence of *Griswold*. Building on *Loving* and *Eisenstadt*, they should have better explained the connection between equality and private decision making. They should have anticipated and laid the groundwork for rejecting indirect and often pretextual restrictions on abortion. They should have laid the groundwork, too, for public funding for poor women's abortions. I fear the "undue burden" standard is too malleable and have written an opinion designed to foreclose some of the restrictions permitted by Justice O'Connor's "compromise."

I completely disagree with, but have long admired, Justice White's dissenting opinion (joined by Justice Rehnquist) in the 1986 *Thornburgh* case. (*Casey* partly overruled *Thornburgh*.) My concurrence and my effort to explain why abortion rights are fundamental and required by "ordered liberty" is an attempt to place myself in conversation with Justice White and other members of the Court who have disparaged the idea that access to abortion could be a requirement of ordered liberty and democratic citizenship.

I include privacy discourse in my opinion in self-conscious rejection of the view of some feminist legal theorists that *Roe* would have been better off decided solely by reference to equality. In other places I have argued that the liberty and equality cases for abortion are intertwined and that abortion rights are vital for women's citizenship. See A. Allen, "The Proposed Equal Protection Fix for Abortion Law: Reflections on Citizenship, Gender and the Constitution," *Harvard Journal of Law and Public Policy* 18 (1995): 419–55. In my mock opinion, I point to the fact that privacy was in the air in the 1960s as an exciting new express legal value implicit in the Bill of Rights and the Fourteenth Amendment. Privacy was an important and emerging legal value in the 1960s and 1970s, along with equality. For the first time in history, government and private-sector invasions of informational and decisional privacy were a frequent focus of policy debates, lawsuits, and scholarship. Viewed in this light, it should come as no surprise that privacy discourse found its way into abortion jurisprudence.

Akhil Reed Amar

Although I have styled this imaginary concurrence/dissent as a response to the imaginary opinion of Chief Justice Balkin and fellow members of the fictional Balkin Court, in a few places I have in effect alluded to Justice Blackmun's actual opinion in the real *Roe*. For example, my opening paragraph in Part I aims to remind the reader that, in the real *Roe,* Justice Blackmun devoted considerable attention to the Hippocratic Oath and modern AMA pronouncements, while never so much as quoting the actual language of the Due Process Clause. In another passage, I borrow two words from Blackmun—namely his concession that the abortion issue was *inherently different* from the issues addressed by previous cases. *Roe* at 159. And, in passing, I criticize the real *Roe*'s rush to constitutionalize the trimester framework. Readers who desire to see my further thoughts about real *Roe* may wish to consult Akhil Reed Amar, "Intratextualism," 112 *Harv. L. Rev.* 749, 773–78 (1999), and Akhil Reed Amar, "The Supreme Court, 1999 Term. Foreword: The Document and the Doctrine," 114 *Harv. L. Rev.* 26, 76, 109–14 (2000).

Many of the specific historical and textual claims summarized in my imaginary concurrence/dissent are elaborated elsewhere. In addition to the two articles cited here, see generally Akhil Reed Amar, *The Bill of Rights: Creation and Reconstruction* (1998).

In discussing the fact that no women sat on the Court in *Griswold,* I was tempted to state explicitly that no women sat on the *Roe* Court, either. However, I omitted this historically accurate truth from my concurrence/dissent in order to stay within the alternative universe of the imaginary Balkin Court, four of whose eleven members are women.

Jack M. Balkin

I wrote the first draft of my opinion before the other participants in order to give them something to work against. Because *Roe v. Wade* and *Doe v. Bolton* raise a number of difficult and complicated procedural issues, I tried to discuss and resolve most of them in my opinion as Chief Justice, allowing the other participants to focus on the substantive issues that interested them most.

The contributors presented their draft opinions at a conference held at Yale Law School on January 31, 2003; this gave me an opportunity to rethink my arguments in light of the conversations I had with my colleagues. I am grateful to them for the discussions we had, which have caused me to recast substantial portions of what I originally wrote.

I had three basic goals in writing my opinion.

First, I thought it was important to explain why *Roe* was not a departure from the Court's post–New Deal jurisprudence. The standard story is that after the New Deal revolution, courts no longer protected fundamental rights outside the Bill of Rights, so that *Roe* and *Griswold* were somehow illegitimate. I wanted to show that this is a misreading of our nation's constitutional history. *Skinner v. Oklahoma*, which recognized a fundamental interest in procreative liberty, was decided at the same time that the Roosevelt Justices were overturning *Lochner*-era precedents.

From the country's founding to the present day, there is an enduring tradition of recognizing and protecting basic human rights. The nature of these rights changes over time, not simply because of the whims of individual Justices, but because we live in a democracy. The rights Americans believe to be fundamental change over time because of social movement mobilization and contestation. For this reason, it is a mistake to see constitutional rights as essentially opposed to democracy. Calls for protection of fundamental rights arise out of democratic politics.

Second, I believed that the abortion right should be grounded in the principle of sex equality. Before *Roe,* the Supreme Court had decided only one sex equality case, *Reed v. Reed.* But treating *Roe* as a sex equality case in 1973 is not as far-fetched as it might appear. The Supreme Court heard arguments in *Frontiero v. Richardson,* 411 U.S. 677 (1973)—one of the central cases guaranteeing sex equality—the same Term as it heard the second round of arguments in *Roe v. Wade,* and *Frontiero* was decided in the same Supreme Court Term as *Roe.* In addition, as the Court itself noted in *Frontiero,* Congress had already passed the Equal Rights Amendment in March 1972. The women's movement was changing the way that Americans thought about the Constitution's basic commitments to equality. The story of the women's movement is an excellent example of how our Constitution gains its meaning through the practices of democracy, not in opposition to them.

Although sex equality arguments were presented to the Justices in the briefs of amici, the Justices were not prepared to engage with them or to take their implications seriously. Nevertheless, the opportunity was there: the Court could have used abortion as the central case to articulate the nature of sex equality. If it had, the course of sex equality jurisprudence—

and abortion jurisprudence—might have been different. My arguments in this portion of the opinion owe a considerable debt to scholars in the anti-subordination tradition, and, in particular, to the work of my colleague Reva Siegel.

Third, I felt it was important to come up with a better solution to the balance between the state's interest in potential human life and a woman's right to abortion. Most people think that Justice Blackmun's solution in *Roe v. Wade*—the trimester framework—was unsuccessful. It appeared to be too legislative and not sufficiently grounded in the reasons for the abortion right.

My opinion argues that balancing the interests and drawing appropriate lines is a legislative task and therefore should be left to legislatures. Courts should articulate what the abortion right is, give legislatures guidance about how to take that right into account in drafting their own laws, and explain how courts will exercise judicial review in evaluating the choices that legislatures make. As I researched the history of how *Roe v. Wade* was decided, I discovered that Justice Brennan had actually proposed something quite similar—although ultimately he decided to join Justice Blackmun's majority opinion, which imposed a fixed set of judicial rules on all legislatures.

My opinion holds that the purpose of the abortion right is to give pregnant women a fair and realistic opportunity to decide whether or not to become mothers. Hence, the legislature must demonstrate that its statutory scheme has provided such a fair and realistic opportunity. The opinion is what I call "discourse shaping"—it requires legislatures to justify their choices in terms of how they affect women's practical equality in civil society and their practical ability to choose whether to become mothers, rather than in terms of the development of the fetus. This is a point that my colleague Jed Rubenfeld particularly emphasized in our conversations, and I have adopted it in my opinion.

There is a rough analogy between my "discourse shaping" approach and the Vermont Supreme Court's decision in *Baker v. State*, 744 A. 2d 864 (Vt. 1999), which held that the Vermont Legislature had a "constitutional mandate" under the state's constitution to find a way to give same-sex couples the "same benefits and protections afforded by Vermont law to married opposite-sex couples." The *Baker* court explained the constitutional principles that the legislature had to comply with, but it left appropriate enforcement of those constitutional principles to the legislature in the first instance, noting that the legislature could extend marriage rights to same-sex couples or create a form of "domestic partnership" with similar rights and benefits. In response, the legislature created the nation's first civil unions law. By inviting legislative participation and innovation in enforcing constitutional guarantees, the Vermont Supreme Court diffused much of the political backlash that might have flowed from its groundbreaking and controversial decision.

In some ways my discourse-shaping opinion makes even fewer demands on the legislature than the *Baker* court, because it does not specify when the cutoff point for abortions must take place. It merely requires that legislatures make findings about what period of time is sufficient to give pregnant women a fair and realistic chance to end their pregnancies. My opinion is not minimalist in Cass Sunstein's sense of the word because it offers an extensive discussion of the liberty and equality principles that should guide legislatures. But it also leaves plenty of open space for legislative response and democratic innovation.

The key point is that judges do not have to write minimalist opinions to respect democratic processes or to avoid a political backlash. To the contrary, giving a legislature guidance about what constitutional principles are at stake may be a better way of facilitating a legislative solution that is both constitutionally and democratically acceptable. If the court says nothing, or very little, about what principles guide its decision, and simply throws the issue back to legislatures without explanation, legislatures may respond with solutions that courts must repeatedly strike down, and *that* experience may well exacerbate political tensions and lead to backlash effects. Instead of hiding the ball, courts should explain why the constitutional rights they seek to protect are important, and what they will be looking for when they review the legislature's work.

The effect of my opinion in *Roe* would be to sweep old abortion laws off the books and to require states to create new ones. In the political climate of the early 1970s, total restrictions on abortion would be the exception rather than the rule. There is good reason to think that if state legislatures in the early 1970s had been required to justify their abortion laws in the ways I describe, most of them would have guaranteed a basic right to abortion somewhere around twenty weeks, halfway through the term of a normal pregnancy, along with various regulations and exceptions. For example, before *Roe*, in February 1972, the relatively conservative ABA had advocated repeal of restrictions on abortion up to the first twenty weeks, midway between the end of the first and second trimesters.

After several states passed new abortion laws and created legislative records justifying them, the Supreme Court would be able to evaluate legislative decisions and fix upon a minimum set of standards. Because it would be reviewing comprehensive schemes that legislatures themselves had devised, the Court would be exercising less of a traditionally legislative and more of a traditionally judicial role. The legislative decisions would also possess a greater democratic legitimacy than a one-size-fits-all requirement imposed by a court. This would not end all controversies over abortion, but it would give the abortion right a firmer, more democratic grounding than the actual decision in *Roe* did.

To be sure, a small number of states would insist on virtually no abortion rights even after the Court struck down Texas's and Georgia's statutes, but precisely because they would be outliers, it would be easier for the Court to hold their restrictions unconstitutional. The Court could and should have waited to see how most states responded to its initial opinions in *Roe* and *Doe* and after some period of years struck down the statutes that were the most restrictive. As my colleague Akhil Amar points out in his opinion, the Court is on safest ground in protecting fundamental rights when it follows this course. The subsequent history of abortion law shows that courts will eventually gravitate toward the center of public opinion in protecting fundamental rights like abortion no matter how assiduously they insist that they are above everyday politics. Given that fact, the Court could have saved itself a great deal of needless trouble, put abortion rights on more secure footing, and shown greater respect for democracy had it followed a path like the one I have advocated here.

Teresa Stanton Collett

I came to this project belatedly, not having the benefit of the exchanges that occurred at the conference and that gave rise to the other opinions in this book but benefiting immensely from reading the opinions in their final form. My contribution was written over the course of two weeks and designed to fit within tight word limits to accommodate the fact that the manuscript was already at the publisher. This necessitated leaving certain key points unexplored and presenting other arguments in an abbreviated fashion. Notwithstanding these constraints, I believe the opinion fairly represents my view that abortion does not advance the interests of women and involves the taking of human life.

I am indebted to the work of Feminists for Life, which has published various essays over the years exploring the historical record of early feminists' opposition to abortion. It was through this organization that I was first encouraged to read such texts as Mary Wollstonecraft's *A Vindication of the Rights of Woman* and Prudence Allen's *The Concept of Woman*. Early discussions of the needs of women to be included in political and economic life were often cast in terms of advancing the interests of families—an argument I find more compelling than those of radical individualism and self-interest so often heard today.

As I noted in my opinion, many of the early feminists recognized that abortion was the product not of choice but of pressure, particularly from the men in women's lives. The current regime of abortion on demand that *Roe* instigated has not changed this sad fact. A 1998 study published by the Guttmacher Institute, a research affiliate of Planned Parenthood, indicates that relationship problems contributed to the decision to seek abortions by 51 percent of American women who had abortions.

> Underlying this general reason are such specific ones as that the partner threatened to abandon the woman if she gives birth, that the partner or the woman herself refuses to marry to legitimate the birth, that a break-up is imminent for reasons other than the pregnancy, that the pregnancy resulted from an extramarital relationship, that the husband or partner mistreated the woman because of her pregnancy, or that the husband or partner simply does not want the child. Sometimes women combined these reasons with not being able to afford a baby, suggesting the importance of having a partner who can offer both emotional and financial support.[1]

The simple fact is that, today as in the nineteenth century, for many women abortion is the man's solution for what he views as the "woman's problem."

What I was not able to include in my opinion, because we were limited to materials available to the members of the Court in 1973, is the medical evidence that has emerged regarding the harmful effects of abortion on women's health. It seems clear that depression and preterm birth for any subsequent pregnancies are risks of abortion.[2] It is equally clear that by aborting their pregnancies, women lose the health benefits that successful pregnancies bring, including reduced risk of breast, ovarian, and endometrial cancer.[3] Cancer is the third leading cause of death for women.

One of the things that shocked me when I read the briefs presented to the *Roe* Court was the amount of detail concerning the development of the unborn child, even in 1973. While there were no pictures as compelling as tiny Samuel Armas's hand apparently grasping the finger of the perinatal surgeon who was repairing his spine while Samuel was still in his mother's womb[4] or those currently available from a 4-D ultrasound system, our common humanity was made clear by the Attorney General of Texas from the medical materials available, even at that time. The failure of the Court to engage, or even allude to, this material in its opinion deeply troubles and grieves me.

Being limited to materials available in 1973, when *Roe* was decided, also precluded any discussion of the mounting evidence that abortion has contributed to the reemergence of the idea of children as possessions. In 1972, one year before the *Roe v. Wade* decision, there were 2.05 reported child abuse cases per 1,000 children, according to the U.S. Bureau of the Census. In April 2004, the U.S. Department of Health and Human Services reported that 12.3 out of every 1,000 children were victims of abuse or neglect. In the six short years from 1986 to 1993, the total number of children endangered quadrupled.[5] While many factors contribute to this increase, the attitude that we are free to dispose of human life that is "unwanted" certainly must be among them.

With the advent of in vitro fertilization, technology that only became available only five years after *Roe v. Wade*, some would-be parents began to dream of "custom-order" children, resulting in today's debate regarding the morality of selecting the sex and other characteristics of a child. The parameters of this debate have expanded so far as to include those who defend the right of two deaf lesbians to intentionally create a deaf child.[6]

All of these facts lead me to agree with Judge Edith Jones of the United States Court of Appeals for the Fifth Circuit:

> Hard and social science will of course progress even though the Supreme Court averts its eyes. It takes no expert prognosticator to know that research on women's mental and physical health following abortion will yield an eventual medical consensus, and neonatal science will push the frontiers of fetal "viability" ever closer to the date of conception. One may fervently hope that the Court will someday acknowledge such developments and re-evaluate *Roe* and *Casey* accordingly.[7]

I pray that day comes sooner, rather than later.

Michael Stokes Paulsen

Like other contributors, I hereby step out of role to offer some "program notes" on my opinion.

I begin with the ending, which is rather harsh in its condemnation not only of *Roe* itself but of those who would defend it or acquiesce in it. The late Professor Robert M. Cover, whose pre-1973 work I cite, was my teacher and mentor at Yale Law School in the early 1980s. His work, his style, and his prophetic passion influenced me greatly—so much so that I try to keep them in mind as a model, both with respect to my own writing and with respect to my interactions with my own students. I do not know whether Cover would have agreed with me on abortion and *Roe,* but I am sure he would have insisted that, given my analysis and conclusions about the decision, I must condemn not only the decision but those who made it and continue to support it. It is in a Coverian spirit of incitement, one that I feel naturally but that was also nurtured by his teaching and writing, that I have written section II of my opinion. The phrase "——— is a man of violence" is borrowed from Cover's article "Violence and the Word." Even more influential on me has been his book on slavery, *Justice Accused,* which is addressed largely to the theme of complicity in violence and injustice inflicted by the legal system. I know that my words will offend many, and the conflict expressed in the opinion over condemning people whom you (otherwise) respect and call friends is a real one, but in the end I feel I cannot do otherwise.

Reading the actual *Roe v. Wade* dissents once again in preparing to write my own, I was struck by how rather weakly critical of the majority they were, given the enormous stakes and the enormity of the Court's outrageous act of lawlessness. It makes me wonder whether decorum, in the face of evil, is really a virtue. What if Byron White had gone nuclear? What if he had stormed into a few offices and threatened to crack a few (numb)skulls, figuratively, or to resign in protest, condemning the Court, rather than offer a standard dissent? For those who today are persuaded that *Roe* is an atrocity, passivity, quiescence, and decorum probably ought not to be thought acceptable responses. But such are the conventions surrounding the writing of judicial opinions, perhaps even more so in 1973 than today. As Cover wrote in *Justice Accused:* "If a man makes a good priest, we may be quite sure he will not be a great prophet."

On the merits of the legal arguments themselves: *Roe*'s wrongness was as evident in 1973 as it is today, and I have referred in the opinion only to legal materials available at the time. *Katzenbach v. Morgan,* concerning Congress's section 5 enforcement power, has been limited rather severely by *City of Boerne v. Flores* (1997), but I think that *Boerne* is wrongly decided on this point, and so I stick with *Morgan,* despite evident weaknesses in the Court's analysis.

The point that *stare decisis* never justifies according generative effect to a prior wrong decision anticipates the Supreme Court's holding in *Planned Parenthood v. Casey* (1992), reaffirming *Roe.* What *Roe* held to be required by substantive due process *Casey* held to be required by *stare decisis,* even assuming the original analysis of *Roe* to be wrong. As I have written elsewhere, such an understanding of *stare decisis* is not only mistaken but affirmatively *unconstitutional,* substituting judicial misunderstanding for the text's actual commands and giving effect to the former rather than the latter. Readers interested in this argument might refer to an article I wrote a few years ago, "Abrogating Stare Decisis by Statute: May Congress Remove the Precedential Effect of *Roe* and *Casey*?" 109 *Yale L. J.* 1535 (2000). For a satire of *Casey*'s reasoning with respect to *stare decisis,* transposing the Court's analysis to a mythical reaffirmation of *Plessy v. Ferguson* by the Court in *Brown v. Board of Education,* see Michael Stokes Paulsen & Daniel N. Rosen, "*Brown, Casey*-Style: The Shocking First Draft of the Segregation Opinion," 69 *N.Y.U. L. Rev.* 1287 (1994). *Roe* is not the worst constitutional decision of all time, but it was in 1973. That dishonor must now go to *Casey.* I have developed the reasons for this conclusion at length in another anniversary article, "The Worst Constitutional Decision of All Time," 78 *Notre Dame L. Rev.* 995 (2003).

Finally, I have also written elsewhere in support of the proposition (which I employ in the opinion) that a clear judicial misinterpretation of the Constitution should not be respected and enforced by the political branches. "The Most Dangerous Branch: Executive Power to Say What the Law Is," 83 *Georgetown L. J.* 217 (1994). *Roe* is the perfect example of a case where other actors in our constitutional system should exercise independent constitutional review of the lawfulness of the actions of the Supreme Court and strike down the Court's decision as contrary to the Constitution.

Not available to the Court in 1973 was the evidence of how harmful abortion is to women. For informative recent studies, see Elizabeth Ring-Cassidy & Ian Gentles, *Women's Health after Abortion: The Medical and Psychological Evidence* (deVeber Inst. 2002), and John M. Thorp, Jr., Katherine E. Hartmann, & Elizabeth Shadigan, "Long-Term Physical and Psychological Health Consequences of Induced Abortion: Review of the Evidence," 58 *Obstetrical and Gynecological Survey* No. 1 (2002). For those inclined to view abortion as strictly a woman's health issue, or who favor abortion rights as a way to promote the interests of women, this evidence should unsettle their assumptions.

My opening footnote quips about the "packed Court" here—the only moment of mild levity in an otherwise somber opinion. But there is truth in this jest. There is a danger that the reader of this volume will come away with the impression that the overwhelming weight of informed constitutional scholarly opinion strongly supports the result in *Roe*. Such a conclusion would be based on a sharply skewed, and highly misleading, slice of opinion. The reader of this volume should be aware how atypical law professor opinion is, and how skewed even this particular sample of law professor opinion is. Most Americans, polls show, oppose abortion in most circumstances. Even in 2003, after years of judicial and media conditioning to think of abortion as a valued right, fewer than 40 percent think abortion should be legal in all or most circumstances (the dominant opinion among the participants in this project). Sixty percent think abortion should be legal in no or only a few circumstances. More particularly, 68 percent think abortion should generally be illegal after the fetus is three months old, and 85 percent think abortion should generally be illegal after the fetus is six months old. Under the regime of *Roe v. Wade* and subsequent opinions—the regime defended by nearly everyone in this symposium—abortion may be had for essentially any reason throughout all nine months of pregnancy, up to and including the point of birth, as the Supreme Court's very recent decision in *Stenberg v. Carhart* (2000), the partial-birth abortion case, makes clear.

The composition of this symposium is quite unrepresentative of American opinion, representing a self-selected elite group. It is unrepresentative even of law professor legal opinion. *Roe v. Wade* is widely regarded as a running joke among legal academics—an example of the lawlessness that has come to define the field of constitutional law. Still, it is undoubtedly the case that support for abortion rights is the dominant *political view* of most American law professors today. But, even within this group, there are few who will labor so hard as the members of this panel to attempt to generate a *legal justification* for their political preferences. These arguments are not typical, or well accepted. They are the ingenious efforts of some of the most brilliant, but also most determinedly pro-abortion, constitutional law theorists of our age. They represent not a consensus but the best arguments that the best legal minds in America today can offer in support of the result in *Roe*.

A short illustrative story, and then I will quit. I recount this not so much to embarrass Jack Balkin as to offer an anecdote in support of the preceding point. A few weeks (or perhaps months) after Jack called me, inviting me to participate, he called me again, asking if I knew any pro-life women who are constitutional law professors. I chuckled a little. I knew the reason for the call: I've organized symposia and conferences, and one likes to have a diversity of views and voices and not to appear too greatly to have stacked the deck in favor of one's own preferred views. And I also knew that the pool of pro-life law professors, women and men, is much shallower and smaller than that of pro-abortion law professors. But what was also slightly amusing is this: while Jack and I are acquainted each other, we do not know each other well. We share mutual friends and have crossed paths, but we don't hang in the same circles. For Jack to have come *to me* for suggestions means that not only did he not know any pro-life female law professors but that he didn't know very many people who *might know* any pro-life female law professors! This symposium thus reflects a narrow slice of a narrow elite that is not personally or professionally acquainted with very many people who hold pro-life views. They of course know such people are out there. They just don't know any of them. (I gave Jack some names, but none participated in the symposium at Yale. That is not necessarily Jack's fault: many folks are just too busy, others might not like to be type-cast, and others actually may fear subtle or overt professional reprisal for expressing views that are very strongly disfavored in legal academia. I note that Professor Teresa Collett, one of the most distinguished and respected pro-life law professors and educators in the nation, was added at the book publication stage.)

And so the resulting mock judicial opinions, interesting though they may be, are perhaps most interesting as case studies of the way legal academics these days tend to think and write. This project may, in the end, reveal more about what constitutional law professors in 2003 tend to think and say than about "What *Roe v. Wade* Should Have Said."

Jeffrey Rosen

In playing the Ely and Bickel role here, I don't expect to win lots of converts: liberal advocates of judicial restraint have even fewer fans today than they did when *Roe* was decided (thanks in part, to the constitutional polarization that was set in motion by *Roe* itself.). But the meat and potatoes dissent is easy enough to write—despite three decades of attempts by the finest constitutional minds in the country, none of the attempts to justify *Roe* on alternative grounds strike me as substantially more convincing than Justice Blackmun's famously artless opinion itself. Most of the historical material that I've used in this piece was available to the Court in 1973, although I've helped myself to insights from two more recent articles: Reva Siegel's "Reasoning from the Body: A Historical Perspective on Abortion Regulation and Questions of Equal Protection," 44 *Stan L. Rev.* 261 (1992) and (for the summary of the laws on the books when *Roe* was decided, as well as the discussion of nineteenth-century medical history) Paul Benjamin Linton's "*Planned Parenthood v. Casey*: The Flight from Reason in the Supreme Court," 13 *St. Louis U. Pub. L. Rev.* 15 (1993).

Jed Rubenfeld

I want to thank Professor Jack Balkin for all the work he did putting this book together and for inviting me to contribute to it. Because my contribution is based on arguments I have made at length elsewhere,[8] I will add little more here.

In my opinion, I refer to other "members of this Court" who "today describe a woman's interest in terminating an unwanted pregnancy as mere 'convenience, whim, or caprice.'" The reference is not to any of the opinions in this volume. It is, rather, to Justice White's dissent in *Roe,* in which he was joined by Justice Rehnquist.[9]

I mention "brain birth" in my opinion. I am not sure the term existed in 1973. The idea was probably in the air, however, and *Roe* quickly prompted considerable examination of it, in both the medical and the legal literatures. Early proponents of "brain birth" argued that the critical moment is the one when the fetal brain first emits electrical activity, often said to occur around the eighth week.[10] This seems to me the wrong concept; a transistor radio produces electrical activity. The better question, I think, is when the cerebral cortex—that part of the human brain distinguishing it from all others and responsible for our higher capacities—first comes into neurological existence and first begins emitting minimally organized electroencephalographic activity. Although the matter is hardly free from doubt, this apparently occurs no earlier than the twentieth week.[11]

A word should be said about the recently decided *Lawrence v. Texas*.[12] On the whole, I do not think *Lawrence* strengthens *Roe*. True, it commits five justices to the view that the Constitution protects some kind of unwritten right of privacy having something to do with sex. But *Lawrence*'s right of privacy does not seem to be *Roe*'s.

The *Lawrence* Court speaks of laws that "demean" and "stigmatize." These terms do not seem to apply to abortion laws, at least not in the way they apply to laws prohibiting homosexual sex. The *Lawrence* Court also comes close to embracing the view that activity cannot be prohibited merely because a majority views the activity as immoral. This proposition could certainly be said to vindicate *Roe*, but it would also constitutionalize the libertarian shibboleth that government "cannot legislate morality," an idea that I never saw in *Roe* and cannot believe is part of our Constitution.

A very great deal of law rests on majority views of morality. Title VII is an example. That is why libertarians say antidiscrimination law is unconstitutional. I have always believed that *Roe* stands for a stronger, more specific, more interesting principle, truer to the Constitution. I will not repeat that principle here; the short of it can be found in my opinion, and the long in my article *The Right of Privacy*.

Reva B. Siegel

This opinion presents the abortion right as grounded in the equal citizenship principle, a principle that we have come to understand through the social movement struggles that produced the Fourteenth and Nineteenth Amendments. At the time the Court decided *Roe*, the women's movement was arguing that equal citizenship required effective access to abortion. In a line of cases decided just after *Roe*, the Court interpreted the Fourteenth Amendment's Equal Protection Clause to prohibit sex discrimination, but declared that regulation directed at pregnant women was not the kind of sex-based state action that could violate the Equal Protection Clause.[13] This opinion demonstrates how the constitutional jurisprudence of abortion and equal protection might differ had the Court developed sex discrimination doctrine with laws prohibiting abortion as its paradigm, rather than excluded, case.

I have elsewhere argued that the abortion right can be understood on sex-equality grounds.[14] This opinion draws on that earlier work but differs in that it grounds the abortion right in equality arguments under the

Fourteenth and Nineteenth Amendments that were actually advanced by the women's movement in the 1960s and 1970s. The sex equality arguments for abortion rights circulating at the time *Roe* was decided were an integral part of the movement's demands for equal citizenship.[15] Modern sex discrimination doctrine has adopted the movement's understanding of equal citizenship in significant part. For this reason, an understanding of the abortion right that has not been incorporated into equal protection doctrine nonetheless resonates plausibly within it.

The second-wave feminist movement understood sex equality as a question rooted in the roles, practices, and institutions of family life. By 1973, the movement's constitutional lawyers argued that regulation of the pregnant woman was presumptively unconstitutional when it enforced stereotypes and sex role prescriptions of the separate-spheres tradition. A classic expression of this understanding is an equal protection brief that Ruth Ginsburg filed in 1972 in a case involving a woman who faced an involuntary discharge from the Air Force because she was pregnant. See Brief for Petitioner, *Struck v. Sec'y of Def.*, 409 U.S. 1071 (1972) (No. 72-178); Ruth Bader Ginsburg, "Remarks for the Celebration of 75 Years of Women's Enrollment at Columbia Law School," 102 *Colum. L. Rev.* 1441, 1447 (2002). Ginsburg's brief in the *Struck* case has been neglected because the Court disposed of the case by remanding it to the Court of Appeals on mootness grounds and soon thereafter ruled that regulation directed at pregnant women was not the kind of "sex-based" state action that would trigger heightened scrutiny under equal protection principles.

In this early period, women advanced sex equality arguments for the abortion right in the streets and in a number of cases. Briefs tied sex equality claims to different provisions of the Constitution—in particular, the Fifth, Eighth, Thirteenth, Fourteenth, and Nineteenth Amendments. See Brief of Amici Curiae Human Rights for Women, Inc. at 11–12, *United States v. Vuitch*, 402 U.S. 62 (1971) (No. 84) (arguing that the statute denies women, as a class, the equal protection of the law guaranteed by the Fifth Amendment in that it restricts their opportunity to pursue higher education, to earn a living through purposeful employment, and, in general, to decide their own future, as men are so permitted, and also arguing that the abortion statute violates the Thirteenth Amendment, on grounds that "[t]here is nothing more demanding upon the body and person of a woman than pregnancy, and the subsequent feeding and caring of an infant until it has reached maturity some eighteen years later"); Brief of Amici Curiae Joint Washington Office for Social Concern et al. at 10–11,

Vuitch (No. 84) (arguing that the abortion statute discriminates against women in violation of their right to equal protection).

Then-attorney Nancy Stearns expressed the equality claim for abortion rights in Nineteenth Amendment as well as Fourteenth Amendment terms. See First Amended Complaint at 6–7, *Women of Rhode Island v. Israel* (D.R.I. June 22, 1971) (No. 4605) (arguing that "denial of the vote represented maintenance of the dividing line between women as part of the family organization only and women as independent and equal citizens in American life"; contending that "[t]he Nineteenth Amendment recognized that women are legally free to take part in activity outside the home. But the abortion laws imprison women in the home without free individual choice").

In *Roe v. Wade* itself, Stearns submitted an amicus brief challenging the Georgia and Texas abortion statutes in explicit sex equality terms on Fourteenth Amendment, due process, equal protection, and Eighth Amendment grounds. There she argued, with respect to the due process claim, that "restrictive laws governing abortion such as those of Texas and Georgia are a manifestation of the fact that men are unable to see women in any role other than that of mother and wife." See Brief of Amici Curiae New Women Lawyers et al. at 24, 32, *Roe v. Wade*, 410 U.S. 113 (1973) (No. 70-18). She further argued, with respect to the equal protection claim, that "laws such as the abortion laws presently before this court in fact insure that women never will be able to function fully in the society in a manner that will enable them to participate as equals with men in making the laws which control and govern their lives," id. at 32, and she contended, with respect to the Eighth Amendment claim, that

> [s]uch punishment involves not only an indeterminate sentence and a loss of citizenship rights as an independent person . . . [and] great physical hardship and emotional damage "disproportionate" to the "crime" of participating equally in sexual activity with a man . . . but is punishment for her "status" as a woman and a potential child-bearer.

Id. at 42; see also Brief for Plaintiffs, *Abramowicz v. Lefkowitz*, 305 F. Supp. 1030 (S.D.N.Y. 1969) (No. 69 Civ. 4469), *cited in* Diane Schulder & Florynce Kennedy, *Abortion Rap* 218 (1971) (attacking New York abortion laws under a Fourteenth Amendment due process claim and asserting that abortion laws are "both a result and symbol of the unequal treatment of women that exists in this society").

While many in the movement argued for abortion rights in the language of equality, by the time of *Roe* the movement had increasingly come to speak about abortion in the language of liberty, privacy, and choice—not only to litigate the question under *Griswold v. Connecticut*, 381 U.S. 479 (1965), but also to protect the ERA from the abortion controversy. Even so, several years after *Roe*, when the Court attempted to exclude regulation of pregnant women from the nation's employment discrimination laws, the women's movement secured an amendment to the Civil Rights Act of 1964 that provided pregnant workers protection against sex discrimination in employment and benefits. See Post & Siegel, supra, at 2011–13. During the 1980s, as critics of *Roe* challenged the opinion's constitutional basis in liberty and privacy values, *Roe*'s proponents increasingly came to defend the abortion right on sex-equality grounds. And when the Court reaffirmed and revised the *Roe* framework in *Planned Parenthood of Southeastern Pa. v. Casey*, 505 U.S. 833 (1992), these sex equality arguments appeared throughout the justices' opinions. See Kenneth Karst, "Constitutional Equality as a Cultural Form: The Courts and the Meanings of Sex and Gender," 38 *Wake Forest L. Rev.* 513, 531–35 (2003); Reva B. Siegel, "Abortion as a Sex Equality Right: Its Basis in Feminist Theory," in *Mothers in Law: Feminist Theory and the Legal Regulation of Motherhood* (Martha Fineman & Isabel Karpin eds., 1995) (surveying equality arguments for the abortion right in law review literature and in *Casey*).

This opinion synthesizes sex equality arguments for the abortion right advanced in the years before *Roe* was decided and in the decades during which it was under siege. It shows how the Court could have started sex discrimination jurisprudence in an opinion striking down laws that criminalize abortion, and suggests how this approach would alter our understanding of the abortion right and equal protection law more generally. In reconstructing social movement arguments advanced in the era before the Court decided *Roe*, the opinion also reflects on the relation of judicial and popular constitutionalism. While courts generally work to efface connections between judicial and popular constitutionalism, this opinion aspires to a kind of counter-factual transparency. The opinion reflects on the role that people play in shaping judicial interpretation of the Constitution—and on the ways that judge-pronounced constitutional law can intervene in and shape constitutional culture.

In deriving and enforcing the abortion right, the opinion demonstrates that courts do not merely defer to popular understanding; they identify conflicts between the nation's evolving understandings of its constitutional commitments and its long-standing beliefs and practices and call upon the nation to revise its customs in the light of its commitments. The opinion suggests how the abortion right is grounded in this dialogic understanding of judicial review. The opinion is drafted on the assumption that the right it enunciates will have to be taken up, defended, and elaborated in judicial and popular fora and that this process is an integral part of the practice of declaring rights—a collaborative process through which the nation's understanding of its constitution evolves.

Cass R. Sunstein

Roe v. Wade accomplished many things at once. In one bold stroke, it gave American women the right to choose abortion. At the same time, it raised serious and enduring issues about judicial legitimacy. Over the past three decades, *Roe* has symbolized, more than any other case, the risk that constitutional law might be nothing more than judicial value judgments. *Roe* has attained this status partly because the right to choose abortion seemed, to many, to lack clear constitutional roots and to come as a kind of bolt from the blue. But part of the controversy over *Roe* stems from the substance—from the Court's legitimation of a practice that millions of Americans consider, in good faith and on the basis of deep moral convictions, to be morally objectionable and even a form of murder. To its enduring discredit, the Court gave extremely short shift to this belief.

The Court had several plausible routes in *Roe*. One of the least plausible, I think, was the route it took: a broad ruling, in its very first confrontation with the abortion question, that invalidated an extraordinary range of judgments by the states. This route seems to be among the least plausible of the options for one reason: it went so far so fast. It is highly relevant, in this connection, that the democratic process was in a state of flux and that states were in the midst of increasing the availability of abortion. Indeed, and it is worth lingering over this point, *there was a greater increase in lawful abortions in the three years before Roe than in the three years after.* Since the overwhelming majority of all abortions were lawful after *Roe,* this simple statistic suggests that the nation was moving, quite rapidly, toward legalizing abortion. And since the Court ran roughshod over the deep moral commitments of countless Americans, it created new questions about the legitimacy of the Court's role in American government. These new questions have played a big part, and a damaging part, in numerous elections.

We shouldn't oversimplify here. I think it unquestionable that *Roe* has become our generation's *Lochner*, that is, the preeminent symbol of judicial overreaching. At least this is *Roe*'s meaning within much of the legal culture and for many (not all) Americans. But *Roe* could also have become our generation's *Brown*, that is, a correct, stirring, even heroic reading of the Constitution to invalidate a practice that was a source of unacceptable injustice. Decades after it was issued, *Roe* has not acquired the kind of solidity and security that *Brown* has long enjoyed. But might not the system of racial segregation have some resemblance to the system of forced childbirth to which *Roe* spelled an end? The question should not be dismissed. Through an accident, a mistake, or much worse, many girls and young women might, in the pre-*Roe* years, find themselves facing a dangerous, illegal abortion or involuntary motherhood at a far too early stage of their life. The equal protection challenge, to that situation, seems to me quite plausible. If the equal protection clause forbids states from turning people into second-class citizens—if there is no caste system here—then the problem of sex discrimination is serious.

But there were several problems with accepting this argument at the time of *Roe*. First, the constitutional law of sex equality was poorly developed. Second (and this problem exists even today), the interest on the other side—the protection of fetal life—could not possibly be rejected with the certainty and moral clarity with which the Court could dismiss the interest in continuing racial segregation.

In these circumstances, I believe that it would have been quite plausible for the Court to uphold the Texas and Georgia statutes, bracketing the question whether the right to choose abortion qualifies as fundamental and simply concluding that the interest in protecting the fetus adequately justified the intrusion on that right. But one consideration above all others seems to me to undermine this approach: as everyone knew, laws banning abortion were violated every day, producing countless dangerous, illegal abortions. These laws did not, in practice, promote their intended goal— or at least they promoted that goal far less in reality than on paper. This point does not mean that the Constitution is offended by laws that are regularly violated. But it does raise serious doubts about the constitutional validity of the life-protecting justification for intruding on what does seem, to me, to qualify as an interest with constitutional support (that is, the interest in reproductive freedom).

All this is by way of explaining the particular option my opinion se-
lects: a narrow, minimalist ruling that brackets the hardest questions and
that strikes down two laws that seem to me highly unusual and quite draconian. This kind of ruling would have represented an exceedingly small
step. It would have reflected some of virtues of judicial silence, which, it
seems to me, is often a constructive force. Such an opinion would also
have invited a kind of dialogue between the political process and the
courts in which the judges were not necessarily senior partners.

On purely political grounds, the opinion I have sketched is far from
entirely satisfactory to me. With most Americans, I think that abortion
should be safe, legal, and rare. On purely legal grounds, the opinion I have
sketched is also not entirely satisfactory to me: it extends the overbreadth
doctrine in a way that the Court had not yet done. But on institutional
grounds, the Court should have proceeded far more slowly and incrementally than it did, and I think that an overbreadth ruling was its best available option.

Mark Tushnet

The discerning reader will see that this opinion is a lightly edited version
of the substantive portions of Justice Douglas's concurring opinion in the
1973 abortion cases. In taking this course, I had in mind Borges's story
"Pierre Menard, Author of Don Quixote." For present purposes, the "lesson" I draw from Borges's story—if a work of imaginative literature can
be said to have a lesson—is that authorial creativity is in fact strongly
constrained. (I acknowledge that this lesson is in some ways inconsistent
with one interpretation of Borges's story. According to that interpretation,
authorial creativity *consists in* acting subject to strong constraints.)

My point in appropriating Justice Douglas's opinion for myself is to
emphasize that it may be impossible, and certainly is unfair—to the historical record, at least—to think ourselves back into the position of the
judges who decided *Roe*, acting as if we had available to us only the legal
materials they had available yet knowing what has happened between 1973
and today, and then to produce "opinions" different from the ones they
produced. The opinions written by the Court's members were, in this
sense, the opinions they *had* to write. Of course, there were other options,
in the sense that the legal materials available in 1973 *could* have supported
other opinions. It's just that the real people who occupied positions on the

Supreme Court would not have chosen those options. And, of course, there were reasons why those people and not others were sitting on the Court at that time. The constraints that operated in real history put into question the value, other than as a truly academic exercise, of rewriting *Roe v. Wade.* (And, even as an academic exercise, it may be only an occasion for participants to show off.)

In some ways, my point is the obverse of a standard point made about originalist constitutional interpretation: if we managed to revive James Madison, made sure he knew everything that had happened between 1787 and today, and asked him how he would resolve a contemporary constitutional question, the answer he would give us would be one of the answers that someone today would give, because—on the assumptions I have made—Madison would *be* one of us. Similarly, I think, with the enterprise here: if we try to think ourselves back to 1973, we would *be* people of 1973, with all their strengths and weaknesses. Of course, we can't be sure which of those people we would be, although I'm pretty sure that few of us would have been justices on the Supreme Court.

Although one of us—me—actually did have something to do with producing the opinions in *Roe v. Wade.* I was the law clerk in Justice Thurgood Marshall's chambers with responsibility for overseeing the opinions in *Roe.* Here I would like to make a few observations in retrospect about the *Roe* opinions. The first, embodied in the opinion I have provided, is that, in my view, Justice Douglas's opinion stands up quite well. Following the model of his often derided but actually quite intelligent opinion in *Griswold,* the opinion pulls together doctrinal strands from a variety of areas and argues (demonstrates?) that, taken cumulatively, they show why the woman's interest should prevail in the abortion context: similar interests prevailed in prior cases against interests similar to those asserted by the states in the abortion context. It is, to my mind, a fine example of constitutional adjudication in the common law mode.

My second and third observations come from my reading of the Court's internal papers, now available in several manuscript collections. Justice Harry Blackmun drafted an opinion after the first round of argument in the abortion cases, which argued that the Texas and Georgia statutes were unconstitutionally vague because they failed to provide doctors with sufficient guidance to allow the doctors to perform legally permitted abortions without at the same time reasonably fearing prosecution. At the time, the opinion was—I think nearly universally within the Court—regarded as grossly unsatisfactory. The difficulty was that, less than a year before the argument in *Roe*, the Court had upheld the District of Columbia's abortion statute against a vagueness challenge after construing it to include substantive criteria quite similar to those in the Georgia statute. And, how could the even more restrictive Texas statute be unconstitutionally vague if the District of Columbia statute (and by inference the similar Georgia one) wasn't? Justice Byron White circulated a draft dissent that was regarded as devastating in making this point.

Reading Justice Blackmun's draft opinion and Justice White's draft dissent twenty years later, I concluded that Justice Blackmun's draft wasn't nearly as bad as people thought at the time. Or, put another way, the criteria people used to evaluate the draft apparently were simply *different* from the ones I brought to the opinion twenty years later. And yet, if those *were* the evaluative criteria people had, they (we) could not have been misapplying them. The legal materials available in 1972, that is, *defined* what a good legal argument was (then). It seems to me that we (today) ought to entertain the possibility that opinions that we draft today would in 1973 have seemed quite strange, resting on assumptions about the legal culture that had not yet developed. Again, to put the point another way, we ought to entertain the possibility that opinions not written in 1973 might fall outside the set of professionally respectable opinions according to the criteria of respectability present in 1973. My re-presentation of Justice Douglas's opinion is designed in part to raise that possibility.

Here I have in mind specifically the intimations in many efforts to revise *Roe* that considerations of woman's equality ought to play a significant role in the decision. The Court had barely begun to recognize women's equality interests as constitutionally significant, and I suspect that a draft opinion that gave substantial weight to equality interests would have been derided nearly as strenuously as Justice Blackmun's vagueness opinion was. The Court in 1973 couldn't muster a majority for a rule that statutes that use gender as a classification should be given particularly careful examination (*Frontiero v. Richardson*), and it hasn't even yet done so as to laws that have a disparate adverse impact on women, a major theme in the gender-based defense of *Roe*'s outcome. "Opinions" that use materials available in 1973 to support a women's-equality theory for *Roe*'s outcome would have been regarded in 1973 as outside the bounds of professional respectability—as, indeed, were the advocates who were actually making such arguments.

My third observation also involves the constraints on the opinions as they developed in 1973. The prevailing historical account of how the opinions developed is this. Justice Blackmun's second version abandoned the vagueness argument and developed the privacy one that ultimately prevailed. The draft of this version divided pregnancy into two stages. Before fetal viability states had no power to regulate abortions, and after viability they could regulate it fully, to the point of making it a crime to perform an abortion after viability. (The draft may not have said this quite so specifically, but that was its clear import.) Again, according to the standard historical account, as a law clerk, I was bothered by the rigidity of this distinction and persuaded Justice Marshall to send a letter to Justice Blackmun. That letter, which I drafted, noted essentially policy-based concerns about the line Justice Blackmun drew. As pregnancy proceeded, the medical risks to women of abortions increased. Even before the point of fetal viability, some abortion procedures might be justifiably regulated to ensure that those risks were minimized. But, previability regulation couldn't be too severe. The reason, according to Justice Marshall's (my?) letter, was that many women, particularly young women in distressed circumstances, might deny to themselves and everyone else that they were pregnant until their pregnancies were reasonably well advanced. Justice Blackmun's all-or-nothing approach didn't seem to allow for the sensible policy response of allowing regulation in the service of the woman's medical interests at some point before fetal viability. Responding to the letter, Justice Blackmun revised his opinion, giving us its final form and the division of pregnancy into three, not two, stages.

So the story goes. I remember some details differently. I did draft the letter, and Justice Marshall did send it, and after receiving the letter Justice Blackmun did revise his opinion. But, my recollection is that, within Justice Marshall's chambers, it was the Justice himself who raised concerns about the rigidity of the draft we were working with and specifically adverted to the situation of the young women who denied that they were pregnant. Further, I recall—and there are hints in the documentary record —that Justices William Brennan and Potter Stewart had raised similar concerns with Justice Blackmun. Attributing Justice Blackmun's revisions to Justice Marshall's letter, or to me, seems to me to overstate the importance of the letter, and certainly of my personal role.

Even more, it seems to me that the concerns the Justices expressed are best understood as based on constitutional rather than policy concerns. The structure of the response to Justice Blackmun's draft was that, while it acknowledged an asserted state interest in preserving the possibility that a fetus would become a (full) person, it did not acknowledge a state interest in protecting the woman's health against unjustified risks. The viability line was Justice Blackmun's accommodation of the woman's interest with the state's interest in preserving the potential of life, as the opinion put it. That line, though, did not allow regulation in the interest of the woman's health before viability. Once Justice Blackmun was persuaded that the state had such an interest, the trimester scheme he developed followed quite naturally. The risks to the woman's health from abortion procedures increased as pregnancy advanced, and just as the state's interest in preserving potential life eventually overcame the woman's interest, so too would the state's interest in protecting the woman's health. Where to draw the lines? Some degree of arbitrariness was inevitable, but doctors themselves thought in terms of the trimesters of pregnancy. Once the justices had moved from acknowledging one state interest to acknowledging two, dividing pregnancy into three stages rather than two made sense. The trimester distinction replaced the viability line in the ultimate opinion.

My point here is not simply to correct the story historians have come to tell; after all, I am relying on my recollections, which may be inaccurate (and shaped by various contemporary concerns, rather than—or in addition to—the facts themselves). It is in addition to suggest that some of the features of *Roe* and *Doe* that seem questionable today seemed quite natural then. Given the constitutional concerns as the justices saw them, the structure of the opinions was either entirely sensible or even inevitable.

My appropriation of Justice Douglas's opinion is thus designed to raise several questions. How could those men (the gender here is one of the points) actually have done anything different? And, what's the point of imagining that they could have produced opinions other than the ones they actually did? Perhaps the conceit is that we—the folks contributing to this collection—can do better. But, of course, we are academics, not judges, and we have lived through thirty years of social, cultural, political, and legal (if there are differences among these) experience since then. I have no idea, and I think my colleagues have no idea, what constraints we would face were we to be in a position to write real opinions in a real abortion case. And, to make an obvious point, the political coloration of the contributors to this collection is such that most of us are unlikely in the extreme to be in a position to do so. So—and this is a serious question —what's the point of the exercise?

Robin West

The specific arguments for the unconstitutionality of abortion laws put forward in the first two parts of this opinion were not developed at the time of *Roe*. A closely related argument regarding the *morality* of abortion decisions was put forward around the time *Roe v. Wade* was litigated, in Professor Judith Jarvis Thompson's classic article, "A Defense of Abortion," which appeared in the *Journal of Philosophy and Public Affairs.* 1 *Phil. & Pub. Aff.* 47 (1971). A few years later, the basic argument I propose toward the end of this opinion, that the criminalization of abortion constitutes a violation of the equal protection clause because it imposes obligations of good samaritanism unmatched by any obligation imposed by our legal regime, was argued at length by Donald H. Regan, in "Rewriting *Roe v. Wade,*" 77 *Mich. L. Rev.* 1569 (1978–1979). Most recently, and I think persuasively, Eileen McDonagh has carried this deeply liberal argument for abortion rights forward in her groundbreaking book, *Breaking the Abortion Deadlock: From Choice to Consent* (1996). Beginning with the same basic insight as Regan and Thompson, Professor McDonagh goes on to present the important claim that not only is criminalization of abortion a violation of equal protection on these grounds, but also the failure of the state to fund safe abortions for poor women unable to afford them is unconstitutional. The arguments in this fantastical opinion draw heavily from her insights.

Likewise, the potential unconstitutionality of the common law's marital rape exemption was not actively considered anywhere, at the time of *Roe v. Wade,* so the possibility that laws that attribute different consequences on the basis of whether the pregnancy was the result of a rape, and hence marital rape, might themselves be unconstitutional, could not have been made at the time of *Roe.* Since *Roe,* in the 1980s and 1990s, most states did reform their rape law so as to abolish at least some part of the marital rape exemption, some citing federal constitutional grounds for doing so. Georgia was in fact in the foreground of this development. The Supreme Court of Georgia, in *Warren v. State,* 336 S.E.2d 221, a progressive 1985 decision, held that the common law's marital rape exemption violated the Georgia constitution and for that reason, as well as others, could not be construed as a part of the Georgia law of rape, and the Georgia legislature, in 1996, amended its rape law so as to explicitly disavow the marital rape exemption. Ga. Code Ann. § 16-6-1 (1996). Again, this development, under way by the early 1980s, was not visibly on the horizon in the late 1960s or early

1970s, by anyone other than rape law reformers. Virtually all states at that time embraced some version of the common law "marital rape exemption," by explicitly defining rape so as to exclude wives (the Model Penal Code took this route), by enacting separate and less punitive regimes for sexual violence within families, or by simply following the common law tradition. For a thorough history of both nineteenth- and twentieth-century feminist movements' efforts to abolish the marital rape exemption, see Jill Elaine Hasday, "Contest and Consent: A Legal History of Marital Rape," 88 *Cal. L. Rev.* 1373 (2000). More generally, no court or commentator had explicitly addressed the connections between unwanted pregnancies and domestic violence—indeed, the very phrase "domestic violence" still struck many legal decision makers in courthouses or statehouses as either oxymoronic or comical. For histories of attempts by feminists and policy makers to criminalize domestic violence, see Reva Siegel, "'The Rule of Love': Wife Beating as Prerogative and Privacy," 105 *Yale Law Journal* 2117 (1996); Susan Schechter, *Women and Male Violence: The Visions and Struggles of the Battered Women's Movement,* 20–24 (1982); and Linda Gordon, *Heroes of Their Own Lives: The Politics and History of Family Violence* (1988).

Like many commentators and like many contributors to this volume, I wish the actual Court in *Roe v. Wade* had employed an equal protection analysis rather than a privacy analysis in addressing the issues surrounding abortion. Unlike perhaps most contributors to this volume, however, I wish they had struck the statute on "classic" equal protection grounds that anti-abortion laws treat similarly situated persons differently, in a way that violates basic moral norms of decency. Of course pregnancy is different from other physical states, but that hardly renders the classic equal protection question inappropriate or inapplicable: the question, as always, could be or should be whether these laws that criminalize abortion wrongly treat women who are pregnant differently from other similarly situated—not identically situated—persons, and to that question I think the answer is a clear "yes." Of course, we must determine who and what is similarly situated, and of course, that requires normative judgments, but if we keep in mind the basis for this inquiry—whether the state is treating all citizens with equal dignity and respect—these questions are not unanswerable, nor are they invariably irrational or emotional. There is no reason this "classic," jurisprudential understanding of equal protection law has to be constrained by artificial and at bottom illogical inquiries about various categories: suspect classifications, levels of scrutiny, and the like. Had the

Court pressed this claim, it seems to me, it could have developed a body of equal protection law regarding not only pregnant women but also women generally that might have been deeper and more consistent with the judicial role and less preemptive than the various "antisubordination" equality arguments that have been put forward on behalf of abortion rights since Roe. It might also have been able to produce a jurisprudence that would not invite the range of problems—constitutional and political—that have plagued attempts of the court and others to locate rights to abortion in the Court's privacy jurisprudence. And, as I argue in the text, it might also avoid the very real twin dangers of truncating a full and congressional exploration of the constitutional ramifications of the subordination of women within the traditional family and, even worse, of legitimating that subordination through the expediency of providing a legal means for avoiding it.

Methodologically, the Court could have taken a different route, in the abortion and reproduction cases, than it chose: it might have signaled to the country and to Congress that Congress has a central role to play in implementing the grand and far-reaching promises of the Fourteenth Amendment and restrained its own rhetorical impulses so as to not impede that role. Had it done so, perhaps we would have a Congress more actively engaged in the work of legislating toward the end of liberty and equality, no matter how defined, and a Court less paranoically inclined to strike back every time Congress attempts to do so. Even more ambitiously, had it done so, we might have a body of "equal protection legislation" authored and implemented by Congress, pursuant to its section 5 powers, that would reflect the possible "antisubordinationist" meanings of that phrase suggested by Professors Balkin and Siegel in their draft opinions. I believe not only that Congress, not the Court, is the *appropriate* branch of government to develop such a body of legislative law under the Fourteenth Amendment but that it is also the *only* branch of government that could possibly do so. The egalitarian and antisubordinationist interpretation of the Clause elaborated in different ways by Siegel, Balkin, Allen, and Rubenfeld, all of which I fully endorse, will be realized only through legislation, not through adjudication. Congress, not the Courts, must take the lead in delineating the content of the Equal Protection Clause so understood.

Finally, with all due respect to Mark Tushnet, I too have some sense of the oddity of this entire project: I can't possibly project myself imaginatively onto the Court at the time *Roe* was decided, or any other time. Nor can I imagine the Supreme Court of that day deciding the case in the way already suggested: in the late 1960s and early 1970s, domestic violence was still for the most part treated as material for late-night television comics, there was no movement afoot to challenge the constitutionality of marital rape laws, and there was little or no concern on the Court's part about not treading on Congress's Section 5 powers. But Mark's alternative conception of time travel—If "I" had been on the Court, "I" would have been one of "them"—also reads like metaphysical nonsense: who's the "I" that would be one of "them"? Why does he imagine "he" would have been Douglas, rather than Blackmun? *Invasion of the Body Snatchers* is hardly more realistic or plausible than *Back to the Future*. I took the assignment question to be "What do you wish the Court had done, with benefit of hindsight?" rather than how the Court might have better decided the opinion, or how I might have written the opinion had I been on the Court at the time. My answer is that I wish that the Justices had written a decision more tied to basic constitutional principles, that they'd focused on the clearly unconstitutional facet of the phenomenon of patriarchy but that has *never* been held to be such by the Supreme Court, and that is the state's failure to protect women from sexual violence within the family and from the consequences of that violence, including unwanted pregnancies, and that they had planted the seeds of a jurisprudence that would accommodate and welcome multiple, and even conflicting, constitutional interpretations and aspirations. Contrary to the fear of interpretive uncertainty at the heart of Justice O'Connor's decision in *Casey*, it seems to me that we can live with a constitutionally complex world with multiple actors, interpreters, and meanings. I think we all would be better off for it if the Court had long ago signaled its willingness to participate in one.

NOTES

1. Akinrinola Bankole, Susheela Singh, and Taylor Haas, "Reasons Why Women Have Induced Abortions: Evidence from 27 Countries," 24 *International Family Planning Perspectives* 117 (1998) citing statistics from Aida Torres and Jacqueline Darroch Forrest, "Why Do Women Have Abortions?" 20 *Family Planning Perspectives* 169 (July-August 1988).

2. John M. Thorp et al., "Long-Term Physical and Psychological Health Consequences of Induced Abortion: Review of the Evidence," 58 *Obstetrical & Gynecological Survey* 67 (2003).

3. See id.; V. Beral et al., "Does Pregnancy Protect against Ovarian Cancer?," *The Lancet* (May 20, 1978) at 1083 ("pregnancy—or some component of the child-bearing process—protects directly against ovarian cancer"); and G. Albrektsen et al., "Is the Risk of Cancer of the Corpus Uteri Reduced by a Recent Pregnancy? A Prospective Study of 765, 756 Norwegian Women," 61 *Int'l. J. Cancer* 485 (1995).

4. The photo and story can be found at "Doctors Give Little One a Hand," *The Tennessean* (Sept. 7, 1999) available at http://www.tennessean.com/sii/99/09/07/fetus07.shtml.

5. Andrea J. Sedlak and Diane D. Broadhurst, *Third National Incidence Study of Child Abuse and Neglect* (1996).

6. Liza Mundy, "A World of Their Own," *Washington Post*, March 31, 2002, p. W22.

7. *McCorvey v. Hill,* 385 F. 3d 846, 852–53 (5th Cir. 2004) (Jones, J., concurring) available at http://www.ca5.uscourts.gov/opinions/pub/03/03-10711-CV0.wpd.pdf.

8. See Jed Rubenfeld, "The Right of Privacy," 102 *Harv. L. Rev.* 737 (1989); Jed Rubenfeld, "On the Legal Status of the Proposition That 'Life Begins at Conception,'" 43 *Stan. L. Rev.* 599 (1991).

9. *Doe v. Bolton,* 410 U.S. 179, 221 (1973) (White, J., dissenting) (opinion applicable to *Roe* and *Doe*) (criticizing the Court for taking the position that "the Constitution of the United States values the convenience, whim, or caprice of the putative mother more than the life or potential life of the fetus").

10. See, e.g., Joseph W. Dellapenna, "Nor Piety Nor Wit: The Supreme Court on Abortion," 6 *Colum. Hum. Rts. L. Rev.* 379, 408 (1974–1975). Some have continued to argue for this view. See Donald Hope, "The Hand as Emblem of Human Identity: A Solution to the Abortion Controversy Based on Science and Reason," 32 *U. Tol. L. Rev.* 205, 216–17 (2001); John M. Goldenring, "The Brain-Life Theory: Towards a Consistent Biological Definition of Humanness," 11 *J. Med. Ethics* 198, 200 (1985).

11. See, e.g., Raymond D. Adams & Maurice Victor, *Principles of Neurology* 458 (4th ed. 1989) (synaptogenesis in cerebral cortex begins between 150th and 180th day); N. Herschkowitz, "Brain Development in the Fetus, Neonate, and Infant," 54 *Bio. Neonate* 1, 10 (1988) ("The earliest synapses within the cortical plate are seen between 19 and 23 weeks gestation."); J. Korein, "Ontogenesis of the Fetal Nervous System: The Onset of Brain Life," 22 *Transplantation Proc.* 982, 983 (1990) (cortical formation occurs and brain life begins no earlier than week 20); Cherry Thompson, "Cortical Activity in Behavioural Development," in *Brain and Behavioural Development* 131, 136 (J. Dickerson & H. McGurk, eds. 1982) (electrical activity "is random, irregular, unresponsive and dissociated" in the fetal cerebral cortex until at least the twenty-second week of gestation). For more, see John R. Hughes, *EEG in Clinical Practice* 69–70 (1982); K. J. S. Anand & P. R. Hickey, "Pain and Its Effects in the Human Neonate and Fetus," 317 *New Eng. J. Med.* 1321, 1322 (1987); D. Gareth Jones, "Brain Birth and Personal Identity," 15 *J. Med. Ethics* 173, 177 (1989); Gary B.

Gertler, Note, "Brain Birth: A Proposal for Defining When a Fetus is Entitled to Human Life Status," 59 *S. Cal. L. Rev.* 1061 (1986). For the view that disanalogies between brain birth and brain death render the former concept problematic, see D. Gareth Jones, "The Problematic Symmetry Between Brain Birth and Brain Death," 24 *J. Med. Ethics* 237 (1998).

12. 539 U.S. 558 (2003) (striking down a Texas statute criminalizing homosexual sodomy).

13. Immediately after *Roe* was decided, Justice Brennan authored his pathbreaking plurality opinion in *Frontiero v. Richardson,* 411 U.S. 677 (1973), making the case for heightened scrutiny of sex-based state action under the Fourteenth Amendment; the following year, the Court handed down *Geduldig v. Aeillo,* 417 U.S. 484 (1974), holding that the regulation of pregnant women was not sex-based state action within the meaning of the Fourteenth Amendment's Equal Protection Clause.

14. See Reva B. Siegel, "Reasoning from the Body: An Historical Perspective on Abortion Regulation and Questions of Equal Protection," 44 *Stan. L. Rev.* 261 (1992) (demonstrating, through an analysis of the nineteenth-century campaign to criminalize abortion, the kinds of gender-, race-, and class-based concerns that can shape "physiological" arguments for prohibiting the practice).

15. For an account of the equal citizenship claims of the second-wave women's movement as they focused on the family, see Robert C. Post & Reva B. Siegel, "Legislative Constitutionalism and Section Five Power: Policentric Interpretation of the Family and Medical Leave Act," 112 *Yale L.J.* 1943, 1984–2020 (2003). This account also demonstrates how the second-wave women's movement drew upon the Nineteenth Amendment in the period before enactment of the ERA and litigating successes under the Fourteenth Amendment. The role that the Nineteenth Amendment played as midwife to modern sex equality claims has been completely erased in equal protection jurisprudence. See Reva B. Siegel, "She the People: The Nineteenth Amendment, Sex Equality, Federalism, and the Family," 115 *Harv. L. Rev.* 947, 953–65 (2002).

The Constitution of the United States of America
Selected Provisions

Amendment I (1791)

Congress shall make no law respecting an establishment of religion, or prohibiting the free exercise thereof; or abridging the freedom of speech, or of the press; or the right of the people peaceably to assemble, and to petition the Government for a redress of grievances.

Amendment II (1791)

A well-regulated militia, being necessary to the security of a free State, the right of the people to keep and bear arms, shall not be infringed.

Amendment III (1791)

No soldier shall, in time of peace be quartered in any house, without the consent of the owner, nor in time of war, but in a manner to be prescribed by law.

Amendment IV (1791)

The right of the people to be secure in their persons, houses, papers, and effects, against unreasonable searches and seizures, shall not be violated, and no warrants shall issue, but upon probable cause, supported by oath or affirmation, and particularly describing the place to be searched, and the persons or things to be seized.

Amendment V (1791)

No person shall be held to answer for a capital, or otherwise infamous crime, unless on a presentment or indictment of a Grand Jury, except in cases arising in the land or naval forces, or in the militia, when in actual service in time of war or public danger; nor shall any person be subject for the same offense to be twice put in jeopardy of life or limb; nor shall be compelled in any criminal case to be a witness against himself, nor be deprived of life, liberty, or property, without due process of law; nor shall private property be taken for public use without just compensation.

Amendment VI (1791)

In all criminal prosecutions, the accused shall enjoy the right to a speedy and public trial, by an impartial jury of the State and district wherein the crime shall have been committed, which district shall have been previously ascertained by law, and to be informed of the nature and cause of the accusation; to be confronted with the witnesses against him; to have compulsory process for obtaining witnesses in his favor, and to have the assistance of counsel for his defense.

Amendment VII (1791)

In suits at common law, where the value in controversy shall exceed twenty dollars, the right of trial by jury shall be preserved, and no fact tried by a jury shall be otherwise reexamined in any court of the United States, than according to the rules of the common law.

Amendment VIII (1791)

Excessive bail shall not be required, nor excessive fines imposed, nor cruel and unusual punishments inflicted.

Amendment IX (1791)

The enumeration in the Constitution, of certain rights, shall not be construed to deny or disparage others retained by the people.

Amendment X (1791)

The powers not delegated to the United States by the Constitution, nor prohibited by it to the States, are reserved to the States respectively, or to the people.

Amendment XIII (1865)

1. Neither slavery nor involuntary servitude, except as a punishment for crime whereof the party shall have been duly convicted, shall exist within the United States, or any place subject to their jurisdiction.

2. Congress shall have power to enforce this article by appropriate legislation.

Amendment XIV (1868)

1. All persons born or naturalized in the United States, and subject to the jurisdiction thereof, are citizens of the United States and of the State wherein they reside. No State shall make or enforce any law which shall abridge the privileges or immunities of citizens of the United States; nor shall any State deprive any person of life, liberty, or property, without due process of law; nor to deny to any person within its jurisdiction the equal protection of the laws.

2. Representatives shall be apportioned among the several States according to their respective numbers, counting the whole number of persons in each State, excluding Indians not taxed. But when the right to vote at any election for the choice of Electors for President and Vice-President of the United States, Representatives in Congress, the executive and judicial officers of a State, or the members of the legislature thereof, is denied to any

of the male inhabitants of such State, being twenty-one years of age, and citizens of the United States, or in any way abridged, except for participation in rebellion, or other crime, the basis of representation therein shall be reduced in the proportion which the number of such male citizens shall bear to the whole number of male citizens twenty-one years of age in such State.

3. No person shall be a Senator or Representative in Congress, or Elector of President and Vice-President, or hold any office, civil or military, under the United States, or under any State, who, having previously taken an oath, as a member of Congress, or as an officer of the United States, or as a member of any State Legislature, or as an executive or judicial officer of any State, to support the Constitution of the United States, shall have engaged in insurrection or rebellion against the same, or given aid or comfort to the enemies thereof. But Congress may by a vote of two-thirds of each House, remove such disability.

4. The validity of the public debt of the United States, authorized by law, including debts incurred for payment of pensions and bounties for services in suppressing insurrection or rebellion, shall not be questioned. But neither the United States nor any State shall assume or pay any debt or obligation incurred in aid of insurrection or rebellion against the United States, or any claim for the loss or emancipation of any slave; but all such debts, obligations and claims shall be held illegal and void.

5. The Congress shall have the power to enforce, by appropriate legislation, the provisions of this article.

Amendment XV (1870)

1. The right of citizens of the United States to vote shall not be denied or abridged by the United States or by any State on account of race, color, or previous condition of servitude.

2. The Congress shall have the power to enforce this article by appropriate legislation.

Amendment XIX (1920)

1. The right of citizens of the United States to vote shall not be denied or abridged by the United States or by any State on account of sex.

2. Congress shall have power to enforce this article by appropriate legislation.

Roe v. Wade: A Selected Bibliography

The literature on *Roe v. Wade* is enormous. A comprehensive bibliography would take many pages. Instead, I offer a list of works consulted in preparing this book, plus a basic list of works (1) on *Roe* itself; (2) on the history of contraception and abortion; (3) on theories of fundamental rights and sex equality; (4) on constitutional interpretation; and (5) on constitutional theory generally.

ABC News–*Washington Post*. Poll. "Public Support for Abortion Depends on Why It's Done," January 21, 2003, available at http://abcnews.go.com/images/pdf/909a2Abortion.pdf.

Abortion Access Project. "Fact Sheet: The Shortage of Abortion Providers," available at http://abortionaccess.org/AAP/publica_resources/fact_sheets/shortage_provider.htm.

Ackerman, Bruce. *We the People: Foundations*. Cambridge, MA: Harvard Univ. Press, 1991.

Alan Guttmacher Institute. "Facts in Brief: Induced Abortion," available at http://www.guttmacher.org/pubs/fb_induced_abortion.html.

———. "State Policies in Brief," available at http://www.guttmacher.org/pubs/spib.html.

Allen, Anita L. *Uneasy Access: Privacy for Women in a Free Society*. Totowa, NJ: Rowman & Littlefield, 1988.

———. "The Proposed Equal Protection Fix for Abortion Law: Reflections on Citizenship, Gender and the Constitution." 18 *Harvard Journal of Law and Public Policy* 419 (1995).

———. *Why Privacy Isn't Everything: Feminist Reflections on Personal Accountability*. Totowa, NJ: Rowman & Littlefield, 2003.

Amar, Akhil Reed. *The Bill of Rights: Creation and Reconstruction*. New Haven: Yale Univ. Press 1998.

———. "Intratextualism." 112 *Harv. L. Rev.* 749 (1999).

———. "The Supreme Court, 1999 Term. Foreword: The Document and the Doctrine." 114 *Harv. L. Rev.* 26 (2000).

Arkes, Hadley. *First Things: An Inquiry into the First Principles of Morals and Justice*. Princeton: Princeton Univ. Press, 1986.

Balkin, Jack M., ed. *What* Brown v. Board of Education *Should Have Said: The*

Nation's Top Legal Experts Rewrite America's Landmark Civil Rights Decision. New York: N.Y.U. Press, 2001.

Balkin, Jack M., and Levinson, Sanford. "Understanding the Constitutional Revolution." 87 *U. Va. L. Rev.* 1089 (2001).

Blasi, Vincent, ed. *The Burger Court: The Counter-Revolution That Wasn't.* New Haven: Yale Univ. Press, 1983.

Bork, Robert H. *The Tempting of America: The Political Seduction of the Law.* New York: Free Press, 1989.

Brest, Paul, Levinson, Sanford, Balkin, J. M., and Amar, Akhil Reed. *Processes of Constitutional Decisionmaking: Cases and Materials.* 4th ed. New York: Aspen, 2000.

Bronner, Ethan. *Battle for Justice: How the Bork Nomination Shook America.* New York: W. W. Norton, 1989.

CNN/*Time.* Poll on *Roe v. Wade* conducted by Harris Interactive, July 17–18, 2001, available at http://www.pollingreport.com/Court.htm.

Craig, Barbara Hinkson, and O'Brien, David M. *Abortion and American Politics.* Chatham, NJ: Chatham House, 1993.

Critchlow, Donald T. *The Politics of Abortion and Birth Control in Historical Perspective.* University Park: Pennsylvania State Univ. Press, 1996.

Cott, Nancy. *The Grounding of Modern Feminism.* New Haven: Yale Univ. Press, 1987.

Devins, Neal. *Shaping Constitutional Values.* Baltimore: Johns Hopkins Univ. Press, 1996.

Devins, Neal, with Watson, Wendy L. *Federal Abortion Politics: A Documentary History.* 5 vols. New York: Garland, 1995.

Dickson, Del, ed. *The Supreme Court in Conference (1940–1985): The Private Discussions behind Nearly 300 Supreme Court Opinions.* New York: Oxford Univ. Press, 2001.

Dunne, Finley Peter. *Mr. Dooley at His Best.* Elmer Ellis ed. New York: Charles Scribner's Sons, 1938.

Dworkin, Ronald. *Life's Dominion: An Argument about Abortion and Euthanasia.* New York: Alfred A. Knopf, 1993.

Ely, John Hart. "The Wages of Crying Wolf: A Comment on *Roe v. Wade.*" 82 *Yale L.J.* 920 (1973).

———. *Democracy and Distrust: A Theory of Judicial Review.* Cambridge, MA: Harvard Univ. Press, 1980.

Finer, Lawrence B., and Henshaw, Stanley K. "Abortion Incidence and Services in the United States, 2000." *Family Planning Perspectives,* 35:1 (Jan.-Feb. 2003) 6–15 (available at http://www.agi-usa.org/pubs/journals/3500603.pdf).

———. "The Accessibility of Abortion Services in the United States." *Family Planning Perspectives,* 35:1 (Jan.-Feb. 2003): 16–24 (available at http://www.agi-usa.org/pubs/journals/3501603.pdf).

Fried, Charles. *Order and Law: Arguing the Reagan Revolution—A Firsthand Account.* New York: Simon & Schuster, 1991.

Fried, Marlene. "Abortion in the United States." *Health and Human Rights* 4 (2000): 174–94.

Friedman, Leon, ed. *The Supreme Court Confronts Abortion: The Briefs, Argument, and Decision in* Planned Parenthood v. Casey. New York: Farrar, Straus & Giroux, 1993.

Gans Epner, Janet E., Jonas, Harry S., and Seckinger, Daniel L. "Late-term Abortion." *Journal of the American Medical Association* 280 (Aug. 26, 1998): 724–29 (available at http://eileen.250x.com/Main/PBAinfo/jsc80006.htm).

Garrow, David J. "Justice Souter Emerges," *New York Times,* September 25, 1994, Sec. 6, p. 1.

———. *Liberty and Sexuality: The Right to Privacy and the Making of* Roe v. Wade. New York: Macmillan, 1994.

———. "Abortion before and after *Roe v. Wade*: An Historical Perspective," 62 *Alb. L. Rev.* 833 (1999).

Gilman, Howard. "Constitutional Law as Partisan Entrenchment" (available at http://www.yale.edu/law/ltw/papers/ltw-gillman.pdf).

———. "How Political Parties Can Use the Courts to Advance Their Agendas: Federal Courts in the United States, 1875–1891." *American Political Science Review* 96 (2002): 511–24.

Ginsburg, Faye D. *Connected Lives: The Abortion Debate in an American Community.* Berkeley: Univ. of California Press, 1980.

Ginsburg, Ruth Bader. "Some Thoughts on Autonomy and Equality in Relation to *Roe v. Wade.*" 63 *N.C. L. Rev.* 375 (1985).

———. "Speaking in a Judicial Voice." 67 *N.Y.U.L. Rev.* 1185 (1992).

Glendon, Mary Ann. *Abortion and Divorce in Western Law: American Failures, European Challenges.* Cambridge, MA: Harvard Univ. Press, 1987.

———. *Rights Talk.* New York: Free Press, 1991.

Gordon, Linda. *The Moral Property of Women: A History of Birth Control Politics in America.* Rev. ed. Urbana: Univ. of Illinois Press, 2002.

Gordon, Linda. *Woman's Body, Woman's Right.* Rev. ed. New York: Penguin, 1990.

Gorney, Cynthia. *Articles of Faith: A Frontline History of the Abortion Wars.* New York: Simon & Schuster, 2000.

Graber, Mark A. "The Nonmajoritarian Difficulty: Legislative Deference to the Judiciary." 7 *Studies in American Political Development* 35 (1993).

———. *Rethinking Abortion: Equal Choice, the Constitution, and Reproductive Politics.* Princeton: Princeton Univ. Press, 1996.

Henshaw, Stanley K. "Factors Hindering Access to Abortion Services." *Family Planning Perspectives* 27:2 (Mar.-Apr. 1995): 54–59 (available at http://www.agi-usa.org/pubs/journals/2705495.pdf).

Henshaw, Stanley K., and Host, Katheryn. "Abortion Patients in 1994–95; Characteristics and Contraceptive Use." *Family Planning Perspectives* 28:4 (July-Aug. 1996): 140–47, 158 (available at http://www.agi-usa.org/pubs/journals/2814096 .pdf).

Hull, N. E. H., and Hoffer, Peter Charles. Roe v. Wade: *The Abortion Rights Controversy in American History.* Lawrence: Univ. Press of Kansas, 2001.

Irons, Peter, and Stephanie Guitton, eds., *May It Please the Court.* New York: New Press, 1993.

Jones, Rachel K., Darroch, Jacqueline E., and Henshaw, Stanley K. "Contraceptive Use among U.S. Women Having Abortions in 2000–2001." *Perspectives on Sexual and Reproductive Health,* 34(6) (2002): 294–303 (available at http://www.agi-usa.org/pubs/journals/3429402.pdf).

Justice Harry A. Blackmun Oral History Project (1995).

Karst, Kenneth, L. "The Supreme Court, 1976 Term—Foreword: Equal Citizenship under the Fourteenth Amendment." 91 *Harv. L. Rev.* 1 (1977).

———. "Woman's Constitution," 1984 *Duke L.J.* 447 (1984).

———. *Belonging to America: Equal Citizenship and the Constitution.* New Haven: Yale Univ. Press, 1989.

Kennedy, David M. *Birth Control in America: The Career of Margaret Sanger.* New Haven: Yale Univ. Press, 1970.

Kluger, Richard. *Simple Justice: The History of* Brown v. Board of Education *and Black America's Struggle for Equality.* New York: Alfred A. Knopf, 1975.

Koppelman, Andrew. "Forced Labor: A Thirteenth Amendment Defense of Abortion." 84 *Nw. U.L. Rev.* 480, 486 (1990).

Kurland, Philip B., and Casper, Gerhard, eds. *Landmark Briefs and Arguments of the Supreme Court of the United States: Constitutional Law*—Roe v. Wade (1973). Frederick, MD: University Publications of America, 1990.

Law, Sylvia A. "Rethinking Sex and the Constitution." 132 *U. Pa. L. Rev.* 955 (1984).

Levinson, Sanford. "Redefining the Center: Liberal Decisions from a Conservative Court." *Village Voice* (July 2–8, 2003) (available at http://www.villagevoice.com/ issues/0327/levinson.php).

Luker, Kristin. *Abortion and the Politics of Motherhood.* Berkeley: Univ. of California Press, 1984.

MacKinnon, Catharine A. *Feminism Unmodified: Discourses on Life and Law.* Cambridge, MA: Harvard Univ. Press, 1987.

———. "Reflections on Sex Equality under Law." 100 *Yale L.J.* 1281 (1991).

McConnell, Michael W. "How Not to Promote Serious Deliberation about Abortion." 58 *U. Chi. L. Rev.* 1181 (1991).

———. "Religion and the Search for a Principled Middle Ground on Abortion." 92 *Mich. L. Rev.* 1893 (1994).

———. "The Selective Funding Problem: Abortions and Religious Schools." 104 *Harv. L. Rev.* 989 (1991).

McDonagh, Eileen. *Breaking the Abortion Deadlock: From Choice to Consent.* New York: Oxford Univ. Press, 1996.

Mohr, James C. *Abortion in America: The Origins and Evolution of National Policy, 1800–1900.* New York: Oxford Univ. Press, 1978.

NARAL Pro-Choice America Web site. "Clinic Violence and Intimidation," available at http://www.naral.org/facts/terrorism.cfm.

NARAL Pro-Choice America. *Who Decides? A State-by-State Review of Abortion and Reproductive Rights.* 12th ed. Washington, DC: NARAL, 2003.

National Abortion Federation Web site. "Violence Statistics," available at http://www.prochoice.org.

———. "History of Violence," available at http://www.prochoice.org.

Nomination of Judge Clarence Thomas to Be Associate Justice of the Supreme Court of the United States: Hearings before the Comm. on the Judiciary, United States Senate, 102d Cong., 1st Sess., pt. 1 (1991).

O'Brien, David. *Storm Center: The Supreme Court in American Politics.* 6th ed. New York: W. W. Norton, 2003.

Paulsen, Michael Stokes. "Abrogating *Stare Decisis* by Statute: May Congress Remove the Precedential Effect of *Roe* and *Casey*?" 109 *Yale L.J.* 1535 (2000).

———. "Captain James T. Kirk and the Enterprise of Constitutional Interpretation: Some Modest Proposals from the Twenty-Third Century." 59 *Alb. L. Rev.* 671 (1995).

———. "The Worst Constitutional Decision of All Time." 78 *Notre Dame L. Rev.* 995 (2003).

Paulsen, Michael Stokes, & Rosen, Daniel N. "*Brown, Casey*-Style: The Shocking First Draft of the Segregation Opinion." 69 *N.Y.U. L. Rev.* 1287 (1994).

Perry, Michael J. "Abortion, the Public Morals, and the Police Power: The Ethical Function of Substantive Due Process." 23 *UCLA L. Rev.* 689 (1976).

———. *Morality, Politics, and Law.* New York: Oxford Univ. Press, 1988.

———. *We the People: The Fourteenth Amendment and the Supreme Court.* New York: Oxford Univ. Press, 1999.

Powe, Lucas A. *The Warren Court and American Politics.* Cambridge, MA: Harvard Univ. Press, 2000.

Regan, Donald H. "Rewriting *Roe v. Wade.*" 77 *Mich. L. Rev.* 1569 (1979).

Rosen, Jeffrey. *The Unwanted Gaze: The Destruction of Privacy in America.* New York: Random House, 2000.

Rosenberg, Gerald N. *The Hollow Hope: Can Courts Bring about Social Change?* Chicago: Univ. of Chicago Press, 1991.

Rubenfeld, Jed. "The Right of Privacy." 102 *Harv. L. Rev.* 737 (1989).

———. "On the Legal Status of the Proposition That 'Life Begins at Conception.'" 43 *Stan. L. Rev.* 599 (1991).

———. *Freedom and Time: A Theory of Constitutional Self-Government.* New Haven: Yale Univ. Press, 2001.

Saletan, William. *Bearing Right: How Conservatives Won the Abortion Wars.* Berkeley: Univ. of California Press, 2003.

Sandel, Michael J. "Moral Argument and Liberal Toleration: Abortion and Homosexuality." 77 *Cal. L. Rev.* 521 (1989).

Savage, David G. *Turning Right: The Making of the Rehnquist Supreme Court.* New York: John Wiley, 1992.

Schwartz, Bernard. *The Unpublished Opinions of the Burger Court.* New York: Oxford Univ. Press, 1988.

———. *The Ascent of Pragmatism: The Burger Court in Action.* Reading, MA: Addison-Wesley, 1990.

Siegel, Reva B. "Reasoning from the Body: A Historical Perspective on Abortion Regulation and Questions of Equal Protection." 44 *Stan. L. Rev.* 261 (1992).

———. "Abortion as a Sex Equality Right: Its Basis in Feminist Theory." In Martha Fineman and Isabel Karpin, eds., *Mothers in Law: Feminist Theory and the Legal Regulation of Motherhood.* New York: Columbia Univ. Press, 1995.

———. "She the People: The Nineteenth Amendment, Sex Equality, Federalism, and the Family." 115 *Harv. L. Rev.* 947 (2002).

Simon, James F. *The Center Holds: The Power Struggle within the Rehnquist Court.* New York: Simon & Schuster, 1995.

Smith-Rosenberg, Carroll. *Disorderly Conduct: Visions of Gender in Victorian America.* New York: Alfred A. Knopf, 1985.

Strauss, David A. "Abortion, Toleration, and Moral Uncertainty." 1992 *Sup. Ct. Rev.* 1 (1993).

Sunstein, Cass R. "Neutrality in Constitutional Law (with Special Reference to Pornography, Abortion, and Surrogacy." 92 *Colum. L. Rev.* 1 (1992).

———. *The Partial Constitution.* Cambridge, MA: Harvard Univ. Press, 1993.

———. *One Case at a Time: Judicial Minimalism on the Supreme Court.* Cambridge, MA: Harvard Univ. Press, 1999.

———. *Designing Democracy: What Constitutions Do.* New York: Oxford Univ. Press, 2002.

Thompson, Judith Jarvis. *A Defense of Abortion.* 1 *Phil. & Pub. Aff.* 47 (1971).

Torres, Aida, and Forrest, Jacqueline Darroch. "Why Do Women Have Abortions?" *Family Planning Perspectives* 24(4) (1988): 169–76.

Tribe, Laurence H. "The Supreme Court: October 1972 Term. Foreword: Toward a Model of Roles in the Due Process of Life and Law." 87 *Harv. L. Rev.* 1 (1973).

———. *Abortion: The Clash of Absolutes.* New York: W. W. Norton, 1990.

Turkington, Richard C., Allen, Anita L., and Abbey, Edward L., eds. *Privacy Law: Cases and Materials.* 2nd ed. St. Paul, MN: West, 2002.

Tushnet, Mark. *Abortion: Constitutional Issues.* New York: Facts on File, 1995.

———. *The New Constitutional Order.* Princeton, NJ: Princeton Univ. Press, 2003.

Urofsky, Melvin I., with Urofsky, Philip E., eds. *The Douglas Letters: Selections from the Private Papers of Justice William O. Douglas*. Bethesda, MD: Adler & Adler, 1987.

Weddington, Sarah. *A Question of Choice*. New York: Penguin, 1992.

West, Robin. *Progressive Constitutionalism: Reconstructing the Fourteenth Amendment*. Durham, NC: Duke Univ. Press, 1994.

———. *Caring for Justice*. New York: New York Univ. Press. 1999.

———. *Re-Imagining Justice: Progressive Interpretations of Formal Equality, Rights, and the Rule of Law*. Burlington, VT: Ashgate Press, 2003.

Woodward, Bob, and Armstrong, Scott. *The Brethren: Inside the Supreme Court*. New York: Simon & Schuster, 1979.

Yalof, David. *Pursuit of Justices: Presidential Politics and the Selection of Supreme Court Nominees*. Chicago: Univ. of Chicago Press, 1999.

Yarbrough, Tinsley E. *The Rehnquist Court and the Constitution*. New York: Oxford Univ. Press, 2000.

1980 Republican Party platform, available at http://andrsn.stanford.edu/Abortion/Platform_Planks.html.

About the Contributors

Anita L. Allen is the Henry Silverman Professor of Law and Professor of Philosophy at the University of Pennsylvania Law School. She is the author of books including *The New Ethics: A Guided Tour of the 21st Century Moral Landscape* (Miramax, 2004); *Why Privacy Isn't Everything: Feminist Reflections on Accountability for Private Life* (Rowman & Littlefield, 2003); *Privacy Law* (West, 2002, with Richard Turkington); and *Uneasy Access: Privacy for Women in a Free Society* (Rowman and Littlefield, 1988). Professor Allen has been on the Board of the Family Planning Council of Philadelphia and is a past Chair of the Board of Planned Parenthood of Metropolitan Washington.

Akhil Reed Amar graduated from Yale College in 1980 and from Yale Law School in 1984. After clerking for Judge Stephen Breyer on the U.S. Court of Appeals for the First Circuit, he joined the Yale faculty in 1985, where he is now the Southmayd Professor of Law and Political Science. His books include *The Bill of Rights: Creation and Reconstruction* (Yale Univ. Press, 1998) and *Processes of Constitutional Decisionmaking* (co-edited with Paul Brest, Sanford Levinson, and J. M. Balkin) (4th edition, Aspen, 2000). He is currently at work on *America's Constitution: A Biography,* which will be published by Random House in 2005.

Jack M. Balkin is Knight Professor of Constitutional Law and the First Amendment at Yale Law School and the founder and director of Yale's Information Society Project, an interdisciplinary center devoted to the study of law and the new information technologies. His work ranges over many different fields, from theories of cultural evolution to legal and musical interpretation. His books include *The Laws of Change: I Ching and the Philosophy of Life* (Schocken, Press 2002); *What Brown v. Board of Education Should Have Said* (N.Y.U. Press, 2001); *Processes of Constitutional Decisionmaking* (co-edited with Paul Brest, Sanford

Levinson, and Akhil Reed Amar) (4th ed., Aspen, 2000); and *Cultural Software: A Theory of Ideology* (Yale Univ. Press, 1998).

Teresa Stanton Collett is a Professor of Law at the University of St. Thomas School of Law in Minneapolis, Minnesota, where she teaches bioethics. She has been active as both an academic and a practicing lawyer in the national debate on abortion. As a lawyer, she recently testified before both the U.S. Senate and House Judiciary Committees in favor of the Child Custody Protection Act, which would make it a federal crime to take a minor across state lines to avoid complying with state parental involvement laws related to abortion. She has authored numerous amicus briefs and was counsel of record for an amicus brief before the U.S. Supreme Court in *Stenberg v. Carhart,* 530 U.S. 914 (2000). Her brief was quoted extensively by Justices Thomas and Kennedy. She currently serves as special attorney general for the state of Oklahoma in defending its abortion liability law. She is the vice president of University Faculty for Life, a national multidisciplinary organization supporting scholarship on abortion, infanticide, and euthanasia. She is an elected member of the American Law Institute and the co-author of a textbook on lawyer's ethics and more than thirty professional articles on issues ranging from the vocation of women to the constitutionality of fetal pain legislation.

Michael Stokes Paulsen is the McKnight President Professor of Law and Public Policy, the Briggs & Morgan Professor of Law, and Associate Dean for Research Scholarship at the University of Minnesota Law School, where he has taught since 1991. He is a 1981 graduate of Northwestern University and a 1985 graduate of Yale Law School and Yale Divinity School. Professor Paulsen has served as an Assistant U.S. Attorney and as an Attorney-Adviser in the Office of Legal Counsel in the U.S. Department of Justice. He has served as Staff Counsel for the Center for Law and Religious Freedom. He has written and published more than fifty scholarly articles and book chapters in the fields of constitutional law, has written numerous briefs and argued in numerous cases in the federal courts on constitutional issues, and is regularly called on to provide testimony for congressional and other legislative committees on constitutional questions concerning separation of powers, the First Amendment, religious liberty, abortion, presidential election law, and the constitutional law of war. He is co-author of a forthcoming new casebook on the Constitution of the United States.

Jeffrey Rosen is a law professor at the George Washington University Law School and the legal affairs editor of *The New Republic*. He is the author of *The Unwanted Gaze: The Destruction of Privacy in America* (Vintage, 2001) and *The Naked Crowd: Preserving Liberty and Security in an Anxious Age* (Random House, 2004). His essays and commentaries have appeared in many publications, including the *New York Times Magazine*, the *Atlantic Monthly*, and the *New Yorker*.

Jed Rubenfeld is Robert R. Slaughter Professor at Yale Law School. He is the author of many articles on constitutional law and theory and of *Freedom and Time: A Theory of Constitutional Self-Government* (Yale Univ. Press, 2001). He serves as the U.S. Representative to the Council of Europe's Commission on Democracy through Law.

Reva B. Siegel is Nicholas deB. Katzenbach Professor of Law and Professor of American Studies at Yale University, where she teaches constitutional law, antidiscrimination law, and legal history. Her writing analyzes law's role in challenging and preserving status inequality, in areas including the regulation of reproduction, family, work, and suffrage in the nineteenth and twentieth centuries. Much of her recent work draws on the civil rights conflicts of the 1960s and 1970s to examine the life of the Constitution outside the courts, considering the role of the political branches and social movements in securing constitutional change. Professor Siegel is the co-editor with Catharine A. MacKinnon of *Directions in Sexual Harassment Law* (Yale Univ. Press, 2003).

Cass R. Sunstein is Karl N. Llewellyn Distinguished Service Professor, Law School and Department of Political Science, University of Chicago. His books include *The Second Bill of Rights: FDR's Constitutional Vision and Why We Need It More Than Ever* (Basic Books, 2004); *Why Societies Need Dissent* (Harvard Univ. Press, 2003); *Designing Democracy* (Oxford Univ. Press, 2002); *Republic.com* (Princeton Univ. Press, 2001); and *The Partial Constitution* (Harvard Univ. Press, 1993). He has participated in law reform and constitution-making activities in many nations and testified before Congress on a number of constitutional issues.

Mark Tushnet is Carmack Waterhouse Professor of Constitutional Law at the Georgetown University Law Center. He is the co-author of four casebooks, including the most widely used casebook on constitutional law; has written twelve books, including a two-volume work on the life of Justice Thurgood Marshall; and has edited four others. He was President of the Association of American Law Schools in 2003. In 2002, he was elected a fellow of the American Academy of Arts and Sciences.

Robin West is Professor of Law at Georgetown University Law Center. She is the author, most recently, of *Re-Imagining Justice: Progressive Interpretations of Formal Equality, Rights, and the Rule of Law* (Ashgate Press, 2003) and *Caring for Justice* (N.Y.U. Press, 1999). She lives in Baltimore, Maryland, with her husband and three children.

Table of Cases

Index